1 MONTH OF
FREE
READING

at

www.ForgottenBooks.com

By purchasing this book you are eligible for one month membership to ForgottenBooks.com, giving you unlimited access to our entire collection of over 1,000,000 titles via our web site and mobile apps.

To claim your free month visit:

www.forgottenbooks.com/free94463

ISBN 978-1-5285-7269-9
PIBN 10094463

NAPOLEON
AND THE INVASION
OF ENGLAND VOL. I

PLAYING at BUBBLES

GEORGE III AND NAPOLEON. THE HEROES OF THE GREAT TERROR

NAPOLEON
AND THE INVASION OF
ENGLAND
THE STORY OF
THE GREAT TERROR

WITH NUMEROUS ILLUSTRATIONS FROM
CONTEMPORARY PRINTS, CARICATURES, ETC.
EIGHT IN COLOUR.   TWO VOLUMES.   VOL. I

NEW YORK   JOHN LANE COMPANY   MCMVIII

W 5
v. 1

INTRODUCTION

THE probabilities and possibilities of a successful foreign invasion of England by sea have afforded abundant occupation for political and polemical writers, as well as naval and military experts, ever since the first rumours of the approach of the Armada, called Invincible by its vainglorious contriver. If one takes the incursions of the two Stuart Pretenders in 1715 and 1745 out of the category of foreign invasions, very few of the many projected descents on our shores went further than the stage of preparation, while signal victories like that of La Hogue put an end for a lengthy period to what was looked on almost as a standing menace. During the first nine decades of the eighteenth century Louis XIV, XV, and XVI and their advisers were in turn, directly or indirectly, responsible for the hostile designs of 1708, 1718, 1722, 1745, 1755, 1756, 1759, 1779, and 1782, although Sweden, Spain, and Holland were in some instances adroitly made use of to further the aggressive policy of France. Tradition has, almost from time immemorial, played an important part in French diplomacy, and the invasion of England had come to be regarded in that light long before the birth of Napoleon or the first inception of those grandiose and elaborate plans of conquest which culminated in the Great Terror of 1796–1805. Defence associations, volunteering, the calling out of the *posse comitatûs*, camps of observation, and stirring appeals to arms, both in prose and verse, are in reality an inheritance of the Great Terror of 1588. They figure in the history of the greater part of the eighteenth century. Ralph Allen of Bath, the friend of Pope, whose favourite niece Gertrude Tucker had married Bishop Warburton, organized a local volunteer corps when the menaces of Louis the Well-Beloved and his *protégé* the Pretender took the place of the threats of Louis the Great.[1] Badges given by the commanding officers as rewards for efficiency are occasionally to be found in the cabinets of collectors, and equally interesting are the medals of the loyal associations formed for the

---

[1] "We hear that Ralph Allen Esq. of Widcomb near this City, intends to raise One Hundred Men, at his own Charge for the Service of his Majesty and the Nation, at this critical Juncture, when we are threatened with a powerful Invasion from abroad, and disturbed by a Rebellion at home. On Wednesday last Sixty Men (for the Purpose above mention'd) were sworn before John Cogswell, Esq: our present Mayor; And we are credibly informed that several Young Men in the neighbourhood intend to offer themselves, voluntarily, to compleat the body of Men the said Gentleman proposes to raise: They will be cloath'd, arm'd, and maintain'd at Mr. Allen's own Expence; their Cloath's to be Blue, turn'd up with Red, and they are now learning their Exercise, a Person of Experience, being lately come from London for that purpose." [*Bath Journal*, Monday, February 3, 174⅞.]

And again :—

"On receiving the News Yesterday Morning of the precipitate Retreat of the Rebels from Stirling, on the Approach of the Army under his Royal Highness the Duke of Cumberland the Mayor order'd the Bells to be immediately rung; about One-o-clock our Cannon were fir'd, and in the Evening some curious Fire Works were play'd off, on the Parade by order of Mr. Nash, amidst a very great Concourse of People. The Corporation assembl'd in the Evening at the Guildhall (which was illuminated) and drank several Loyal Healths. There was likewise a Ball at Mrs Wiltshire's for the Ladies and Gentlemen, and the Night concluded with great Joy among all Degrees of People.

"Mr. Allen's House at Widcomb was finely illuminat'd, a large Bonfire was made near it; *and his Men, lately rais'd*, fir'd several Vollies on the above Occasion." [*Bath Journal*, February 10, 174⅞.]

defence of the country and the support of the House of Hanover at the critical epoch when France was actively aiding the Stuarts, and England and Austria were allied in the war occasioned by the dispute concerning the succession to the imperial throne. "Where Hearts are right, let Hands unite," is the inscription on the reverse of those tokens, while on the obverse one reads, "These banners spread are Gallia's dread." The heraldic supporters and colours of Austria and England appear on either side of an oval charged with a figure of St. George in the act of slaying the dragon, surmounted by that of Britannia, with the words "For our Country ' on a scroll below. Within the first device are full-length portraits of the two monarchs with clasped hands. A superb enamel badge of this kind, elaborately set in exquisite paste, is still in existence, and was in all probability worn by the president of the Association.

We have, however, no present concern with the invasions of England attempted or projected prior to the Revolution, which, by the irony of fate, made the heirs of our would-be invaders our fast friends and allies, while their former subjects became our relentless foes. It is merely essential to correct the popular error which makes Napoleon the *fons et origo* of the invasion idea, which originated nearly two centuries before he saw the light, was rampant when he was still in the cradle, recurred in an acute form long after his death, and has a certain actuality at this very moment, when the revival of the Channel Tunnel scheme has already brought a new defence association into existence.

The story of the Great Terror, which for a whole decade turned "Merry England," Scotland, and Ireland into one vast camp, has found little favour with English historical or military writers. Although dealt with incidentally and superficially in a vast number of works, no book devoted entirely to the subject has ever appeared. In 1852 the excitement born of Louis Napoleon's *coup d'état* was evidently responsible for Sir E. S. Creasy's *The Invasions and the Projected Invasions of England from the Saxon Times, with Remarks on the Present Emergencies.* Of the 312 pages it contains, only 61 tell the story of those eventful years when the "Corsican Ogre" was our national bogey. In 1876 appeared two bulky volumes by Captain H. M. Hozier, entitled *The Invasion of England; a History of the Past, with Lessons for the Future.* Ninety pages were deemed sufficient to dispose of the protracted duel between Napoleon and Nelson for the mastery of the sea, and they include a narrative of the three abortive expeditions to Ireland, and the landing at Fishguard in 1797 of Colonel Tate at the head of a band of felons and galley-slaves, dubbed by Wolfe Tone "La Légion Noire." Both books wholly lack an index of any kind, and their self-confessed and transparent incompleteness presents a striking contrast to the monumental work—a veritable *magnum opus*—which Captain Édouard Desbrière has given to France and the world at large under the title *1793-1805 Projets et Tentatives de Débarquement aux Iles Britanniques.* The five volumes from the pen of Captain Desbrière contain an aggregate of 2636 pages. Their publication under the direction of the "Historic Section of the French Staff" began in 1900 and ended in 1902. The illustrations are confined to a few plans and diagrams, and notwithstanding the graceful lucidity of the author's style, the mastering of the contents of these five closely printed

volumes is a task of considerable difficulty. Captain
Desbrière has had access to official archives both in London and Paris, and his knowledge of English is supposed
to have specially qualified him for an undertaking which
was evidently a labour of love. It must be confessed that
the text contains frequent and perplexing errors, many of
which are doubtless attributable to the carelessness or
inexperience of the proof-reader; but it is sometimes
evident that the author himself lacks system and clear-
ness, which is much to be regretted in what is beyond
question a great and valuable contribution to the history
not only of France, but of Europe at large. Proper names
and place-names are frequently mutilated beyond recogni-
tion—e.g. we have Frey-Harock for Grays-Thurrock and
Green-hill for Greenhithe; totals of troops refuse to tally—
on one page it is a half-brigade, on the next the half has
dropped out and the brigade paradoxically has become a
whole one; and dates are often wrongly given owing to the
puzzling intermixing of the Gregorian and Revolutionary
calendars. An index should certainly have been provided
for each volume. As it is, Desbrière, like Creasy and
Hozier, has committed the capital error of dispensing with
it altogether; but even this does not prevent our gratefully
acknowledging the colossal industry, the patient research,
the sound judgment, and the shrewdness of observation
displayed by him during his four years' toil. Captain
Desbrière always writes of England in a spirit of courtesy
and conciliation.

The absence of English textbooks relating to the Great
Terror is more than atoned for by the richness of other
sources of information, many of them hitherto unknown
and unexamined, from which the writers have endeavoured

to reconstitute as it were the political, military, naval, and social history of the crises of 1797–8, as well as those of 1801 and 1803–5. From the beginning of 1797 until the end of 1805 (if we except the brief respite given to men's minds on both sides of the Channel by the Peace of Amiens) the "to be or not to be" of the invasion was the all-absorbing and all-pervading topic of correspondence and conversations, and that from the palace to the cottage. It was an age of letter-writing, diary-keeping, and pamphleteering, and Napoleon's projects are constantly mentioned in the journals of women like Fanny Burney, then the wife of one of the French *émigrés*, Mary Berry, Hannah More, Hester Lynch Piozzi, and others. Elizabeth Montagu was alive in 1797, but her reign as Queen of the Blue Stockings was over. Bishops at their visitations; judges on the bench; politicians in both Houses of Parliament; preachers in their pulpits; dramatic authors in their plays; poets in their verses; actors on the stage; Freemasons in their lodges; magistrates at their county meetings; merchants on 'Change; shopkeepers at their counters; and labourers at the plough all held the same language as to the common danger. If some dissentient voices were heard in 1797–8 when the aftermath of the Revolution still lingered in the land, there was increased enthusiasm in the patriotism of 1801, and burning ardour coupled with absolute unanimity in that of 1803–5.

The writers have had access to many unpublished letters of the period, in which the great subject of the hour is discussed or alluded to by Fox and many of his English and French contemporaries. It has long been the fashion to decry the intelligence of George III, who at the time when the invasion cloud appeared most threatening had passed the meridian of life, and was already subject to frequent attacks of the mental disease so soon to become permanent. During the Great Terror George III showed himself to be every inch a patriot, and he may fairly be credited with having personally suggested some of the most practical measures of defence. Neither he nor the Queen nor their sons and daughters ever tired of attending the reviews and military parades, which, between 1797 and 1805, were often of daily occurrence. Never did George III show the smallest sign of fear, although it was felt that his visit to Weymouth and excursions in the Channel were attended with personal risk, on account of the possible proximity of some of Napoleon's cruisers. His Majesty's letter to Bishop Hurd, dated Windsor, November 30th, 1803, only came to light in 1849, and is quite worth reprinting as one of the human documents of the later phase of the Great Terror. It runs as follows: " We are here in daily expectation that Bonaparte will attempt his threatened invasion; the chances against his success seem so many that it is wonderful he persists in it. I own I place that thorough dependence on Divine Providence that I cannot help thinking the usurper is encouraged to make the trial that the ill-success may put an end to his wicked purposes. Should his troops effect a landing, I shall certainly put myself at the head of my troops and my other armed subjects to repel them.[1] But as it is impossible to foresee the events of such a conflict, should the enemy approach too near to Windsor, I shall think it right the Queen and my daughters should cross the Severn, and send them to your Episcopal Palace at Worcester; by this hint I do not the least mean they shall

[1] George III was now in his sixty-sixth year.

be any inconvenience to you, and shall send a proper
servant and furniture for their accommodation. Should
this event arise, I certainly would rather have what I value
most in life remain, during the conflict, in your diocese and
under your roof than in any other place in the island."[1]
In May, 1797, three months after the Fishguard incident,
an attempt was made to shake the loyalty both of the
regular troops and the militia by the widespread distribution of a seditious circular.[2] At this juncture the King was
in daily communication with his son the Commander-in-
Chief,[3] who also displayed the greatest activity in grappling
with a danger, traced to the act of foreign emissaries.
The following are examples of the numerous unpublished
letters[4] written by the King during this particular period
of agitation.

"WINDSOR, *May 28th*, 1797.
m p^t A.M.

"MY DEAR FREDERICK,

"I highly approve of your attention in having wrote
to me that Woolwich continues quiet and consequently no
reason occurred for detaining the Coldstreams beyond the
limits of this Field day.

"The idea of Marquis Cornwallis to remove one of the
discontented Companies from the Barracks seems very
proper provided it can be to some place where their conduct can be properly watched. Sir Charles Grey's presence at Sheerness cannot be but proper and M. G. [Major
General] Fox's returning to Chatham where his presence

---

[1] Richard Hurd (1720–1808) had been preceptor to the Prince of Wales
and Duke of York from 1776 till 1780. From 1774 till 1781 he held the
bishopric of Lichfield, and in the latter year was translated to Worcester. In
1783 he declined the primacy. George III and Queen Charlotte visited him
at Worcester in 1788. He was an intimate friend of both and enjoyed their
entire confidence.   [2] See *post*, p. 203.   [3] Frederick, Duke of York.
    [4] Mr. Broadley's collection of MSS. relating to the Great Terror.

is necessary not less so ; in which case Colonel Fisher may have the momentary command at Sheerness. Major General Sheriff as he is well thought of by some Generals may undoubtedly be added to the staff in Sir Wm Pitts' district.

> " I ever remain
>   Your most affection father
>   . " GEORGE R."

> " WINDSOR, *May* 29, 1797.
>
> $\frac{m}{40}$ p^t 7 A.M.

" MY DEAR FREDERICK,

"I am happy to find things remain quiet at Woolwich, tho as yet no real confidence can be placed in it, and this must not abate the Attention of the Officers.

"The having sent Colonel Nesbitt to Gravesend is a proper precaution, but undoubtedly he ought to have some Guns to command the passage of the River, without which he cannot ensure examining suspicious ships, that come up the River, or prevent the Lancaster from falling down to the Nore.[1]

> " I ever remain,
>   Your most Affectionate Father
>   " GEORGE R."

Eleven months later the volunteer associations are in process of rapid formation. The King is busy signing warrants, but he again takes an opportunity to make suggestions, on this occasion to the Prime Minister.

" I have lost no time in signing the warrants prescribed by Act of Parliament for the Defence of the Kingdom ;— these being drawn up in general words I think perfectly right, as otherwise with some to whom they are addressed enumerable [*sic*] correspondence would have arisen on

---

[1] The Mutiny of the Nore had broken out two days previously.

every trifling alteration the necessity of the Service might occasion. The Instructions which accompanied the Warrants seem judiciously drawn, as also the private instructions to the Board of Admiralty.

"It occurs to Me it would be highly necessary the Commanding General in each District should be informed as nearly as possible of the Naval force on his Coast, as the concurrence of the Navy might be frequently highly essential.

"GEORGE R.

"QUEEN'S HOUSE,

April 8th 1798 $\frac{m}{48}$ p^t 8 A.M."

Here is certainly a proposal of some real value. For a man of mature age, King George was at his desk at an unusually early hour.[1] The King throughout this interesting correspondence showed a keen appreciation of the relative value of every officer about whom he wrote.

Three years later he thus conveys a timely hint to the Commander-in-Chief as to the inexpediency of a proposed " command " for his nephew and future son-in-law, Prince William of Gloucester, the " Silly Billy " of contemporary satirists :—

" WEYMOUTH, *Sept.* 25, 1801.

" MY DEAR FREDERICK,

" The usual papers came this morning and the recommendations to vacant Commissions, which I approved of.

" Your statement in favour of Brigadier Scott makes his appointment to the Command of the Royal Somerset Reg^t of Fencibles on the death of Colonel Forbes very proper.

" I cannot say I very willingly would put Prince William in any Command where much tallents [*sic*] were required, but there is little probability of any attempt on the North West District that he will there be most out of the way.

" My dear Frederick,
" Your most affectionate Father,
" GEORGE R."[2]

Between the 17th and 20th September, 1805, Pitt had an interview with King George at the Royal Lodge, Weymouth. It is with this, the latest phase of the Great

[1] Another of his letters to the Commander-in-Chief at this juncture is dated " 35 p 9 P.M.," and a third " 50 m p 7 A.M."

[2] The correspondence between George III and the Duke of York, 1797–1805, was only quite recently sold pell-mell to various autograph dealers. Another letter of great importance bearing on the acute crisis of 1804 will be found in Vol. II, chap. xv.

Terror, that Thomas Hardy opens the first part of his wonderful dramatic poem *The Dynasts*. With rare skill he depicts the events which occur in rapid succession in Wessex, London, Paris, and Boulogne. The meeting at Weymouth of Pitt and the now purblind King is thus related :—

KING.
We've had alarms
Within this few weeks past, as you may know,
That Bonaparte has landed close hereby.

PITT.
Such rumours come as regularly as harvest.

KING.
And now he has left Boulogne with all his host.
Was it his object to invade at all,
Or was his vast assemblage here a blind?

PITT.
Undoubtedly he meant invasion, Sir,
Had fortune favoured. He may try it yet.

On the 4th October, a fortnight later, the Royal Family left Weymouth, and returned to Kew. The King no longer wrote legibly as he did in 1798, and even in 1803. Four days before Trafalgar he thus writes to Lord Mulgrave :—[1]

" KEW, *October* 17, 1805.

" The information by the mail just arrived is so important that Lord Mulgrave has judged very properly in instantly communicating it, though at an irregular hour. The violence of Bonaparte is highly advantageous to the good cause, and probably has effected a decision in the line to be pursued by the King of Prussia that will be more efficacious than the interview with the Emperor of Russia would have produced without it.

" GEORGE R."

[1] The three letters are in Mr. Broadley's collection of MSS.

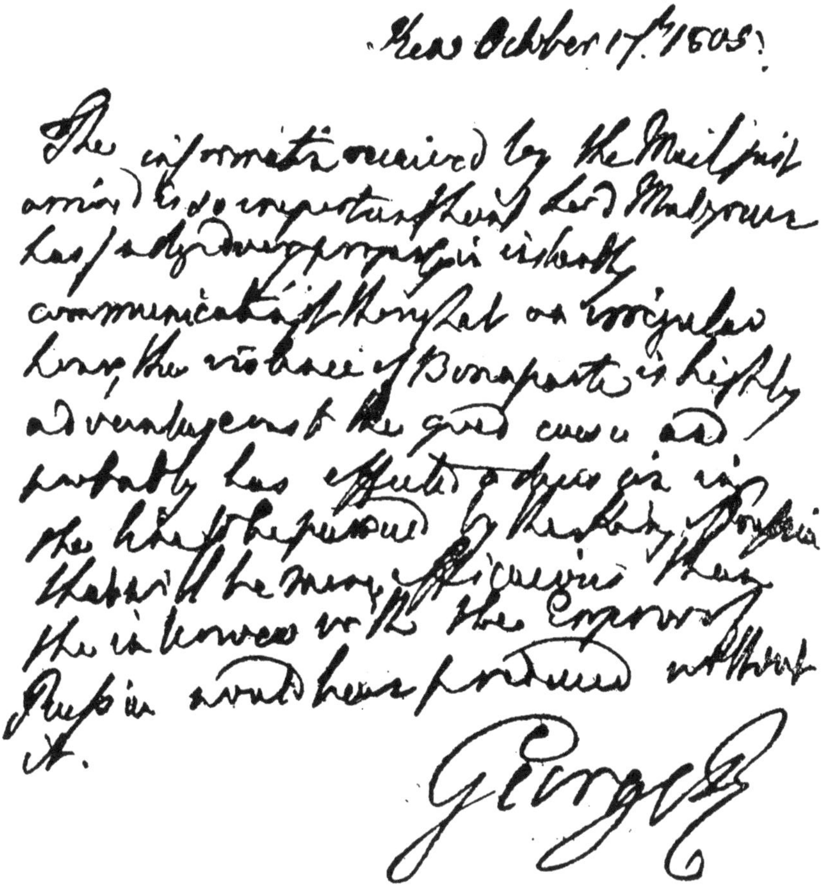
Kew October 17th 1805.

George R.

Only a few hours later Mack signed the capitulation of Ulm; four days afterwards Nelson died at Trafalgar, having by a great naval victory once again saved England from the possibility of invasion in the near future, and virtually freed her from the shadow of the Great Terror.

Many of the unpublished letters which are referred

to in the text are scarcely less interesting than those
of King George. We have Richard Cumberland com-
posing a song to stimulate the patriotism of the
volunteers, Charles James Fox discussing the real object
of Bonaparte's movements with his brother the General,
Mrs. Piozzi giving her views as to the remuneration of our
naval protectors, and Bruix making an appointment for
the purpose of examining a torpedo newly invented by
Fulton, and so forth. It is but quite recently that the
Fishguard despatches of Lords Milford and Cawdor were
found in the shop of a Birmingham curiosity dealer. They
will be reproduced in the chapter which relates the almost
farcical prologue to the ambitious dreams of Bonaparte
and the later evolutions of the Army of England.

By far the most important source of information, now
utilized for the first time, is the MS. *Memoirs on the Defence
of Great Britain and Ireland,* compiled in 1803 and 1804 by
General Charles François Dupérier Dumouriez, in many
respects one of the ablest and most far-seeing statesmen
and soldiers whose latent powers were developed by the
exigencies of the French Revolution. Although Dumouriez
outlived Napoleon, he was thirty years his senior. If they
had been contemporaries, the course of European history
might have been very different. As it was, few Frenchmen hated "the Corsican upstart" more intensely than the
man who was Governor of Cherbourg while the future
Emperor was still a child. Dumouriez broke with the
Convention in the very year which witnessed the arrival
in France of Bonaparte and the other members of his
family as unknown and obscure Corsican refugees. There
was little in Napoleon's leadership of his ultra-democrat
compatriots against the Paolists to betoken the prowess

he was to display a few months later as Commandant of the Artillery of the Army of the South. The two men were never fated to meet face to face in the arena of practical politics. If they had ever come in contact, a death-struggle for the supreme power between the victor of Jemappes and the winner of Marengo and Austerlitz would have been inevitable. Born at Cambrai in 1739, Dumouriez endured for some years the tortures which in those days fell to the lot of a rickety child. He was released from the heavy metal frame used to support his emaciated limbs only just in time to save his life. Before he reached man's estate, however, he could bear any amount of fatigue, and he became as robust in body as he was alert in mind. He had won name and fame in the Seven Years' War, and had seen a whole decade of active service before in 1768, the year which immediately preceded Napoleon's birth, he went through the Corsican campaign under Marshal de Vaux, whom he regarded not only as his leader, but as his friend and patron. In 1772 a suspicion of secret relations with Poland and Hamburg entailed on Dumouriez a lengthy period of detention in the Bastille. During the years 1774, 1775, and 1776 he was the head of an official mission to examine and report upon the Channel harbours and their defences. In 1775 it was Dumouriez who selected Cherbourg in preference to Havre as the great naval centre of the future, and he was almost immediately entrusted with the superintendence of the necessary works there. In 1777 he was appointed Commandant of Cherbourg, and in the following year entered on the active discharge of his functions in that capacity. It was at this juncture that he planned hostile expeditions against the

Channel Islands and the Isle of Wight. In 1790 Dumouriez became an active politician, and joined the ranks of
the Girondists. His published pamphlets were as bellicose and highly flavoured as his speeches, but speedily
led to promotion, and the dashing captain of the. Seven
Years' War became first Minister of Foreign Affairs and
then Général en Chef des Armées Françaises. Over
the death of the king Dumouriez fell out with his former
political friends, who denounced him as a traitor. Shortly
after the battle of Neerwinden—his only defeat—he went
over to the Austrians, and never more set foot on French
soil. In 1794 the *Vie Privée et Politique du Général
Dumouriez, Pour servir de suite à ses Mémoires* was published at Hamburg, where six years later he met Nelson
on his way to England. Between 1793 and 1803 he
wandered from Court to Court as the propagandist of
Bourbon restoration. That he was a philosopher and
deep thinker as well as a born general and one of the
greatest military experts of the warlike age in which he
lived is abundantly evident from his numerous published
works, and still more so from the MS. commenced late in
1803 and completed in May, 1804. In the pages of this
MS. the author frankly alludes to himself as a former
"Commander of Cherbourg," an "Overseer of the Harbour Works of Cherbourg," an officer of the French army
under Louis XV and XVI, a protégé of the Marshal de
Vaux, an Assistant Q.M.G. under Marshal de Vaux in
1779, a refugee in England in 1803, and "a counsellor to
the English Government and Adviser to the Staff." In
1804 no other man alive in any way answered to these
detailed and explicit indications but Charles Francis
Dumouriez.

Some three years ago a thick octavo volume of carefully written MS., bound in stout vellum and provided with a metal clasp, found its way into the shop of a well-known London second-hand bookseller. The description given of it in the catalogue was insufficient and somewhat misleading, but the present owner has no difficulty in identifying it with the work for the preparation of which the author received for just twenty years a pension of at least £1000 per annum from the British Government. From the first word to the last the MS. is, without the shadow of a doubt, in the peculiarly characteristic and easily recognizable handwriting of Dumouriez, which varied little during the last forty years of his life, and of which numerous specimens are available for the purpose of comparison. The calligraphy of the *Memoirs*, begun probably under the auspices of Addington and finished after the return to office of Pitt, is absolutely identical to that of a very remarkable letter written to Nelson by Dumouriez, in English, from Altona on the 20th April, 1801, which was sold by Messrs. Sotheby on the 8th July, 1905. Dumouriez was a linguist of no mean order, and the missive in question demonstrates the fact that he possessed a very sufficient knowledge of our language before he began his twenty years of continuous residence on British soil. "My dear and glorious Nelson," wrote the illustrious exile, "Victory is ever bounded [*sic*] to your name, as my friendship to your character. I hope the Peace with the Northern Powers will give another turn to your constant successes, more profitable for the public cause. Paul's foolish brain destroyed our hopes, they revive with the successor. If you have the charge of the Mediterranean Sea, we can together deliver Italy and France of the democratic

Conclusion.

23

Au reste il est tems de couper le cheveu qui tient le glaive de Buonaparte suspendu sur l'Angleterre. Il est tems de faire cesser cet état d'anxiété qui concentre dans cet empire d'immenses moyens de guerre, qui comprime l'énergie nationale, qui la laisse exposée en spectacle à l'inquiète curiosité des puissances continentales, sans amener aucun résultat utile, sans déterminer la fin de cette guerre.

Rien n'est plus dangereux qu'une perpétuelle deffensive. Rien n'ouvre un champ plus vaste aux attaques de toute espece, raprochées, ou eloignées, de la part de l'ennemi. On veut bien croire que chaque année ajouterait un degré de perfection, s'il n'était pas dans la nature de l'homme de décroître en énergie, lorsqu'elle a été d'abord poussée au plus haut point, & lorsqu'elle s'émousse par une trop longue attente.

Mais au bout du compte, quand on aurait perfectionné les mesures prises pour la sûreté de la Patrie, à quoi aboutirait cette éternelle guerre deffensive, dont la longueur pourrait endormir ou attiédir l'énergie nationale, & qui continuerait à donner à l'Empire Britannique l'attitude humiliante d'une place assiegée par une armée moins forte que sa garnison? Quelle confiance pourraient reprendre les Puissances du Continent, si ce systême, qui ressemble à la peur, se prolongeait, & cet armement exageré & ruineux ne devenait dangereux.

tyranny. I desire nothing else. After that, take your leave, and spend the remnant of your life in the calmness shadowed with the laurels you for yourself implant'd. Farewell, dear Nelson, and be constant in friendship as you are in triumphing of [over] internal foes and external enemys."

Seven years before John Gillray had portrayed the future friend of Nelson and "Counsellor of England" as dining at St. James's Palace on May 15th, 1793, the *plat de résistance* being the head and battered crown of Louis XVIII served up by Fox and Sheridan, both wearing Phrygian caps adorned with tricolour cockades. The founder of Cherbourg had evidently been held responsible for one of the earliest post-French Revolution invasion panics. In 1803 and 1804 Dumouriez, Fox, and Sheridan were all three to be found amongst the most eloquent and stalwart champions of English national defence and war to the knife with the "democratic tyrant" now on the high road to the imperial throne.

References will be frequently found in the text to the remarkable essay of Dumouriez, who during the time he was compiling it was constantly in communication with the Duke of York and Lords Melville and Camden. It is hoped, however, that the whole of the MS. will, as it richly deserves, be carefully translated and edited for publication as a supplemental volume to the present work. The high character, transcendent ability, and exceptional position of Dumouriez demands it, and assuredly there is no other instance in history of the Foreign Minister of one country, and that within twelve years of his having held the office, living to draw up in every detail a scheme for the defence of the country of which he once planned the invasion. Sir John Bowring, who was Dumouriez's literary executor and the composer of the Latin epitaph in Henley Church, so unpardonably misquoted by the General's German biographer, tells us[1] that "Dumouriez died on 2nd March, 1823, at Turville Park, aged eighty-four, his last days having been made comfortable by an allowance from the Duke of Orleans, which enabled him to keep a carriage. The General had, I believe, a pension of £1000 a year from the British Government, with whom he was in intimate communication, and *for whom he drew up a plan of defence against the menaced French invasion. At his death his papers were purchased by the Government from his executors.*" As far as can be ascertained, there is no trace of another copy of the whole or any portion of the MS., to which the author made additions in 1805, 1806, and 1808, either in the Record or War Offices.[2] Shrewdness and common sense are the characteristics of Dumouriez's deductions and observations. Much that he writes is prophetic, and, like his anticipation of Napoleon's attack on Austria, strangely verified by subsequent events. It was in May, 1804, that Dumouriez wrote: "It is time for England to cut the thread that holds the sword of Bonaparte above her head. Nothing is so demoralizing as an everlasting defensive. It may be thought that every year would add to the perfection of the measures taken, but it is in human nature to grow less and less energetic, seeing that the first enthu-

---

[1] *Autobiographical Recollections of Sir John Bowring, with a brief Memoir of L. N. Bowring,* pp. 307 *et seq.* London, 1877.

[2] Fragments of Dumouriez's memoranda on the defence of England exist in the library of the Secretary of State for War. See *Napoleonic Studies,* by J. Holland Rose, Litt. D. London, George Bell, 1904.

siastic effort always calls forth the highest degree of that energy. Unless England proceeds to attack she will present the spectacle of a place beleaguered by a weaker force than its own garrison. This will be tantamount to cowardice, and could not inspire the continental powers with confidence. The defensive power is unwieldy, costly, and even dangerous. It will not make Bonaparte abate one jot of his pretensions and projects; it is out of proportion with the danger of the invasion, which 200,000 men could repel with the help of a Navy which alone can meet all the navies of the world collected together. No doubt England had to reach the offensive *viâ* the defensive, but let it be clearly understood that if from this year [1804] an attack does not supersede defence, then his chances will be very much increased." It was to some purpose that Nelson strongly impressed on the British Government the wisdom of utilizing the knowledge of Dumouriez.

In the *Histoire de la Caricature sous la République, l'Empire et la Restauration*, by Champfleury,[1] ample justice is done to the powerful influence on English public opinion exercised by such artists as Gillray and Rowlandson throughout the Great Terror, although, curiously enough, comparatively little notice is taken of the elder Cruikshank, Woodward, and the other artists, great and small, who made the Corsican Ogre and his flotilla the target of their satire. It was to James Gillray that Napoleon owed the *sobriquet* "Little Boney," which will be remembered when the innumerable abusive and depreciative epithets so freely bestowed on our redoubtable adversary are forgotten. "Gillray fut," observes the French historian of caricature, "un véritable excitateur, un remueur de fibres

---

[1] Vol. IV, pp. 247-397. Paris, n.d.

patriotiques, et son nom devrait être donné à une des rues avoisinant la place où se profile la statue de Wellington." The phrase is so particularly happy and appropriate that it would lose half its force by translation. Champfleury places Gillray above Rowlandson, who so frequently defeated the object he had in view by gross exaggeration of form and features. There are comparatively few French invasion caricatures in existence,[1] but the German artists, it will be seen, showed Napoleon little more mercy than Gillray and Rowlandson. For the last two decades of the eighteenth century and the first two of the nineteenth the caricature was a national institution in England. Throughout the Great Terror the satiric prints exhibited in the shop windows of Humphrey in St. James's Street, Fores in Piccadilly, Ackermann in the Strand, and Holland's Museum in Oxford Street, and freely lent out in portfolios for inspection at evening parties, served to intensify the general detestation of our foreign foe and stimulate the spirit of patriotism and dogged determination to resist *à l'outrance* which animated every class of the community. If one learns much of the political side of the Great Terror from Pitt, Rose, Fox, Windham, and the rest of the statesmen of the period, for its side-lights and social aspect, one must go to the pages of Wright and Grego and private collections like that to which the present writers have had access. The ballad and the broadside proved quite as useful in the same direction as the caricature; and, as might be expected, the invasion had its own songs, song-books, and song writers, as well as its own jests, toasts,

---

[1] One of these, however, not only foreshadows the invasion by tunnel idea of 1883, but that by aeroplane as foreshadowed in 1907.

and sentiments.[1] If it has been reserved for the namesake of one of the sturdiest sailors of Trafalgar times to describe in dramatic form, but with true poetic feeling, the fall of the curtain on Napoleon's cherished dream of conquering England, most of the poets of the period made use of the menaced invasion to " improve the occasion," although the birthday and New Year odes of " Poet " Pye and the additional verses to the National Anthem and " Rule Britannia," thoughtfully provided by Miss Anna Seward and others, have long since lost their savour. These remarks will explain the *raison d'être* of the chapters in which the popular literature in prose as well as in verse and the pictorial satire both of the earlier and later phases of the Great Terror are dealt with at length.

The works of Creasy and Hozier on the subject of the invasion of England were each written at a time when the question of national defence was pre-eminently the topic of the hour, although we were neither in 1852 or in 1876 once more singing—

> Thou Who rul'st sea and land,
> Stretch forth Thy guardian hand,
> Potent to save !
> Lead forth our monarch's host
> And proud invasion's boast
> Crush on our warlike coast—
> God save the King.

---

[1] *Account of Gillray's Caricatures*, by Wright and Evans, London, 1851 ; *England under the House of Hanover*, by Wright, 1849 ; and *Rowlandson the Caricaturist*, by Joseph Grego, 1880. The two elder Cruikshanks, both of them volunteers, were already hard at work in the early days of the Great Terror. George Cruikshank's earliest works appeared in 1803, but (see *post*, p. 244) he published in 1860 a crushing retort to General Sir W. Napier's animadversions on the old corps as " Mimic Soldiers."

The pamphlet of General Sir Charles Napier on *The Defence of England by Corps of Volunteers and Militia,* which appeared in the same year (1852) as Sir E. Creasy's book, was the signal for an avalanche of ephemeral brochures emphasizing in some shape or other Coleridge's saying : " If men could learn from history, what lessons it might teach us." Captain Hozier placed on the title page of his first volume the words, " The cry is still they come " ; while on that of the second he inscribes the lines : " Happy England !—happy with a special reference to the present subject in this, that the wise dispensation of Providence has cut her off by that streak of silver sea." If he had chosen he might have substituted Coleridge's charming lines—

> And Ocean, 'mid his uproar wild,
> Speaks safety to his island child.
> Hence for many a fearless age
> Has social quiet loved thy shore ;
> Nor ever proud invader's rage
> Or sacked thy towers, or stained thy fields with gore—

for the more prosaic prose of the *Edinburgh Review.*

The centre of menace may now have shifted itself from Paris to Berlin, but this has only been since the accession of King Edward VII. At the commencement of the century the invasion tradition of the Bourbons and the Bonapartes still held good at the Quai d'Orsay, along with certain other hereditary diplomatic dogmas which it may now be devoutly hoped have been finally cast aside. The immediate consequences of the revival of the Channel Tunnel project, however, abundantly show that the possibilities of an invasion of England from the Continent are still very much within the sphere of practical politics. The reopening of the controversy laid to rest in 1883 is no

sooner mooted than the war of words becomes fiercer than
ever. Sir James Knowles once more unfurls the standard
of uncompromising resistance, which, like William Pitt's
map of Europe, has been rolled up "these ten years";
all sorts and conditions of men and women, from Lord
Wolseley to Dr. Sophia Jex-Blake, sound the shrill note of
alarm; and while the shareholders of one great railway
company applaud the idea as a benefit to the human race,
those of another denounce it as dangerous and destructive
to England's safety. One has only to read the issue of *The
Nineteenth Century and After* for February last to realize
the extent and intensity of the interest centred in everything which relates to the inviolability of our territory.
Indeed, if the cry about the unprotected condition of
our northern and eastern coasts may be taken as an indication, it seems likely that the question of the sufficiency
or otherwise of our home defences will arrest public attention as urgently in 1907 as it did in 1807 and indeed in
1707. There is something strangely reminiscent of Napoleonic times in the verses now quoted from a poem which
lately appeared in the *Pall Mall Gazette.*

> When men stood anxious at their posts,
>   Whilst women sobbed alone ;
> When Fear gazed darkly o'er our Land,
>   The Fear we dared not own :
> The windward sandbanks did their task,
>   The shoals upon their lee—
>
>   Who saved us from the Corsican ?
>   They !—and our sullen Sea !
>
> Loud roars the Watcher of our shores,
>   The Stiller of Alarm !
> The narrow, sand-strewn, storm-swept Straits
>   That guard us from all harm !

> Spirit of sandbank, surf, and spume,
> And spindrift driven free—
> Save us this day, from those, we pray,
> Who would betray our Sea !

During the Great Terror Charles Dibdin was the laureate of the people. The important post now held by Mr. Alfred Austin was occupied by Mr. Henry James Pye, who rarely failed to introduce the subject of the invasion into his official odes. The following may fairly be taken as a specimen of his art. Quoth the " British Muse " :—

> Go forth, my sons, as nobler rights ye claim
> Than ever fann'd the Grecian patriot's flame,
> So let your breasts a fiercer ardour feel,
> Led by your Patriot King, to guard your country's weal.
>
> .   .   .   .
>
> Her voice is heard—from wood, from vale, from down,
> The thatch'd roof village and the busy town,
> Eager th' indignant country swarms,
> And yours a people clad in arms
> Num'rous as those whom Xerxes led,
> To crush devoted Freedom's head ;
> Firm as the band for Freedom's cause who stood,
> And stained Thermopylee [*sic*] with Spartan blood ;
> Hear o'er their heads the exulting Goddess sing :
> These are my fav'rite sons, and mine their warrior King.

The rhyming inanities of those days have long since become things of the past. They have disappeared as completely as the flat-bottom boats and the rest of the complicated machinery which was intended to bring Napoleon and his army—" Gallia's hosts," in the language of Mr. Pye—across the Channel. Although there is no longer a demand for the verses which taxed so severely the resources of Cibber, Whitehead, Warton, and Pye, and the skill of the unfortunate composers who had to set their effusions to music, the Poet Laureate is still occasionally called upon to strike his lyre.   This has already happened as far as the Channel Tunnel is concerned, and Mr. Alfred Austin disposes of the whole matter by repeating three lines written by him just a quarter of a century ago :—

> Nay, England, if thy citadel be sold
> For lucre thus, Tarpeia's doom be thine,
> And perish smothered in a grave of gold.

Be the ultimate decision what it may, it is evident that the story the writers have to tell possesses an interest which regards the present and the future quite as much as it does the past.   They prefer, however, to leave the reader to draw his own deductions from the facts which they venture to think throw a new light not only on Napoleon's projected invasions of England, but on the social and political life of the age to which they belong.

The writers desire to express their gratitude to Sir George White, Bart., of Cotham House, Bristol, for permission to use a contemporary water-colour sketch and MS. song of the Bristol Volunteers of 1797 as well as a rare broadside relating to the military history of the city at that period; to Dr. J. Holland Rose, the latest and greatest of Napoleon's biographers, and Commander Robinson, R.N., the author of *The British Fleet*, for many valuable suggestions; to Mr. H. H. Raphael, M.P., for access to the magnificent collection of engraved portraits formed by him in illustration of the *Memoirs of Barras;* to Mr. Clement Shorter for placing at their disposal his interesting series of invasion handbills, carefully preserved more than a century ago by Madame Tussaud; to Mr.

Edward Laws, the historian of Pembrokeshire, for the communication of several new facts concerning the Fishguard episode of February, 1797; to Messrs. Spink for the loan of the cast of a very rare variety of Napoleon's famous invasion medal of 1804; to Monsieur L. Forrer for many interesting particulars as to the medals and tokens issued in France in connection with the projects of 1796–1805; to Monsieur Godefroy Mayer of Paris, for a note on the French iconography of the invasion, both serious and humorous; to Mr. Sydney Sydenham, of Bath, for information as to the volunteer tokens and badges of the period dealt with; and to Mr. John Lane for the care and taste he has bestowed on the effective reproduction from the scarce originals of the numerous characteristic illustrations now placed before the reader of these volumes. Valuable assistance has also been given to the writers by Mr. G. L. de St. M. Watson in revising the proofs of these pages and preparing a careful analysis of the voluminous information contained in Captain Desbrière's official treatise.

CONTENTS

ILLUSTRATIONS

NAPOLEON
AND THE INVASION
OF ENGLAND VOL. I

NAPOLEON AND THE INVASION OF ENGLAND

CHAPTER I

EARLY PROJECTS OF THE FRENCH REPUBLIC FOR THE INVASION OF THE BRITISH ISLES, 1793–7—ENGLAND ON THE DEFENSIVE

> "He that would England win
> Must with Ireland first begin."—OLD PROVERB.

AN inveterate and exceeding bitter hatred of England was for generations the legacy of every son of France. It was the one connecting link between the *ancien régime* and its successor which was never severed. Napoleon Bonaparte, the apotheosis of the Revolution, in whose person was summed up that vague political creed which set human life at naught and regarded Europe as one great battlefield, was no exception. And yet to England the future Emperor owed accidentally his first step to fame. At the siege of Toulon she gave him a golden opportunity which he grasped, but ever after she dogged his footsteps on land and sea. The genius of England always stood on his threshold, be it palace or camp; she was always in the way.

Given an island and a narrow sea separating it from a continent, the instinct of the soldier on the larger territory prompts its invasion. The precedent set 55 B.C. by Cæsar, who embarked his legions at Portus Itius, supposed by some historians to be Calais, and by others Wissant, between that port and Boulogne, was followed down the centuries by other enterprising individuals representing both official and private interests. Perhaps a modern Froissart will yet pen the chronicles of the innumerable expeditions fitted out with the object of plundering the British Isles. Suffice to say that Louis XVI had contemplated invasion, and that before the infant French Republic declared war against Holland and England in 1793, Monge, the Minister of Marine, sent a note to the Jacobins of all countries and to the inhabitants of the seaports of France urging them to a final effort. Ireland was grumbling over her numerous real or fancied grievances; the storm which ended in the Rebellion of '98 was brewing. "Already these free men show their discontent," writes Monge on the last day of 1792. "Well, we will fly to their succour. We will make a descent on the island; we will lodge there fifty thousand caps of liberty; we will plant there the sacred tree, and we will stretch out our arms to our republican brethren; the tyranny of their government will soon be destroyed. Let every one of us be strongly impressed with this idea." [1]

> Plant, plant the tree, fair freedom's tree,
>   Midst dangers, wounds, and slaughter;
> Each patriot's breast its soil shall be,
>   And tyrants' blood its water. [2]

[1] Quoted by Pitt in his speech in the House of Commons on February 1st, 1793.

[2] Chorus of a song used by those who had republican tendencies, and which took the place of "God save the King." It will be found in the Appendix, No. XXVII, to the Report of the Committee of Secrecy of the Irish House of Commons, presented by Lord Castlereagh on the 21st August, 1798.

Dumouriez, that impetuous, but able and far-sighted, soldier of fortune, who was in turn Constitutionalist, Girondist, Jacobin, and supporter of the British Ministry, having conquered Belgium after a brilliant campaign, was the man of the moment in Paris. He had already prepared plans for the invasion of England in the winter of 1777–8,[1] consequently his ideas on the proposed expedition carried considerable weight. He saw that by subjugating Holland her naval resources would be at the disposal of the Republic. So glittering a prospect could not be resisted. On January 13th, 1793, the Convention accordingly ordered the armament of thirty ships and the construction of twenty-five more, while the total number of troops was to be increased to half a million, 227,000 of whom, consisting of the armies of Belgium, the Moselle, the Rhine, and of " England," were to act on the offensive.[2] There was at first no plan for coast defence. Later some twenty thousand men were assigned for the purpose, for it was thought not unlikely that the British might turn the tables on them and land soldiers on French soil. With the breaking out of the Vendean rebellion faded away all

---

[1] The objective was to be the Isle of Wight, which was then in a poor state of defence, the greater part of the English army being in America. Several thousands of French troops were to be concentrated at Cherbourg, and on a dark November night embark on two hundred *chasse-marées*, thirty of which were to be armed with 24-pounders. French or English smugglers would pilot them across the Channel. This expedition was but the beginning of a general campaign, for in 1779 the Spanish and French fleets were to join forces and proceed to Portsmouth with seventy thousand men, who would either land there and march on London, leaving the original force to attack the naval arsenal, or sail round to carry out the great plan of "a descent on Rye." The preparations for carrying out these schemes are said to have cost eighty million francs.—Dumouriez MS., pp. 27–37.

[2] *Projets et Tentatives de Débarquement aux Iles Britanniques*, Vol. I, p. 21, by Édouard Desbrière.

chances of putting the idea to a practical test. The troops which had marched to the coasts for that purpose were promptly sent to the recalcitrant provinces.

Hostilities between France and Great Britain had now begun, war being declared against the latter Power and Holland on the 1st February, 1793, closely followed by equally drastic measures against Spain on the 7th March. Pitt, who had just completed the tenth year of his unbroken spell of office, shortly afterwards entered into an alliance with Russia, followed by others with Sardinia, Spain, Naples, Prussia, the Empire, and Portugal. Revolutionary France had not a single friend, Denmark and Sweden remaining neutral. It was the policy of the British Minister to set a seal on the friendship of foreign countries by paying heavy subsidies when necessary, the allies fighting in the interior of Europe, aided by whatever troops the non-military Power could put in the field, and her navy narrowly watching the seas. At the beginning of the war which was to be waged so relentlessly, England had a hundred and fifteen sail-of-the-line and France seventy-six ;[1] Spain also had seventy-six, of which twenty were the worse for repair ; Holland boasted forty-nine ; Portugal had six, and Naples four.[2] This array would appear very formidable and imposing, but the navies of Spain and Holland were in a condition of decay, both as regards seamen and actual material strength. There was also an appalling lack of morale in the French service. Mutiny was frequent; everything was in a deplorable state, men and ships, stores and administration. Money was lacking as well as provisions and clothing. Chaos reigned supreme, the wages

[1] *The Influence of Sea Power upon the French Revolution and Empire*, Vol. I, p. 75, by Captain A. T. Mahan, u.s.n.   [2] *Ibid.*, p. 78.

of systematic neglect. The mad frenzy of the people for equality had removed many of the best officers, and the opinion of the ordinary seaman carried almost as much weight as that of the commander. The dry rot which set in was not entirely eradicated under the influence of Napoleon, and for years the French navy continued to pay the price of a purely theoretical belief that patriotism was the alpha and omega of statesmanship.

The defeat of the fearless Royalist peasants of La Vendée at Savenay[1] encouraged the Convention to an expedition against the Channel Islands, but the smoking flax of civil war was not quenched, and soon broke into flame again. English squadrons also appeared off the coasts and a small engagement took place near Havre. It remained for General Hoche,[2] Bonaparte's most formidable rival, to propose and organize a definite and infinitely more comprehensive plan of action. This was in 1796, by which time the Batavian Republic[3] [Holland], Prussia, Sweden, and Spain had come to terms with France, to be followed in October by Naples; Pitt had also made overtures for peace, but without success. Three years before, Hoche had approached the Committee of Public Safety with an offer to carry over an army to England in trading vessels.

[1] December 23rd, 1793.

[2] Hoche, Lazare (1768-97), the son of the keeper of the royal staghounds at Montreuil. Having successfully pacified La Vendée and Brittany, and proved successful at Quiberon, he was appointed to the command of the expedition against Ireland (see *post*, p. 7) which left Brest on December 15th, 1796. His victories over the Austrians in the spring of the following year were only arrested by the peace of Leoben (April 19th, 1797). Five months later he died at the age of twenty-nine.

[3] On the conquest of the United Provinces by France in 1795, the Stadholder took refuge in England, and the country was constituted the Batavian Republic. The States-General at once formed a close alliance with France.

"I want neither place nor rank! I'll be the first to tread the soil of these political brigands!"[1]   In this later and saner effort the protection of the coasts by means of gunboats constantly cruising to and fro was to be his first care, followed by an attack on Jersey and Guernsey, and a *chouannerie* carried on in England. Hoche's attention was again diverted, and it was not until he had earned for himself the title of "the peacemaker of La Vendée" that he was able to give further attention to the matter. By this time General Humbert[2] had taken up the cause of Irish independence, which Hoche supported enthusiastically. They went apace with the preparations. Six small vessels and a similar number of transports were placed at their disposal, and arms were provided for several hundred jail birds whom they proposed to release from the prison at Brest. An "independent legion" of fifteen hundred men was also recruited, but at the last moment the newly elected Directory cancelled everything, and turned a more willing ear to the proposal of Lieutenant Muskeyn, whose experience in the navigation and strategy of small craft such as might be of service in crossing the Channel was considerable. By birth a Fleming, he had seen service as naval lieutenant with the Swedes in their war against the Russians.[3] He repaired to Dunkirk and set about forming a flotilla. Yarmouth and Newcastle were to be the objec-

---

[1] Desbrière, I, p. 31.

[2] Jean Joseph Amable Humbert (*b.* 1767) was the son of a small farmer. He became a volunteer at the outbreak of the French Revolution, and eventually secured the command of his regiment. He was appointed General of Brigade in 1794. After considerable experience in La Vendée he became senior officer of the "Legion of France" which sailed with Hoche in the Bantry Bay Expedition of 1796. — See *Studies in Irish History and Biography*, pp. 257–8, by C. Litton Falkiner.

[3] Desbrière, I, p. 71.

tives in this new plan, with the Humber[1] as an alternative should it be more easy of access. Beginning with some likelihood of success so far as actually leaving port was concerned, it gradually dropped out like the rest. Twenty-two gunboats were built, and eight troopships secured for the transport of five thousand infantry, but so great was the repugnance of the soldiers to the voyage in small boats that in two days no fewer than six hundred men deserted. An attempt to get under weigh was certainly made, but in such unpropitious weather that one of the vessels sank in sight of the shore.

His rival's preparations having ended so ignominiously, Hoche again came forward, and was able to enlist the sympathies of Truguet, the new Minister of Marine. On June 23rd, 1796, the General was informed by the Directory that it relied upon him to put the plans previously matured into execution. The despatch of a relief expedition to the Irish patriots was to be the signal for an armed rising by them, the arrangements being in the hands of the Society of United Irishmen, the leaders of which, having formed themselves into a Junta (Directory), had entered into negotiations for French assistance to enable the thousands of men they represented to cast off the English yoke.[2] The communication averred that the independence of Ireland would cause England to lose her naval supremacy, but it frankly admitted that the French

---

[1] "Rivers are difficult and dangerous for landing, because they can be easily defended, and the land is less open and gives scope for more batteries. The wind which brought a flotilla would also allow the defenders' squadron to sail up."—Dumouriez MS., p. 8.

[2] The Society of United Irishmen was formed at Belfast in 1791. The Junta consisted of five members, Lord Edward FitzGerald, O'Connor, Emmet, McNeven, and Bond.

Marine was still under a cloud, and three small expeditions only could be fitted out. A flotilla was to take five thousand picked men and land them on the coast of Connaught, if possible in Galway Bay, and then proceed at once to the East Indies. This force was to sail in six weeks, and ten thousand muskets were to be stowed away for the use of the Irish. By the 1st September, 1796, a second expedition was to be ready at Brest, with a complement of six thousand independent troops, including some ex-Chouans and a sprinkling of "undesirables"; while a third expedition from Holland, with a force of five thousand men, chiefly foreign deserters under French officers, was to augment the former.

So vague a method of warfare did not appeal to Hoche, who drew up a more business-like scheme after a conference with Wolfe Tone and E. J. Lewens, the accredited agents in Paris of the Irish Junta. Experiencing some discouragement, the General finally went to Brest and found the ships there in a disgraceful condition. Lorient was little better, and Admiral Villaret-Joyeuse, who had been appointed Naval Commander of the fleet, Hoche being in supreme authority, was forced to leave three ships out of five in that port when he wished to take them to Brest. Villaret-Joyeuse still looked upon the Irish part of the cruise as a mere episode, and prepared for a voyage to the East Indies, which Hoche most vigorously opposed, and he soon secured the Admiral's dismissal. He was succeeded by Admiral Morard de Galles, whose previous record would have fitted him well for the task had he not been both aged and infirm. Almost on the eve of departure the Directory decided that as a British squadron of fifteen sail-of-the-line under Admiral Colpoys was cruising in the Channel, it would be wise to make use of five ships which had recently returned to Rochefort from North America. These were brought to Brest under the command of Admiral Richery, but were in so rickety a condition that two only were found to be serviceable, and even these needed repairs. Villeneuve was expected with five ships from Toulon, and Spanish help was also anticipated, but neither was utilized.[1] The total military force under Hoche now consisted of some fourteen thousand men, forming a vanguard, a main body, a rearguard, and a supplementary body. With the vanguard sailed Admiral Bouvet in the frigate *Immortalité*, with Grouchy in military command, and included Richery's two ships. Hoche and Admiral Morard de Galles went with the main body in the frigate *Fraternité*. The rearguard was under Admiral Nielly. Seventeen sail-of-the-line, thirteen frigates, five corvettes, six transports, and two "flutes" comprised the French fleet—a notable armament had the crews been of full strength and the officers well trained.

The day before sailing Hoche issued a proclamation to his troops.[2] It contains less rodomontade than is to be found in the addresses of most Republican generals, but it is worthy of note that he had previously circulated "official" statements to the effect that his troops were destined for Portugal, copies of which were in the hands of the British authorities and put them off their guard. The following was printed at Pau, nearly two hundred miles from Brest.[3]

---

[1] Mahan, *Influence of Sea Power upon the French Revolution*, Vol. I, p. 348. By the Treaty of St. Ildefonso, signed on the 19th August, 1796, Spain concluded an offensive and defensive alliance with France. In the following October Spain declared war against Great Britain.

[2] *Popular Songs, Illustrative of the French Invasions of Ireland*, part iii, p. 13, edited by T. Crofton Croker (Percy Society, 1847). [3] *Ibid.*, p. 7.

" *To the French Army destined to Assist the Irish Revolution.*

" Republicans,

" Proud of having made you victorious on many occasions, I have obtained permission from Government to lead you to fresh successes.   To command you is to be assured of victory.

" Eager to give back liberty to a people worthy of it, and ripe for revolution, the Directory sends us to Ireland with the object of assisting the revolution that some excellent republicans have just undertaken.

" It will be a splendid task for us, who have conquered the myrmidons of the kings armed against the Republic, to break the fetters of a friendly nation, and to help it to recover the rights usurped by the odious English Government.

" You will never forget, brave and faithful companions, that the people amongst whom we are going are the friends of our country, that we must treat them as such, and not as a conquered people.

" On arriving in Ireland you will find hospitality and fraternity ; soon thousands of its inhabitants will come to increase our battalions.   Take good care then never to treat any of them as an enemy.   Like ourselves, they have to be avenged on the perfidious English ; the latter are those alone on whom we have to wreak a striking revenge. Be sure that the Irish sigh no less than you for the moment when, together, we shall march to London to recall to Pitt and to his friends what they have done against our liberty.

" By friendship, by duty, by the honour of the French name, you must respect the persons and the property of the country to which we are going.

"If by constant effort I provide for your needs, be sure that, jealous of preserving the reputation of the army which I have the honour to command, I will severely punish whoever neglects that which he owes to his country. Laurels and glory will be the portion of the Republican soldier; death will be the price of rapine and of pillage.

"You know me sufficiently to believe that, for the first time, I will not fail in keeping my word. I have duly warned you, fail not to remember.

"GENERAL HOCHE.

"BREST, the (blank in text) year of the Republic."

A start was made on the 15th December, 1796, and by the following day the ships were moving towards the open sea. Fate dealt unkindly with the expedition, which began and ended with disaster, for the *Fougueux* (74) and the *Indomptable* (80) collided, while the *Séduisant* (74) struck a reef and foundered. It would have been well if the orders cancelling the whole plan which the Directory had sent to Hoche had been delivered, but they arrived too late. The bad weather caused the various divisions to part company at the very outset, and they were never completely reunited. It was only by the merest luck that Bouvet, Richery, and Nielly came together on the 19th December. Hoche, with one sail-of-the-line and three frigates, on being informed that his scattered fleet had preceded him in getting away from Brest, crowded on all sail, and missed Bouvet's division owing to a dense fog. On the morning of the 21st, by which time his force had been reduced to one sail-of-the-line, the *Nestor*, and the

Fraternité, the Commander-in-Chief gazed on the Irish coast with eager eyes, and drew near to Bantry Bay. During the night the lights of numerous vessels were observed, which he surmised were British, whereas they belonged to his own missing fleet. A storm arose and played havoc with the frigate, and two days after the *Fraternité* had lost her consort. The *Romaine* came in sight for a short time later and disappeared. On the 28th Bouvet's *Immortalité* was reported, and on the following day Hoche knew that the expedition which he had planned with so much care had turned out a fiasco. Two ships remained to tell the tale, the *Scevola*, which was rapidly sinking, and the *Révolution*, which was engaged in rescuing the crew of the former, although she herself was in an almost disabled state owing to a collision.

Meanwhile the other admirals had arrived off the Irish coast on the 21st December with thirty-five sail.[1] Un-favourable weather again precluded them from keeping together, and on the 22nd Bouvet anchored at Bear Haven with eight sail-of-the-line and seven other vessels. The remainder were afterwards blown to sea.[2] The admiral and Grouchy held a council of war, the former being of opinion that a search should be made for Hoche ; but Grouchy, who as military commander-in-chief was supreme once the fleet was at anchor, gave orders that the 6500 troops under him should be landed at Bear Island,[3] and then altered his plans, making Bantry his objective. Bouvet, however, made not the slightest attempt to carry out the command, and Grouchy did not enforce it as he

---

[1] Mahan, Vol. I, p. 355. [2] *Ibid.*, 356.
[3] In Bantry Bay, thirteen miles west of Bantry. The remains of several martello towers, erected after Hoche's expedition, may still be seen.

ought to have done, for which negligence censure has been justly passed upon him. Bad weather again set in that night, and on Christmas Day Bouvet sought the open sea, whither Nielly and Richery followed him, and made for Brest. Bedout's vessels, on board of which were some four thousand men, still remained. Not until he and the military officers with him had discussed the situation, and decided that a landing would serve no useful purpose, did they set sail for Brest, which was reached on January 1st, 1797. The *Trajan* waited off the mouth of the Shannon in the hope of forming a junction with Hoche, and on her captain being told that the *Fraternité* had been seen off the Irish coast on December 26th, he made for Bantry Bay once more. On the 7th January the solitary vessel was sighted by two British sail-of-the-line and two frigates, and a thirty-six hours' chase began, the *Trajan* managing to effect an escape.[1] A division under Commodore Linois had left Bantry Bay the day before. On the 13th it reached home waters. Hoche landed at La Rochelle on the 14th.

Another solitary ship, the *Droits de l'Homme*, acquitted herself with honour, and the stubborn fight she made with Sir Edward Pellew's *Indefatigable* and the *Amazon*, both frigates, is the most noteworthy incident in Hoche's attempt to invade Ireland. The French ship did not set out on the homeward voyage till January 5th, and all went well until the 13th, when the Britishers came up with her. A fierce conflict ensued, which continued far into the night, heavy seas frequently dashing into the portholes and preventing the proper working of the guns. The men on both sides fought with the courage of desperation, and

[1] Desbrière, Vol. I, pp. 193-212.

the carnage on the *Droits de l'Homme* was terrible, partly
due to overcrowding.   At dawn both the *Amazon* and the
Frenchman ran aground in Audierne Bay, thirty-five miles
south of Brest,[1] and eventually became total wrecks.
Many willing peasants appeared on the beach, but were
helpless to lend their aid owing to the tempestuous
weather.   The waves broke over the ships, and many a
poor wretch found a watery grave.   There were a number
of English prisoners on board the *Droits de l'Homme,* and
on the second day nine of them lowered a boat and
reached the shore in safety.   Other attempts were made to
launch small craft and rafts, but they were all swamped.
Writes a British officer who was saved :—

"Weak, distracted, and wanting everything, we envied
the fate of those whose lifeless corpses no longer needed
sustenance.   The sense of hunger was already lost, but a
parching thirst consumed our vitals.   Recourse was had
to wine and salt water, which only increased the want.
Half a hogshead of vinegar floated up, and each had half
a wineglass full.   This gave a momentary relief, yet soon
left us again in the same state of dreadful thirst.   Almost
at the last gasp, every one was dying with misery; the ship,
which was now one-third shattered away from the stern,
scarcely afforded a grasp to hold by to the exhausted and
helpless survivors.   The fourth day brought with it a
more serene sky, and the sea seemed to subside; but to
behold from fore and aft the dying in all directions
was a sight too shocking for the feeling mind to endure.
Almost lost to a sense of humanity, we no longer looked
with pity on those who were the speedy forerunners of our
own fate, and a consultation took place to sacrifice some

[1] Mahan, Vol. I, p. 358.

End of the Irish Invasion:— or — The Destruction of the French Armada.

END OF THE FRENCH INVASION OF IRELAND IN 1797 AS DEPICTED BY GILLRAY

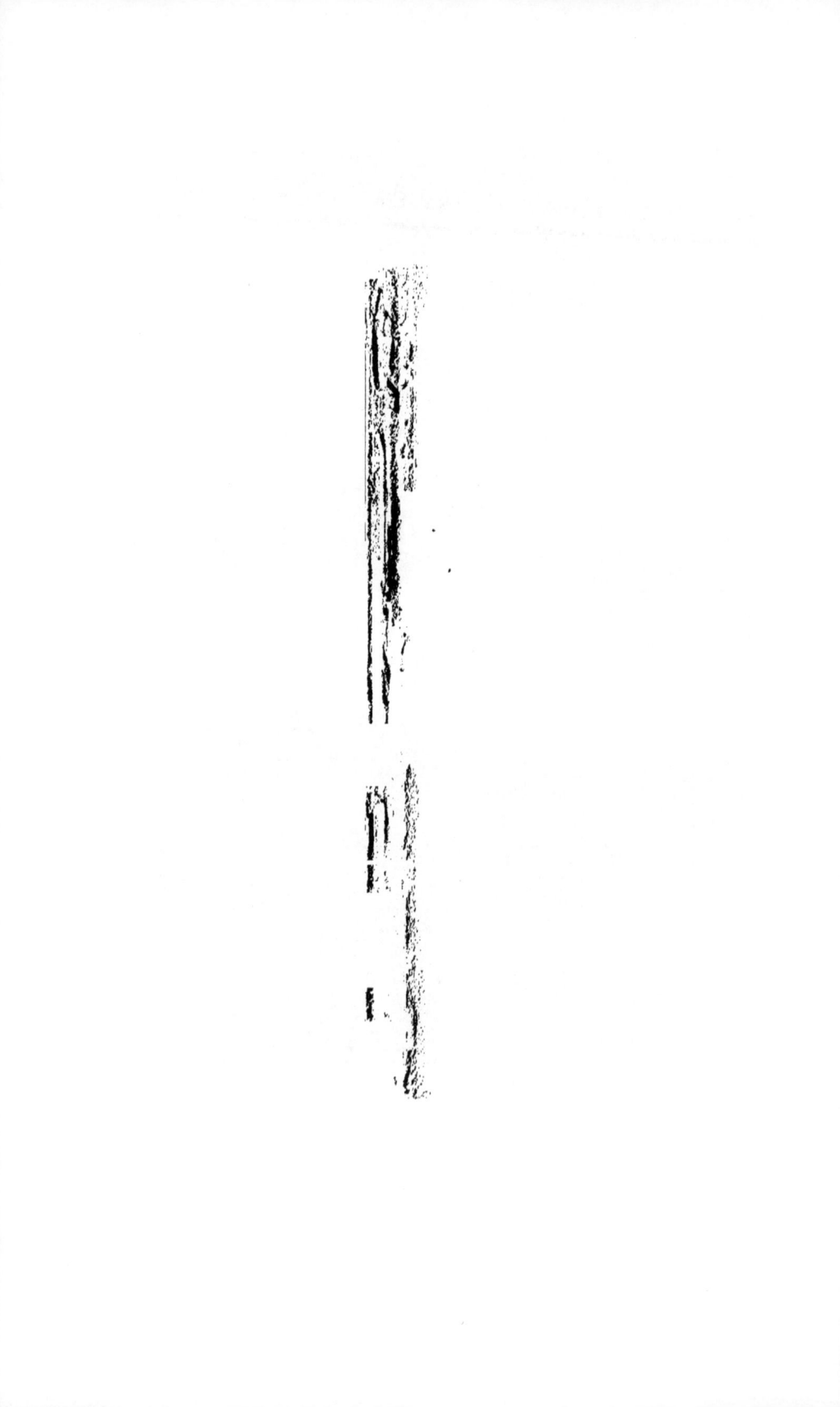

one to be food for the remainder. The die was going to be cast, when the welcome sight of a man-of-war brig renewed our hopes. A cutter speedily followed, and both anchored at a short distance from the wreck. They then sent their boats to us, and, by means of large rafts, about 150, of nearly 400 who attempted it, were saved by the brig that evening; 380 were left to endure another night's misery, when, dreadful to relate, above one-half were found dead next morning."[1] The British losses amounted to three killed and thirty-four wounded. The crew of the doomed *Amazon*, with the exception of six men who attempted to get to shore in the ship's cutter, were saved and made prisoners. Of the 1750 men on board the *Droits de l'Homme* probably only a comparatively small proportion survived both the fight and the wreck, but as to this records are silent.[2] Suffice to say that General Humbert effected his escape, and lived to command a similar expedition a little later.[3]

It has been repeated again and again that an "act of God" alone prevented the invasion of Ireland in the winter of 1796. The weather was certainly against the French part of the time, but Grouchy's dilatoriness was as conspicuous at Bantry as it was at Waterloo, and must be taken into account. Napoleon gave it as his opinion that had Hoche been able to land his "fine army" he would have been successful.[4]

Where was the main British fleet all this time, while the fate of Ireland trembled in the balance? The fifteen sail-

---

[1] James's *Naval History*, p. 81. Epitomized by Robert O'Byrne, f.r.g.s.
[2] *Ibid.*, pp. 81-2.   [3] See *post*, p. 140.
[4] Creasy's *Invasions of England*, Vol. II, p. 209. Dumouriez says that had Admiral Bouvet sacrificed his ships and General Hoche not been parted from his army by a storm, the expedition would not have failed.—MS., p. 267.

of-the-line under Admiral Colpoys, which usually cruised off Brest, had been blown thirty miles to the westward, and two or three frigates under Sir Edward Pellew alone remained to watch the enemy. Colpoys was not aware that the expedition had sailed until the day after the majority of the ships had reached the mouth of Bantry Bay, and then he made for Spithead. The fleet at Portsmouth under Lord Bridport, which was " at home to relieve the fleet off Brest, if necessary, or to pursue the enemy, if he should sail,"[1] got under weigh when nearly all the scattered units of the French fleet were on their homeward voyage. This unsatisfactory method of watching an enemy contrasts strongly with Lord St. Vincent's (formerly Sir John Jervis) later injunction to "hermetically seal up" the French fleets in their harbours. Blockade duty at this time was almost entirely entrusted to a few ships, and occasionally to frigates only; there was seldom a squadron before Brest in winter.[2]

As to what would have happened had Hoche landed in Ireland can only be surmised, but that Earl Camden, the Lord Lieutenant, was satisfied with the precautions taken is shown in his letter to the Duke of Portland, dated January 10th, 1797. " I have the satisfaction to reflect that the best spirit was manifested by His Majesty's regular and militia forces ; and I have every reason to believe that, if a landing had taken place, they would have displayed the utmost fidelity." The regiments trudged many weary miles in the snow, which was cleared away in some parts by the peasantry so as not to hinder the march. " In the

---

[1] Speech by Dundas in House of Commons, 3rd March, 1797 ; *Parliamentary History*, Vol. XXXIII, p. 12.

[2] *The Great Campaigns of Nelson*, p. 19, by William O'Connor Morris.

town of Galway, which for a short time was left with a very inadequate garrison, the zeal and ardour of the inhabitants and yeomanry was peculiarly manifested, and in a manner to give me the utmost satisfaction. In short, the general good disposition of the people through the south and west was so prevalent that, had the enemy landed, their hope of assistance from the inhabitants would have been totally disappointed. From the armed yeomanry Government derived the most honourable assistance. . . . The merchants of Dublin, many of them of the first eminence, marched sixteen Irish miles with a convoy of arms to the north, whither it was conducted by reliefs of yeomanry. The appearance in this metropolis has been highly meritorious. The corps have been formed of the most respectable barristers, attorneys, merchants, gentlemen, and citizens; and their number is so considerable, and their zeal in mounting guard so useful, that I was enabled greatly to reduce the garrison with perfect safety to the town. The number of yeomanry fully appointed and disciplined, in Dublin, exceed 2000, above 400 of whom are horse. The whole number of corps approved by Government amount to 440, exclusive of the Dublin corps. The gross number is nearly 25,000." [1]

The narrative of the Bantry Bay invasion has been handed down in song and story, and the following verse records in rhyme what the latter part of the above despatch conveys in prose :—

TUNE.—*Joy and health to the Duchess wherever she goes.*

All ranks, all professions, shall greatly unite,
    The lawyer, the student, the farmer, the trader,
In one armed host for their country to fight,
    Their rights to preserve and repel the invader :

[1] *London Gazette*, January 17th, 1797.

By this valiant band
Protected we'll stand,
Long as the sea round the shores of Ireland shall flow ;
To them let us raise
The due tribute of praise,
Success to our yeomen wherever they go.[1]

No less interesting is the effort of another minor poet, which also supports the view that the Irish were not afraid that the French might land, but rather that they would fail to do so :—

TUNE.—*Lilliburlero.*

Oh ! brother soldier, hear you the news,
    Twang 'em, we'll bang 'em, and hang 'em up all ;
An army's arrived without breeches or shoes,
    Twang 'em, we'll bang 'em, and hang 'em up all.

            To arms, to arms !
            Brave boys, to arms !

    .   .   .   .   .   .

The French to invade us prepared a great fleet,
    Twang 'em, etc.
And now since they're come, we shall very soon meet.
    Twang 'em, etc.

            To arms, to arms ! etc.

They come the true cause, they say, to advance,
    Twang 'em, etc.
But what is more rare they bring freedom from France,
    Twang 'em, etc.

            To arms, to arms ! etc.[2]

    .   .   .   .   .   .

A ballad of sixteen verses, entitled, " The Invasion," [3]

[1] *Popular Songs, illustrative of the French Invasions of Ireland,* part iii, p. 65.   [2] *Ibid.,* part iii, p. 60.
[3] *Ibid.,* part iii, p. 47.   " This ballad, which was probably first printed in a newspaper of the time, appears in *A Collection of Constitutional Songs,* Vol. I, p. 80, published by A. Edwards, Cork, 1799, and is entitled ' The Invasion ' (written in January, 1797)."

calls to task the British admirals for not having annihilated the French fleet :—

> Nor skill nor courage aught avail
>   Against high Heaven's decrees,
> The storm arose and closed our ports,
>   A mist o'erspread the seas.
>
> For not to feeble, mortal man
>   Did God His vengeance trust ;
> He raised His own tremendous arm,
>   All powerful as all just.
>
> Now fair and strong the south-east blew,
>   And high the billows rose ;
> The French fleet bounded o'er the main,
>   Freighted with Erin's foes.
>
> Oh ! where was Hood, and where was Howe,
>   And where Cornwallis then ;
> Where Colpoys, Bridport, or Pellew,
>   And all their gallant men?

Several other effusions contain references to the same effect, as witness the following from the pen of O'Kelly, whose name is immortalized by Lockhart in his *Life of Sir Walter Scott*. The lesser light paid a personal visit to the author of *Marmion* when the great Scottish writer was in Ireland in 1825. The poem appears to have been founded on one entitled "General Wonder in our Land." [1] O'Kelly's rhyme runs thus :—

> While Admiral Bridport lay at rest,
>   And Colpoys everywhere was peeping,
> Admiral de Galle stole from Brest,
>   And thought to catch the Irish sleeping.
>
> But a rare Admiral, General Gale,
>   Oh may the gods give him a blessing !
> Appeared in time with crowded sail,
>   And gave to frog-eaters a dressing.

[1] *Ibid.*, part iii, p. 70.

Then here's a health to General Gale,
And to Momonia's friends another,
Oh may their union never fail
Invading foes to blast and smother.

Although the French had escaped so lightly in the
Bantry Bay expedition, British admirals had acquitted
themselves with honour from the beginning of the war.
In 1793 Hood burnt part of the Toulon fleet, but had to
evacuate the harbour through the skill of Napoleon
Bonaparte, then a young captain of artillery.　Howe
struck a more decisive blow on "the glorious first of June,"
1794, when seven ships of the French fleet, commanded
by Villaret-Joyeuse, lowered their colours, six being taken
as prizes.　The following year Admiral Hotham prevented the enemy from retaking Corsica[1] and captured two
of their ships, while Lord Bridport defeated the Brest
fleet and secured three sail-of-the-line.　On St. Valentine's
Day, 1797, Jervis defeated the Spanish fleet, which was to
have formed a junction with those of France and Holland
for the purpose of taking over a large army to England.
The victory was a signal proof of the skill of the British
admiral, whose efforts were ably seconded by Nelson.
His armament consisted of fifteen sail-of-the-line against
the enemy's twenty-five.

Not satisfied with the severe rebuffs which the French
navy had so recently experienced, and perhaps encouraged
by the fact that Austria, England's last ally, had recently
signed a preliminary treaty of peace at Leoben,[2] thanks to
Bonaparte's overwhelming victories, Truguet, the Minister

---

[1] Corsica had become a British possession in 1793, but was evacuated in
October, 1796.　The French immediately took possession of the island.
[2] April 18th, 1797.

of Marine, outlined in a letter to Hoche, dated 21st June, 1797, the chief features of a plan of campaign for another attempt on Ireland. The Directory had decided to send six thousand Republican soldiers to Holland under General Humbert, who, it will be remembered, had taken part in the Bantry Bay fiasco, to swell the Dutch force of fifteen thousand men which had been held ready for some time by General Daendels. The Batavian Government was so anxious to throw herself against her former ally that it even offered to guarantee the courage of the troops.[1] Admiral de Winter's squadron of sixteen sail-of-the-line and twelve frigates then lying in the Texel was to take over the twenty-one thousand troops thus concentrated and land them in the north of Ireland. At the same time a fleet of twelve men-of-war and several frigates was to leave Brest with from six to eight thousand men, under the undaunted Hoche, and make for the south or west coast. The services of Wolfe Tone and Lewens were again requisitioned, and the "peacemaker of La Vendée" set off for the Hague to make final arrangements. Contrary to Truguet's instructions, he proposed to abandon his part in the project and join the Dutch expedition. The proffered help was refused, but Wolfe Tone managed to curry favour and was accepted. Before the Dutch put to sea, Hoche, after serving for a short time as French Minister of Marine in succession to Truguet, was a dead man.[2] Had De Winter sailed during the early months of 1797, when the mutiny of the sailors at the Nore and elsewhere[3] occupied the attention of Great Britain, success might have been

---

[1] Desbrière, Vol. I, p. 258.
[2] Hoche died on September 19th, 1797.
[3] April–June, 1797.

his. The chance offered by the naval troubles in England
was unaccountably missed. De Winter still clung to
the Texel, although General Daendels urged upon him
the necessity for immediate action, even if he were compelled to fight Duncan, the British admiral, who was
waiting for him to come out. He thought the Firth of
Forth favourable for landing, and after Edinburgh and
Glasgow had capitulated the troops would embark on
the ships, which by that time would have rounded the
north of Scotland, and sail for Ireland. With his dying
breath Hoche dissuaded Daendels from so grandiose a
plan of campaign, but it is significant that shortly before
the following letter had appeared in one of the official or
semi-official provocative pamphlets widely circulated in
Paris :—

"Courageous Citizens,

"England is the richest country in the world—and
we give it up to you to be plundered. You shall march to
the capital of that haughty nation. You shall plunder
their National Bank of its immense heaps of Gold. You
shall seize upon all public and private property—upon
their warehouses—their magazines—their stately mansions
—and gilded palaces ; and you shall return to your own
country loaded with the spoils of the enemy. This is the
only method left to bring them to our terms. When they
are humbled, then we shall dictate what terms we think
proper, and they must accept them.

"Behold what our brave army in Italy are doing.—
They are enriched with the plunder of that fine country ;
and they will be more so, when Rome bestows, what, if she
does not, will be taken by force. Your country, brave
Citizens, will not demand a particle of the riches you shall

CARICATURE OF THE FRENCH INVASION PROJECTS AGAINST IRELAND. BY J. GILLRAY.

[1797]

bring from Great Britain. Take what you please—it shall be all your own. Arms and ammunition you shall have, and vessels to carry you over. Once landed, you will soon find your way to London.

"HOCHE."

On the 10th October, 1797, the Dutch fleet weighed anchor and received so severe a handling off Camperdown at the hands of Admiral Duncan, who took nine ships out of a possible fifteen,[1] that the Irish expedition had of necessity to be abandoned. Pitt, whose hand had been forced to go to war with France, was now the only one maintaining it, but there could be no turning back. It was well for Great Britain that she was supreme on the sea, that her floating bulwarks still protected her coasts, otherwise she must assuredly have perished. In maritime measures alone, so far as Europe was concerned, were her efforts attended with success; but France found that in colonial conquest her antagonist had lost none of her prowess, for Tobago, Martinique, St. Lucia, and Grenada were captured one by one, as well as the Dutch possessions of Ceylon, Malacca, Cochin, and the Cape of Good Hope. The Spanish island of Trinidad also capitulated. The British army in Holland, under the Duke of York, met with nothing but disaster and retreat, although it served as a subsidiary defence of the British Isles, and the military measures taken for the protection of the kingdom itself cannot be regarded as adequate in the serious situation in which England was placed.

At the end of 1792 the militia was embodied, the statutory quota for England and Wales standing at

---

[1] Mahan, Vol. I, p. 255. The battle was fought on the 11th October.

30,740, to be raised by ballot.[1] The regular army at home consisted of not more than 15,000 troops,[2] exclusive of the Irish establishment,[3] but the estimates for 1793 allowed for 17,344 regulars and 17,602 militia and fencibles in Great Britain, and 12,000 in Ireland, including fencibles. The latter were regular troops which enlisted to serve during the war only, and exclusively for home service. Scotland having no militia, was called upon to supply fencibles.

A very wise precaution was taken. In order to defeat any ulterior motives of foreigners arriving in England an Alien Act was passed on January 8th, 1793, before war had been formally declared, whereby travellers from the Continent wishing to land at any British port had to give an account of themselves in writing and obtain a certificate before being allowed to step on shore. Passports were also necessary if they required to move from town to town. It was during a discussion on this Bill in its earlier stages[4] that Burke, whose *Reflections on the Revolution in France* did so much to stir up the national spirit, flung down a dagger, one of three thousand manufactured at Birmingham, as "a sample of the fruits to be obtained by an alliance with France." Republican and Corresponding societies were numerous, for revolutionary principles were by no means confined to the country which openly avowed them. As a consequence the Habeas

---

[1] *Military Forces of the Crown*, Vol. I, p. 283, by Charles M. Clode, ed. Murray, 1869.

[2] *A History of the British Army*, Vol. IV, part i, p. 77, by the Hon. J. W. Fortescue.

[3] Until the Union in 1800 there was both a British and Irish establishment, each of which was kept quite distinct.

[4] Lord Grenville introduced the Bill on the 19th December, 1792.

PITT ARMING JOHN BULL. [A PROPHETIC CARICATURE OF AUGUST, 1790]

Corpus Act was suspended, and the Irish military establishment was largely increased. On the 5th February, 1794, Pitt stated that "the interior strength of the kingdom consisted of 140,000 effective men, and that of the navy near 90,000 ; the artillery had been placed on a footing of great improvement, and amounted to near 6000 ; the foreign troops in our pay were almost 40,000 ; constituting altogether a force of little short of 276,000 men, in the best condition and discipline."[1] A month later a motion was put before Parliament by the same minister for an augmentation of the militia " in order to provide for the better security of the kingdom against a menaced invasion by the French." A levy of horse and foot volunteers in every county, and by private persons, was proposed, the expenses to be met by public subscriptions in the case of the former until estimates could be prepared. Several counties strongly opposed this system of payment, which was declared by those who resented it as "unconstitutional." However, an Act was passed on April 17th, 1794, "for encouraging and disciplining such troops, or companies of men, as shall voluntarily enrol themselves for the defence of their counties, towns, or coasts, or for the general defence of the kingdom during the present war."[2] The command of the local reserve forces was, of course, vested in the Lord Lieutenant of each county.

From henceforth drills, parades, and reviews became frequent all over the country, and Hyde Park was the scene of many a gathering of loyal citizens in warlike array. The premier corps of the metropolis, and the most exclusive, was the Loyal London and Middlesex Light Horse

---

[1] *Annual Register*, 1794, p. 210.
[2] *Ibid.*, 1794, Appendix to the Chronicle, p. 135.

Volunteers, a body which numbered amongst its one hundred and fifty men the scions of several noble families, including the Duke of Montrose, who served in it as a trooper. It had been formed so far back as 1779, but it was disbanded in 1783, and existed in name only until it was again called into being by the Act mentioned above.[1] As time went on and corps became more numerous, it was found necessary to consolidate some of the smaller of them. The Islington Volunteer Cavalry was therefore merged in the L.L. and M.L.H.V., and riflemen and horse artillery found a place in the regiment.

According to the statement put before the House on the 23rd February, 1795, "the service necessary for the guards and garrisons of the kingdom was 120,000 regulars, 56,000 militia, 40,000 for Ireland and the colonies, exclusive of fencibles and volunteers, of foreign troops in British pay, and of embodied French emigrants."[2] The following year (1796) the first serious attempt to cope with the military requirements of the nation at home was made. Not only was a supplementary militia of 63,878 men to be enrolled by ballot and trained for service at the slightest notice, but 20,000 men were to be added to the irregular cavalry. Pitt therefore proposed that "every person who kept ten horses should be obliged to provide one horse and one horseman to serve in a corps of militia ; that those who kept more than ten should

---

[1] The oldest volunteer corps was, and still is, the Honourable Artillery Company, formed in 1537. The interesting proposal of the "Dovor Association" in 1792 will be found in the Appendix.

[2] *Annual Register*, 1795, p. 177. Fortescue draws attention to the fact that in February, 1795, the entire armed force of England and Scotland was in reality 65,500 men only.—See *History of the British Army*, Vol. IV, part i, pp. 406-7.

provide in the same proportion; and that those who kept fewer than ten should form themselves into classes, in which it should be decided by ballot who, at the common expense, should provide the horse and the horseman. These troops were to be furnished with a uniform and accoutrements, formed into corps, and put under proper officers."[1] Pitt also suggested that gamekeepers and other holders of licences to shoot game should be included. A desperate onslaught against the latter proposition was made by Sheridan and others, which was withdrawn, but after some alterations the other measures became laws in December, 1796.[2] In the following July (1797) an Act was passed authorizing the formation of a militia in Scotland. The ballot was dispensed with in those places where volunteers offered their services in sufficient numbers. At first the service was extremely unpopular, and 3,000 regulars from England were sent over the border to enforce order, but the discontent was short-lived, and very soon patriotism reigned supreme.

It remained for Mr. William Clavell, High Sheriff of Dorset, to put into operation the ancient prerogative of raising the *Posse Comitatûs*. He had little or no information as to the exact purport of this old-time measure of King Alfred's, but the right to call out the civil force of the county was vested in the Sheriff by common law. Mr. Clavell succeeded in organizing the men of Dorset in so efficient a manner that in 1798 and 1803 important Acts were framed upon his efforts.[3] He issued a precept to the justices of the peace ordering them to compile lists, with the assistance of "constables and other police

---

[1] *Annual Register*, 1797, p. 120.   [2] *Ibid.*, p. 126.
[3] 38 Geo. III, c. 27 (1798), and 43 Geo. III, c. 55 (1803).

officers," of all persons between the ages of fifteen and
sixty years capable of bearing arms. Those already acting
in some military capacity, clergymen, and others engaged
in any sacred calling, Quakers, and invalids were alone
excepted. An office was established at the King's Arms,
Dorchester,[1] for the transaction of business, "and where
proper assistants will attend, and persons and horses be
ready to be sent express when requisite." From the names
returned the men were divided into regiments of about a
hundred, out of which five petty commanders were chosen,
who were responsible to the chief commander of the
body for twenty or more men. Those who did not
possess firearms were supplied with pikes some eight feet
long. Intense rivalry, usually of a friendly nature, existed
between these petty officers, and each little band of twenty
strove hard for the blue ribbon of the company. The
market cross or parish churchyard was often the place of
assembly.

Returns were also made of all persons owning vehicles
and horses, so that there might be no difficulty in arranging
for the removal of cattle, fodder, corn, or foodstuffs useful
to the enemy, as well as for conveying soldiers and munitions of war. Directors of stock were appointed, each
one being supplied with a complete list of vehicles in the
vicinity and where they were to be found. Fifty waggons
and sixty men comprised a director's full complement.
As in the case of the commanders of armed men, sub-
directors were duly appointed and held responsible for

---

[1] This ancient hostelry, sketched by Rowlandson during the invasion
days, still exists. His spirited picture has been reproduced in *The Three
Dorset Captains at Trafalgar*, p. 56, in connection with Lord Nelson's stay
there.

THE POSSE COMITATÛS TO RESIST INVASION, 1782

ten waggons and their respective drivers, and definite head-quarters were specified. On the removal of stock receipts were to be given "to the proprietors of each article so deposited, assuring them that they will be indemnified by Government for the actual loss which shall be sustained by its removal," and the same rule obtained with those who lent horses and vehicles. Smiths, carpenters, and wheelwrights were enlisted as pioneers, expert horsemen as messengers and guides, while boys were to assist in the removal of women and children, in which the clergy would also lend their aid.[1]

A letter was sent to every officiating clergyman in Dorset, enclosing particulars of the method of organization. "In case the intention should be misunderstood," it ran, "and alarms and jealousies raised, you will have it in your power to explain the plan, and reconcile such persons to that which is so much for the good of every individual, and so essential to the prosperity, and even the safety of the county."[2] In this way the peaceful farmer, the village cobbler, the clerk, the money-making merchant, even the schoolboy, were turned into soldiers. An enemy, bold, brave, and determined, stood on the threshold, but before the door was a Briton equally brave, equally bold, and equally determined. It would

---

[1] In 1796 two Mr. Welds joined the Purbeck troop of Dorset Cavalry Volunteers: Thomas Weld as captain, and Thomas Weld, junior, as cornet. The latter, who was born on the 22nd January, 1773, married Lucy, daughter of the Hon. Thomas Clifford, and had an only child, Mary Lucy, who became the wife of Hugh Charles, Lord Clifford of Chudleigh. Thomas Weld, junior, succeeded to Lulworth Castle on the death of his father, 1810, and on the death of his wife he entered Holy Orders and became Bishop and Cardinal in 1829. He was the first Englishman to have a seat in the Conclave since the Pontificate of Clement IX. He died 10th April, 1837, aged sixty-four. [2] Dated May 1st, 1797.

have been well had every county been so efficiently prepared.[1]

The great volunteer movement, which began to trans-
form the face of the country and make England for some
years a vast camp, will be spoken of in greater detail in
another chapter. Meanwhile it is essential to give a somewhat detailed account of the descent of Tate's " Black
Legion," acting under Hoche's instructions, on the Welsh
coast. Of all the plans and schemes of our adversaries
during the Great Terror, this was certainly the most extraordinary, both as regards its conception and execution.
Its story is now told to a very great extent on the
authority of hitherto unpublished documents.

---

[1] In the Dorchester Museum may be seen a series of maps showing the
county as practically subdivided in accordance with Mr. Clavell's plan
of defence. These maps give in minute detail the working out of the High
Sheriff's popular plan of a general defence of the county.

CHAPTER II

A THREE DAYS' WAR—THE INVASION OF WALES BY
HOCHE'S BLACK LEGION UNDER COLONEL TATE,
FEBRUARY 22ND, 23RD AND 24TH, 1797.

> O Never shall a foreign foe,
>   Isle of the Brave ! thy Rights destroy ;
> Tho' men should meditate the blow,
>   And fiends their damned arts employ.
>   *" The War Whoop of Victory."*
>   *Patriotic Song of the Great Terror.*

"ON the 18th February, *Bantry Bay*, a Musical Piece of one act, was performed for the first time at Covent Garden. The title of this piece sufficiently indicates the subject and situation of the scene; it is a slight effort, well timed, well intended, and well executed, to create a laugh at the spirited conduct of the boys of Bantry Bay, when the French fleet lately made its appearance in the seas nearest the southern coasts of Ireland; on which occasion it is notorious that the peasantry in that part of the sister kingdom displayed infinite loyalty and zeal, which the author has exhibited on the Stage, seasoned with some of the strong but simple humour that forms the marking features in the characters of the lower order of the Irish. It is said to be the first dramatic production of a Gentleman whose name is Reynolds. The Music is selected and composed by Mr. Reeves."

31

The light-hearted chronicler of the *European Magazine*
was probably unaware that before another week had
passed by the public spirit of England was to be shocked
by the simultaneous occurrence of the mutiny at Sheerness and the piratical attempt—"a singular expedition of
jail birds," Captain Desbrière calls it—of Colonel Tate and
his followers to wage war on the unoffending peasantry
of Pembrokeshire. Nine days later (February 27th)
all was over, and we learn under the heading of Parliamentary Intelligence, that on that evening "a Member
rose to call the attention of the House to the late
attempt of the French upon Wales. He said, that he
saw something exceedingly portentous in the manner
in which the enemy had effected a descent upon the coast
of Wales with 1400 men with arms, but without tents or
field-pieces. It was a matter very extraordinary, that such
a number of men should land, form themselves into a
body upon a hill; and, without showing any disposition
to oppose the people, or the force that had marched
against them, surrender themselves at discretion. Fourteen hundred men, with arms in their hands, could un-
questionably have done something; but from their
conduct, it appeared clear to him that they had been
landed for no other purpose than that of being made
prisoners. Under this consideration, he could not help
sounding an alarm to the country; and, as he did not
know how to act upon the occasion, he begged to be
informed what measure was most proper to be adopted
upon the occasion, and what Motion it would be right for
him to propose to the House.

" The Speaker informed him, that it remained for him
to propose some Motion to the House, in the form of an

Address to his Majesty, or in any other manner that his discretion might suggest.

"He then moved an humble Address, but no person seconded it, and the Motion fell to the ground."[1]

The natural sequel to the French disasters in Bantry Bay was the melodrama enacted with an abundance of "comic relief" at that portion of the Welsh coast in the vicinity of Fishguard[2] variously known as Carregwastad, Carrig Gwastad, and Carn Gwastad. The contriver of these two equally futile efforts, to give effect to the popular refrain of the Paris mob—

> Mettons fin à l'ambition
> De tous les rois tyrans du monde,
> De ces pirates d'Albion,
> Qui prétendoient regner sur l'onde :   (*bis*)
> Nous avons tout ce qu'ils n'ont pas,
> Nous avons le cœur & les bras
> D'hommes libres & faits pour l'être ;
> Nous avons du fer, des soldats,
> Ce qu'il nous faut (*bis*) c'est du salpêtre   (*bis*)—

was Lazare Hoche,[3] upon whom the shadow of an untimely death had already fallen.[4] Possibly he failed to appreciate the ludicrous side of the incident which his perverted ingenuity and frank hatred of England had provided for the dual prologue to the Great Terror, which contrasts so strikingly with the grim tragedy of its epilogue, to be enacted eight years later off Cape Trafalgar.

---

[1] *European Magazine*, Vol. XXXI, p. 205.

[2] In 1797, and for a whole century afterwards, an obscure but picturesque Welsh fishing town, but now widely known to all travellers as the starting-point of the splendid turbine steamers of the Great Western Railway, which ply between the Pembrokeshire coast and that of Wexford, and in all human probability one of our great English ports in the near future.

[3] See *ante*, p. 5, note.   [4] See *ante*, p. 21.

Although the *Annual Register* for 1797 disposes of the invasion of Wales in a dozen lines, the contemporary literature on the subject is far more abundant than one would imagine. While the events of that memorable February were still fresh in men's minds were published *A Brief Narrative of the French Invasion near Fishguard Bay*, by J. Baker, author of the *Picturesque Guide through Wales and the Marches* (Worcester, 1797), another pamphlet on the same subject printed for J. Wright, 169 Piccadilly, London (1798), *Some Account of the Proceedings that took place on the Landing of the French near Fishguard on the 22nd February, 1797, and of the Enquiry afterwards held into Lieut.-Colonel Knox's conduct on that occasion*, etc., by Thomas Knox, late Lieut.-Colonel Commandant of the Fishguard Volunteers (London, 1801)[1] and one or two

---

[1] By a strange coincidence, the inhabitants of Fishguard and its immediate neighbourhood were amongst the first to join the volunteer movement of 1793. Colonel Knox claims for the Fishguard Fencibles the distinction of being the second oldest corps in the kingdom. In 1795 it consisted of four companies, with Thomas Knox, of Minwere Lodge, as Lieutenant-Colonel, 12 commissioned officers, 24 non-commissioned officers, 8 drummers, 4 fifers, and 235 rank and file. There was a Newport as well as a Fishguard division. On the night of February 22nd Colonel Knox first heard of the presence of the French ships at a ball given by Mrs. Harries, of Tregwynt. Fishguard, moreover, was defended by a fort to which "three invalid bombardiers had been sent down in 1795 to instruct the volunteers in the exercise of the great guns." From the moment the Colonel became aware of what was happening he displayed a commendable amount of energy ; but the fort did nothing more than fire one gun "in salute" while Tate was flying the Union Jack, and the Colonel deemed it prudent that his fencibles should retire in the direction of Haverfordwest. Lord Cawdor assumed the command, with the approval of Lord Milford, and a good deal of ill-feeling ensued. Colonel Knox was accused of showing the white feather, and although acquitted of all blame, was requested to resign. Both he and his father, Mr. William Knox, strongly insisted on a further official inquiry. On the 23rd May he sent a challenge to Lord Cawdor, who had addressed him a somewhat acrimonious letter, and the latter agreed to meet him at noon on the following day "upon the turnpike road, between Pembroke Ferry and the road that

other tracts, including a narrative by Mr. Williams, of Crachenllwyd, near St. David's, the farmer who sent his servant to give the alarm. These were supplemented in 1842 by the printing by Mr. Joseph Polter, of Haverford-west, of "An Authentic Account of the Invasion of the French Troops (under the command of General [*sic*] Tate) on Carrig Gwastad Point, near Fishguard, Wednesday, the 22nd day of February, 1797, and their Surrender to the Forces of His Britannic Majesty on Goodwick Sands, on Friday, the 24th of February; likewise some occurrences connected therewith, never before published." The writer was H. L. ap Gwilym, and he appends to his statement an attestation of correctness by two eye-witnesses, both Fishguard Fencible men, Peter Davies and Owen Griffith. Most of these early publications are to be found in the Cardiff Free Library, where several interesting engravings of the landing of Tate and his motley following are preserved.

There is one legend, however, connected with the Fish-guard romance which has held its own for many years, and will probably continue to do so for all time, although it is never even faintly alluded to in the first contemporary accounts. There is a charm about the story of Tate and his army of "undesirable aliens" mistaking the red cloaks of the Welshwomen, old and young, who lined the Fish-guard hills, for the uniforms of advancing battalions of soldiers, and that optical delusion very forcibly influencing

turns off to Williamston, with the gentleman who accompanies me." What ensued is not revealed, but Mr. Knox, senior, bitterly laments the abandon-ment of certain libel actions which put an end to the opportunity "of a full display of Mr. Erskine's eloquence, in developing and exposing the malignity of the charge, and in vindicating my son's conduct while commanding the Fishguard Volunteers."

their disposition to surrender, which is almost irresistible. It even commends itself to the practical and matter-of-fact mind of Captain Desbrière, who gives a laconic note on the subject, which would lose much of its unconscious humour by translation.[1] The last survivor of the alleged Amazons of 1797 only died in 1891, six years before the centenary celebration, which revived for a moment the interest felt in Lord Cawdor's bloodless victory. Nelly Phillips was 103 at the time of her death, and ninety and odd years before she was driving cows from a field at Kilshawe when she espied the French frigates in the offing.

It must be confessed, however, that the romance of Fishguard rests upon very questionable grounds, and is regarded as fiction by Mr. Edward Laws, a notable authority on the subject, who points out that the ballad-writer of the period would assuredly have utilized so promising and picturesque a theme if the occurrence had any shadow of foundation in fact.[2]

Much information about the Fishguard incident will be found in Mr. Laws's *Little England beyond Wales*, a standard history of one portion of Pembrokeshire,[3] and part of it has been cleverly utilized in the introduction to an entertaining book published under the double title of *The Fishguard Invasion by the French in 1797* and *The Fishguard Invasion, or Three Days in 1797*.[4] As might be

---

[1] " L'ouvrage cite" [*The Fishguard Invasion, or Three Days in* 1797], "et d'autres auteurs anglais signalent aussi la curieuse version d'après laquelle un rassemblement de femmes galloises venues pour assister au combat et couvertes du traditionnel châle rouge, aurait, de loin, été prises par Tate pour des troupes régulières anglaises. De la part de ce filibustier et de ses bandits, tout est possible."   [2] See *post*, pp. 66–71.

[3] *A History of Little England beyond Wales.* London : George Bell and Sons. 1888.   [4] London : T. Fisher Unwin. 1892.

expected, this proves a great stumbling-block to Captain Desbrière, who has become acquainted with its contents through the good offices of M. Charles Legras, of the *Journal des Débats*.[1] The anonymous writer devotes thirty-nine pages to a useful historical introduction, while the bulk of the volume is given up to the real or supposed diary of a Welsh divine, the name of whose benefice necessitates the use of nineteen letters in the spelling, and who deals largely with the love affairs of two Welsh maidens, Frances and Eleanor Martin, who ultimately become (mainly by the help of the Rev. Daniel Rowlands) Madame Lebrun and Madame Roux, by marrying two of the Tate jail-birds, whose escape, along with that of nearly five score of their fellow-prisoners, they very materially facilitate. With the thread of the fiction, or semi-fiction, is mixed up certain perfectly authentic documents, although no copy is given of the handbill said to have been placarded in every town in the kingdom offering five hundred guineas for the apprehension of the two delinquents.

The story of the Fishguard episode can be best told by giving in order the various documents connected both with its inception and execution, the existence of one portion of which was unknown in 1892, and also in 1900, when the first instalment of Captain Desbrière's book was published. In the introduction of *The Fishguard Invasion, or Three Days in 1797* copious quotations are given in French, presumably from Emile de Bonnechose's life of Lazare Hoche, with the apparent object of throwing light on the line of reasoning which led "the able originator of the invasion to advocate and justify methods

---

[1] *Projets et Tentatives de Débarquement aux Iles Brittanniques*, Vol. I, pp. 244-5.

which comprised the burning of defenceless towns, the laying waste of crops, and the wholesale destruction of life at the hands of *gens perdus, bandits et massacreurs.*" Hoche credited Carnot[1] with the first idea of organizing a *chouannerie* or system of guerilla warfare in England, for the purpose of giving the inhabitants freedom and inducing them to adopt a republican form of government. With this object in view, the invaders, recruited from the galleys and prisons, and promised full enjoyment of their booty, immunity from their crimes, and a remission of all past sentences, were to proclaim themselves the "avengers of liberty and enemies of tyrants." They were to swear destruction to the abodes of the wealthy, but protection to the cottage ; while, on the other hand, as they advanced they were to throw open the prisons and replenish their ranks by a fresh supply of indigenous malefactors. There was to be no quarter ; bridges should be broken down, roads destroyed, public conveyances pillaged, and naval stores burned as soon as captured. No plan was assuredly ever conceived more entirely calculated to defeat its own object.

On the 25th November, 1796, Hoche thus addresses the Directorate :—

" The American Colonel Tate in command of a thousand men should be landed on the coast of England somewhere in St. George's Channel. The men should have no other

---

[1] Carnot, Lazare Nicolas Marguerite (1753–1823). Between 1793 and 1797 (when he was proscribed and fled to Germany) the " organizer of victory " was mainly responsible for the conduct of French military affairs, and his genius was doubtless largely responsible for the successes which marked the early wars of the Republic. Proscribed by Louis XVIII after Waterloo, he settled at Magdeburg, where he died. His grandson Sadi Carnot became President of the French Republic.

provisions than two hundred cartridges, and the two or three boats conveying them should then take up such a position in the Dublin roads as to be able to intercept any vessel attempting to leave them."

Next day an order was given that the vessels required should be provided at Lorient.[1]

On the 11th December, 1796, Hoche again thus writes to the Directory from the frigate *Fraternité*:—[2]

"I have confided to a man of ability, an ex-soldier, the command of the second legion of irregulars, which I have raised as secretly as possible. It is composed of six hundred men from all the prisons in my district, and they are collected in two forts or islands to obviate the possibility of their escape. I associate with them six hundred picked convicts from the galleys, still wearing their irons. They are all well armed and dressed in their Quiberon jackets. This legion, which has cost next to nothing, has intrepid leaders. It must embark on two frigates and a corvette, and land as near as possible to Bristol, upon which I am anxious to make a surprise attack, which will be the easier because it is unfortified, and the troops are stationed some distance from it. Castagnier, *chef de division*, will be in charge of the expedition, and after the landing is effected I shall send him to cruise before Dublin, to effectually blockade those who, on our approach, wish to return to England. If the expedition succeeds I hope to remit to France the contributions I intend levying on Liverpool and other commercial centres, by threatening them, in case of refusal, with the same fate which will befall Bristol. It is certain that if Quantin had acted in the same way the Government would have wrung from our enemies the means of crushing them."

[1] Desbrière, Vol. I, pp. 238–9.
[2] Desbrière, Vol. I, part iv, p. 239. Preserved in the French National Archives, A. F. III, 186 B.

A month before Wolfe Tone had made the following note on the force described by Desbrière as "strange auxiliaries": "I have witnessed a review of the Black Legion, about 1800 strong. These are the bandits destined for England, and are unmitigated blackguards. They remind me of the Dublin 'green boys.'" Desbrière failed apparently to find any trace amongst the French records of the instructions supposed to have been given by Hoche to Tate, and of which Mr. Edward Laws supplies a copy attested as having been "compared with the original on the 4th May, 1798, at the Secretary of State's Office, Whitehall."

INSTRUCTIONS FOR COLONEL TATE

"There will be placed under the command of Col. Tate, a body of troops, completely organized, to the number of one thousand and fifty, all resolute determined men, with whom he may undertake anything: They are to be called 'La Seconde Legion des Francs.'

"The legion is completely armed; he will be likewise furnished with fast-going vessels with which he is to proceed, before, with, or after the squadron; the vessels will be victualled for the passage, but the legion will bring on shore nothing but their ammunition, which is to be musquet cartridges.

"Col. Tate is to have the command in chief of the legion; the Admiral will give the necessary orders to the officer commanding the naval force, which will proceed up St. George's Channel, and the landing is to be effectuated, if possible, in or near Cardigan Bay.

"But should Col. Tate, on arriving opposite the mouth of the Severn, learn that the river is little or not at all defended, and that the wind and tide allow him to sail up, he will endeavour to execute a *coup de main* on Bristol,

which is the second city in England for riches and commerce; the destruction of Bristol is of the very last
importance, and every possible effort should be made to
accomplish it.

"For this purpose, it will be proper to reconnoitre the
mouth of the Severn, in the day time, and to sail up the
Avon at night fall, within five miles of the town, where
the landing should be made, on the right bank, in the
greatest silence, and, the troops being supplied with com-
bustible matter, Col. Tate is to advance rapidly in the
dark, on that side of Bristol which may be to windward,
and immediately to set fire to that quarter. If the enterprize be conducted with dexterity, it cannot fail to produce
the total ruin of the town, the port, the docks, and the
vessels, and to strike terror and amazement into the very
heart of the capital of England.

"This object being fulfilled, Col. Tate will immediately
re-embark, cross the Severn, and land below Cardiff, which
he will leave on his right, and proceed towards Chester
and Liverpool, in the manner to be pointed out in these
instructions.

"During the passage, Col. Tate will take care that the
troops observe the most exact discipline, and will recommend to the naval officers to carry a press of sail.

"At the moment of the landing, each soldier is to be
furnished with one hundred rounds of ammunition, provisions for four days, and a double ration of wine or
brandy, to recruit them after the fatigues of the voyage.

"Not a moment is to be lost in the debarkation, and
the soldiers must carry their ammunition and provisions
un'il they can secure bât horses; they are never to quit
them, and are to take care to supply what may be ex-
pended on every possible occasion. For the first two days
the legion is to keep in one body, observing not to suffer
any to lag in the rear.

"Col. Tate will feel the necessity of gaining a close and

strong country with all possible speed, and before committing any act of hostility, he will take care to avoid the
morasses, as well from regard to the health of the troops
as to avoid being surrounded by the enemy, who would of
course endeavour to profit of such a defect in his position.

"The expedition under the command of Col. Tate has
in view three principal objects: the first is, if possible,
to raise an insurrection in the country; the second is to
interrupt and embarrass the commerce of the enemy; and
the third is to prepare and facilitate the way for a descent,
by distracting the attention of the English government.

"In all countries the poor are the class most prone to
insurrection, and this disposition is to be forwarded by
distributing money and drink; by inveighing against the
government as the cause of the public distress; by recom-
mending and facilitating a rising to plunder the public
stores and magazines, and the property of the rich, whose
affluence is the natural subject of envy to the poor.

"It is, notwithstanding, to be observed, that however
defective may be the morality of the English people, they
have still a respect for the laws and their magistrates, even
in the moment of insurrection; it will be therefore advisable to spare, as much as possible, the property of those
who may be in any civil function, and even of the country
gentlemen; all impositions should be laid on the peers,
the men of rank and high fortune, the clergy, those who
serve as officers, in the army, navy, and especially in the
militia; of all such, the country seats, farms, woods, cattle,
and corn should be given up to be plundered by the
people; these predatory excursions should be made in
different and even distant quarters, by detachments of two
or three hundred men each.

"Extremities, such as these, rendered necessary by
those of the Republic, and justified by the reflection that
our cruel enemy has shewed the first example, will attract
numbers of artizans and workmen, of vagabonds and

idlers and even of malefactors; but especial care must be taken not to incorporate them into the legion; they are to be formed into new companies, commanded by French officers, and to the end that the natives may not be acquainted with the force employed, these companies are to be kept asunder, and in ignorance of the details as far as circumstances will permit; it is principally by these new formed companies that the insurrection is to be forwarded.

" The commerce of the enemy in the country is to be interrupted by breaking down bridges, cutting of dykes, and ruining causeways, which is, at the same time, essentially necessary for the preservation of the army; by plundering all convoys of subsistence, the public stages and waggons, and even private carriages; the cutting off the supplies of provisions from the principal towns, burning all vessels and boats in the rivers and canals, destroying magazines, setting fire to docks and coal yards, rope walks, great manufactories, etc. etc. It is to be observed, likewise, that by these means a crowd of artizans will be thrown out of employment, and of course ready to embark in any measure which holds out to them subsistence and plunder without labour or fatigue.

" The success of the expedition will likewise be materially forwarded by disarming the militia, by burning the arsenals in the seaports, by stopping the couriers of government, by seducing the enemy's troops to desert, and by the terror which the success of the legion and the progress of the insurrection will carry into the bosoms of the unwarlike citizens. The country most favourable for this system is that which is naturally strong, and in which there are forges and manufactures.

" Subsistence is to be seized wherever it can be found; if any town or village refuse to supply it in the moment, it is to be given up to immediate pillage.

" In order to spread the panic as generally as possible,

the legion is to be divided into several columns, having settled a common rendezvous, where they are to assemble every four, six, or eight days; the inhabitants must be obliged to serve as guides, and any who refuse are to be punished on the spot; the magistrates, or some of their families, are always to be employed in preference on this service, that they may not accuse or punish the others.

"All denunciations against those who join the legion are to be punished by death. Wherever the legion or any of its columns is posted, if the neighbouring parishes do not give instant notice of the approach of the enemy, whether by ringing of bells, or otherwise, they are to be given up to fire and sword. For the safety of the troops under his command, Colonel Tate will avoid, as much as possible, all engagements with regular forces, and will, instead thereof, attack detachments, beat up their quarters, surprize their outposts, etc. He will encourage all deserters and prisoners to enter into the new companies before mentioned; should such prisoners refuse, he will shave their heads and eyebrows, and if they are again taken in arms they are to be shot.

"Colonel Tate will not omit to observe, that there are in England numbers of French, who will be eager to join him, such as prisoners of war, soldiers and sailors, privates in the emigrant regiments, and a crowd of others, whom want and the desire of vengeance will draw to his standard; he may admit such Frenchmen into the legion; but he will observe to be on his guard that the newcomers may not raise cabals or factions; especially if there should be among them any nobles or priests, whose ambition is only to be exceeded by their cowardice; should any such attempt be made, he will take care to punish it most severely. Should the militia or volunteers of any district oppose the march of the legion, such district is to be severely punished, the militia or volunteers to be disarmed, their arms to be distributed among the insurgents, and all ammunition carefully preserved.

"Finally, Colonel Tate will always remember to avail himself of the talents of the principal officers who surround him ; he will profit of all favourable circumstances to acquire for his party the force and confidence necessary to ensure success ; he will spare, and even sustain, the poor and the aged, the widow and the orphan, and will force the great, who are the cause of all our evils, to sustain the whole burden of the war.

"(Signed)   Le Gen. L^e Hoche."

COPY OF THE INSTRUCTIONS TO COLONEL TATE, ON HIS MILITARY OPERATIONS AND MARCHES

"It would be imprudent to remain any length of time on the coast, after having effectuated your landing ; you will doubtless see the necessity of penetrating into the country, and especially into the counties of Cheshire and Lancashire, not to speak of the opportunities which those counties afford you, by means of the mountains, to avoid the pursuit of the enemy, the field of your operations will be more extended : with boldness and intelligence combined, you may easily possess yourself of Chester or Liverpool, which you will ruin by burning the magazines, and filling up the ports, or at least you may cut off all communication between those cities and the interior. There is another object which should likewise decide you to enter those counties, as you will be joined there by two other columns of French troops, to which you will unite that under your command, if the general commanding the expedition in chief shall desire it.

"It is therefore of consequence that you direct your march, from the very moment of landing, upon the town of

Chester, where you will pass the Dee, beyond which you are to establish yourself.

"Your march should be rapid and bold ; you must not keep the main roads, but on the contrary proceed by bye paths and hollow ways, which are at a distance from the high road.   Before you enter any village or town, you are to inform yourself whether there be any troops there, and what is their number ; whether there be a river, and if so, whether there be one or more bridges, whether it be enclosed with walls and barriers, etc., and you are to take your measures in consequence.

"You should frequently change your guides, and in order to mislead the enemy as to your destination, you should not take a new one in presence of him whom you dismiss ; you should often make counter marches, and always mention to the guide you quit a road different from that which you mean to take, asking the way to the town or village on which you mean to turn your back, or at least whither you do not mean to go.

" In order to spread the consternation and astonishment as wide as possible, after the destruction of Liverpool (for this point is capital) you must follow your blow, and seize upon some small town or seaport on that coast, which you will lay under contribution.   You may be sure that im- mediately all the principal places will demand for their protection troops from the government, which is in want of them, and will of course be obliged to separate those of which it can dispose, by which means you will be able to destroy a great number, by beating in detail the detach- ments which may be sent against you.   The mobiliary columns can alone be successfully opposed to you, but even in that case it will be easy for you to destroy their effect.   If they be weak, you will unite your forces and crush them ; if they be strong, by scattering yourselves, and committing hostilities in a hundred different quarters ; the towns, which will be terrified by these means, will soon demand the troops which compose the columns to protect them from your parties, who will thereby remain masters of the field, and starve both the troops and the inhabitants. I doubt much whether the English know as yet the nature and use of mobiliary columns, but even if they do, you may find means to render them useless, because the government has not troops in number sufficient to guard all the points at once, and parties like yours may over-run the country in a thousand different directions.

" Your soldiers are to carry with them nothing but their arms, ammunition, and bread : they will find everywhere clothes, linen, and shoes; the inhabitants must supply your wants, and the seats of the gentry are to be your magazines.

" In case the country, being exhausted, should offer you no further resources, or that a strong body of troops should force you to quit the place where you had established yourself, you must depart with promptitude and expedition, make forced marches, and in the night, reposing yourself by day in the woods and mountains ; if you are obliged to halt, in order to procure provisions, you must first choose a strong position, from which you will send detachments into the neighbouring villages ; it is with your cavalry (for you must take care from the first to mount a sufficient number of your troops) that you are to make this kind of excursion ; you will also observe to re-mount your cavalry as often as necessity may require it.

" Marching in this manner, unencumbered with baggage, your troops cannot be overtaken by the enemy ; but if it should so happen that you are obliged to stand an engagement, you must remember that you are now a Frenchman, inasmuch as you command Frenchmen, and let that incite you to attempt a brilliant stroke ; remember, however, that nothing but inevitable necessity should induce you to hazard the issue of a combat, and in that case you must supply by courage the defect of numbers. Should you be forced to clear your way through the enemy, you must commence the attack, but it must be always by night. About eleven o'clock, or midnight, send out two or three patrols of four or six men each, with orders to set fire to a dozen houses in your rear, in different quarters; the enemy, believing that you are running away, will most probably pursue you, in which case you may lay an ambuscade, or you may avoid him, or you may fall on the rear of one of his columns, which you may cut off with facility, in the dark and the confusion of an unexpected attack. If the enemy should run to extinguish the fires, you have the same advantages; you have your choice, either to avoid him, or which is still better, to beat him; if he remains under arms, and sends out patrols to reconnoitre, you must interrupt them, and put them to the bayonet, without firing a shot, and then, after two or three hours, you must form the column, and advance rapidly, *au pas de charge*, on one of his wings, which you will certainly rout, and then, without pushing the affair further, you will pursue your route, and remember to make in that day two or three countermarches.

" In this manner you may, by a brilliant action, surprise in the night time and cut off a post which may be opposed to you: in the day light and open field you ought not, with the force under your command, to hesitate to attack two thousand of the enemy, and in the night, four or even five thousand: you ought to dislodge eight hundred from a post, not being intrenched; but if intrenched, and especially with cannon, you are not to attack them.

" In order to pass a river, where the bridges are guarded or broken down, if you cannot procure boats, you must endeavour to re-mount towards the source, in order to find a passage by means of a ford, a mill dam, etc. If you are hard pressed, you must strain a stout rope from one bank to the other, and pass your troops; those who do not know how to swim, holding fast by the rope, and carrying their firelocks slung over their shoulders, with the muzzle down-wards to avoid wetting the lock ; if trees can be found on the bank long enough to reach across, they are still better than ropes ; in which case you will fell several of them. If the river, though fordable, be so deep as to take the soldiers up to their necks, you must make the best swim-mers pass first, and the others follow by ranks, each soldier holding the next man strongly with the left hand by the skirt of the coat, and carrying his firelock in the right: by these means those who reach the opposite bank first will sustain the others, and assist them in getting out of the water : your horses will also be of use, but you must not reckon upon them.

"In case your position should be at last no longer tenable, or that superior forces should force you to quit the country bordering on the Channel, you must not lose an instant to join two French parties sent into the counties of York, Durham, and Northumberland. In that case you must send me notice into Ireland, that I may be enabled to execute a diversion in your favour. An officer in disguise may reach me, either by seizing a fishing boat on the coast of Wales, or else by route of Scotland.

" I count upon your firmness and your courage; you may equally rely upon the gratitude of the French nation and my esteem and regard in particular.

"My intention in giving you these instructions is less that you should attach yourself to the letter, than to the spirit of what they contain ; and I leave to your judgment to make such modification therein as circumstances may render necessary.

"(Signed)   LE GEN. L^E HOCHE.

"[SECRETARY OF STATE'S OFFICE, WHITEHALL,
   " 4*th May*, 1798.

" Compared with the original.—F. KING.]"

Captain Desbrière next gives an historical document of considerable interest, of which the following is only a summary.

Journal of Commodore Castagnier commanding the frigate *Vengeance*, and having under his orders the corvette *Constance* . and the lugger *Vautour*, which division was commissioned to disembark in England the Second Legion of Irregulars.

The 28th[1] at 7 a.m. to start for the anchorage in the Camaret Roads. Anchored at 9 a.m. On the morning of the 29th a soldier was subjected to summary punishment for endeavouring to sell his coat. Signal to weigh anchor made at 3 p.m. on the 30th. Sighted the English on the 1st Ventôse [February 19th]. Sighted fourteen heavily laden English ships and mistook the Dublin packet carrying numerous passengers of both sexes for a man-of-war. Hoisted the Russian flag. Tacked during the night so as to enter the Bristol Channel. At 7 a.m. on the 2nd Ventôse gave signal for the division to prepare for anchoring. At 7 p.m. gave signal to get under sail and tack so as to continue our course up Channel. Having reached Parlock [Porlock] Bay, the state of the tide, the prevalence of an east wind, and the threatening weather induced me to make for Cardigan Bay, the second point designated for landing the troops. On the 4th Ventôse [February 22nd] at 4 p.m. anchored in Cardigan Bay close to the shore, and at 5 p.m. began the disembarkation of our forces, which was completed at 2 a.m. on the following morning. No kind of resistance was offered to their landing. On that day [February 23rd] at 4 p.m. Colonel Tate and his officers said

---

[1] Desbrière, Vol. I, pp. 242-3. The 28th Pluviôse corresponds with February 16th, 1797.

FISHGUARD IN FEBRUARY, 1797. [FROM A CONTEMPORARY PRINT]

that they had no further need of my help. In conformity with my instructions a *procès-verbal* was drawn up under my direction,[1] and I took the necessary steps for the execution of the other part of my mission. I sent the lugger *Vautour* to Brest with despatches informing General Morard de Galles of the result of the expedition. I then made sail for Dublin Roads, but was unable to remain there longer than 9 p.m. on the 8th Ventôse [February 26th], in consequence of the change of wind, the threatening weather, and our being encumbered by the number of prisoners from the fourteen vessels[2] we had sunk, two of them armed tenders. Moreover, we were informed by our prisoners that a naval force had left Liverpool in search of us. I signalled that we should make for Sorlingues under all sail, by such a course as would obviate the possibility of our being sighted from the English coast.[3]

[1] This was signed by Colonel Tate, and Captains Didier, Faucon, Bremond, Guilleret, Guériel, and Gavel, as well as the naval officers.

[2] Castagnier does not precise the exact time or details of these captures, beyond the sinking of a small cutter at his orders by the *Vautour* on the 1st Ventôse (February 19th).

[3] The *Vengeance* encountered a hurricane, but eventually reached Brest on the 19th Ventôse (March 9th, 1797). The *Vautour* had also reached the same port in safety. The *Résistance* and the *Constance* had failed to obey the signals of the *chef de division*, and were both captured by the English cruisers. A despatch from Sir Henry Neale to Lord Bridport, dated March 10th, 1797, gives the following details of the fate which overtook the French ships: "The ships taken are *La Résistance*, commanded by Monsieur Montague, mounting 48 guns, 18-pounders, on her main-deck, and manned with 345 men. She is only six months old, built upon a new construction, and is in every respect one of the finest frigates the French had, and certainly the largest, measuring 45 feet beam. The other frigate, *La Constance*, commanded by Monsieur Desauney, mounting 24 nine-pounders upon the main-deck, and manned with 189 men: she is two years old, and a very fine ship. These are two of the frigates which landed troops in Wales: it is a pleasing circumstance to have completed the failure of that expedition. I am particularly happy to inform your Lordships, that neither the *St. Fiorenzo*

The *St. Fiorenzo* was appropriately rechristened the *Fisgard* (Fishguard), and in the latter part of the last century was still the receiving ship at Sheerness.

We now return to the march of events in England and Wales. The first intimation we have of the arrival of Colonel Tate in our home waters was the following despatch from Lieutenant-Colonel Orchard, commanding the North Devon Volunteers,[1] to the Duke of Portland, Secretary of the Home Department. It runs thus :—

"HEARTLAND ABBEY,
"*February* 23rd.

"I think it my duty to state to your Grace that I yesterday received an express from Ilfracombe mentioning that there were three French frigates off that place ; that they had scuttled several merchantmen, and were attempting to destroy the shipping in the harbour. They begged that I would immediately order the North Devon regiment of Volunteers under my command to march to their assistance. In consequence of this representation, I ordered the men to get ready to march as soon as possible. I have great satisfaction in saying that in 4 hours I found every officer and man that was ordered on the parade at Bideford (15 miles from home) ready and willing to march to any place they should be commanded to go to. I cannot express the satisfaction I feel on seeing the men so willing to defend their king and country, at the same

---

nor *La Nymphe* have had any men killed or wounded, or the ships hurt ; the *St. Fiorenzo* only having received two shot in her hull. *La Résistance* had ten men killed, the first Lieutenant and eight men wounded ; *La Constance* had eight men killed and six wounded."—*European Magazine*, Vol. XXXI (1797), p. 433.

[1] Nowhere during the Ten Years' Terror did volunteering attain such noteworthy proportions as in the "Shire of the Sea Kings." In the returns of 1804 Devon heads the list with a total of 16,395 ; Lancashire comes next with 14,856 ; and London third with 13,898. The gross total was 379,943.

time as silent, orderly, and sober as might be expected at a morning parade of an old regiment. The greatest exertions were made by all descriptions of people to assist, and to render any service in their power. As I was preparing to march, I received an account from Ilfracombe that the French ships were gone from the coast, and that tranquillity was again restored to the town. How far the report was well founded I cannot possibly say; but, as this affair may be misrepresented and exaggerated, I trust your Grace will excuse my troubling you with this letter; and I flatter myself it must give you pleasure to hear of the loyalty of this neighbourhood, and that the behaviour of the volunteers and inhabitants will meet the approbation of his Majesty."[1]

On the very same day (Thursday, February 23rd) the overseer's accounts for the borough of Tenby show that the modest sum of a shilling was paid to John Upcoat "for going out to the Road for a skiff to go over to the English side [i.e. from the south coast of Wales to the north coast of Somersetshire], to give information concerning the landing of about 1400 French troops at Fishguard, who on the next day surrendered themselves up to the Welsh who went to oppose them as prisoners of war [sic]."[2] From Somersetshire the news was transmitted to London, and the messenger probably came to Tenby from Stackpole, where Lord Cawdor was aroused in the middle of the night to hear the startling intelligence from Fishguard. Colonel Knox, called away from the festivities at Tregwynt by an urgent message from his subordinate, Ensign D. Bowen, gave the alarm in two letters to Major Bowen, commanding the Newport Division of Volunteers, late on

---

[1] *Gentleman's Magazine*, Vol. LXVI (1797), part i, p. 243.
[2] *The Fishguard Invasion*, pp. 12 and 13.

the 22nd, and on the following day Lord Milford, the Lord Lieutenant of the County, wrote as follows :—

"Dear Sir,

"I had ordered the Cardiganshire Militia, Capt. Ackland's corps, and Lord Cawdor's troop[1] to repair to Fishguard as soon as possible previous to the receipt of your letter.

"I am, dear sir,
"Yours, etc.,

"HAVERFORD WEST,   "MILFORD.

"2 o'clock Thursday morning."

On the same day, probably late in the evening, Colonel Knox wrote the following letter, evidently to the Duke of Portland :—

"FISHGUARD,
"24th February, 1797.

"My Lord,

"I have the honor to inform you, that I received intelligence on the afternoon of the 22nd instant, of two frigates, a sloop, and a cutter having made their appearance off this coast. Upon going to view them, I was further told they were French, and were landing troops; I therefore hastened to this place, and was fortunate enough to meet a detachment of about seventy of the corps of Fishguard Volunteers, commanded by Ensign D. Bowen, marching to attack the enemy. I thought it advisable to immediately order them to retire into the fort (where Gov. Vaughan soon joined us), until the whole of the corps could be collected and information gained of the number of the French.

---

[1] The whole force at Lord Cawdor's disposal amounted to 750 men. It consisted of men belonging to the Castle Martin Yeomanry Cavalry, the Cardiganshire Militia, the Cardiff Militia, some fencible infantry (the Fishguard Volunteers), and a few sailors under Lieutenants Mears and Perkins.

"In the course of that night I was joined by many of the corps, who had come in upon the alarm, and by part of the Newport division under the command of Major Bowen. I learnt early in the morning the force of the enemy was so considerable as to make it necessary for me to retreat without delay. I accordingly evacuated the fort, and bringing off the ammunition of the corps, took the road to Haverfordwest, in order to fall in with the reinforcements which were on their march, having written to the Lord Lieutenant to inform him of our situation. We had retreated about nine miles, when we were joined by Lord Cawdor,[1] to whom Lord Milford had given the command. I therefore put myself under his orders. The success which has attended his gallant exertions is not for me to describe, but I hope I may be permitted to express the gratitude this part of the county must feel with myself, in the zeal and alacrity with which the different corps and many gentlemen of the county came forward to our succour. I received much assistance from Mr. Nisbitt, residing in Fishguard, late an ensign in the army; and I have the pleasure to say the corps under my command conducted themselves in a manner which, I trust, has done them credit. I shall to-morrow detach parties in pursuit of any strangers which may not yet be come in; there

---

[1] John Campbell of Castle Martin, Pembrokeshire, born about 1753, was a descendant of John Campbell, younger son of Archibald, second Duke of Argyll, who had married, about 1510, Muriel, daughter and heiress of John Calder of Calder, or Cawdor, Nairn, representative of the old Thanes of Cawdor. Having represented Cardigan in Parliament, he was raised to the peerage of Great Britain as Baron Cawdor on June 21st, 1796. He married in 1789 the eldest daughter of the fifth Earl of Carlisle, and both his sons were born before the Fishguard invasion. His elder son and successor was granted an earldom. The present Earl Cawdor, for many years chairman of the Great Western Railway, is the great-grandson of the Commander of the English forces in February, 1797. He held cabinet rank as First Lord of the Admiralty for a brief period before the dissolution of Parliament in 1906. His son, Lord Emlyn, is married to a great-granddaughter of Sir Thomas Hardy, Nelson's captain at Trafalgar.

are twenty-five sick near the place where the enemy landed, whom Lord Cawdor has left in my charge. I have the honour to be, with the greatest respect,

"Yours, etc. etc. etc.,
"THOMAS KNOX,
"Lieut.-Col., Fishguard Volunteers."

By the same post the Home Secretary must have received Lord Cawdor's account of the events *quorum pars magna fuit :—*

"FISHGUARD,

"*February* 24*th*, 1797.

"My Lord,

"In consequence of having received information on Wednesday night, at eleven o'clock, that three large ships of war and a lugger had anchored in a small roadstead upon the coast, in the neighbourhood of this town, I proceeded immediately with a detachment of the Cardiganshire Militia and all the provincial force I could collect to the place. I soon gained positive intelligence they had disembarked about 1200 men, but no cannon. Upon night setting in, a French officer, whom I found to be second in command, came in with a letter (a copy of which I sent your Grace, together with my answer), in consequence of which they determined to surrender themselves prisoners of war, and, accordingly, laid down their arms this day at two o'clock. I cannot, at this moment, inform your Grace the exact number of prisoners, but I believe it to be their whole force. It is my intention to march them this night to Haverfordwest, where I shall make the best distribution in my power. The frigates, corvette, and lugger got under weigh yesterday evening, and were this morning entirely out of sight. The fatigue we experienced will, I trust, excuse me to your Grace for not giving a more particular detail ; but my anxiety to do justice to the officers and men I had the honour to command, will induce me to attend your Grace with as little delay as possible, to state their merits and, at the same time, to give you every information in my power on this subject. The spirit and loyalty which has pervaded all ranks throughout the country is infinitely beyond what I can express.

> " I am, etc.,
>> " CAWDOR."

The correspondence enclosed by Lord Cawdor speaks for itself.

Colonel Tate to Lord Cawdor.

> " CARDIGAN BAY,
>> " *5th Ventôse,*
>> " *5th Year of the Republic*
>> [*February 23rd*, 1797].

" Sir,

" The circumstances under which the body of troops under my command were landed at this place render it unnecessary to attempt any military operations, as they would tend only to bloodshed and pillage. The officers of the whole corps have, therefore, intimated their desire of entering into a negotiation, upon principles of humanity, for a surrender. If you are influenced by similar considerations, you may signify the same to the bearer, and in the meantime hostilities shall cease.

> " Health and respect,
>> " TATE, *Chef de Brigade.*"

Lord Cawdor to Colonel Tate.

> " FISHGUARD, *February* 23*rd.*

" Sir,

" The superiority of the force under my command, which is hourly increasing, must prevent my treating upon any other terms short of your surrendering your whole force prisoners of war. I enter fully into your wish of preventing an unnecessary effusion of blood, which your speedy surrender can alone prevent, and which will entitle you to that consideration it is ever the wish of British troops to show an enemy whose numbers are inferior. My major will deliver you this letter, and I shall expect your determination by 10 o'clock, by your officer, whom I have furnished with an escort who will conduct him to me without molestation.

"I am, etc.,
"CAWDOR."

These dry as dust official letters give little idea of the consummate skill with which Lord Cawdor played his game of bluff, and the weird picturesqueness of the hastily improvised council of war at the "Royal Oak," the reading of the English ultimatum to the discomfited Frenchmen, the carrying of the flag of truce by M. Millingchamp, and the return of the hoodwinked emissaries. Lord Cawdor's victory was complete, and Lord Milford[1] writes with pardonable inexactness to the Duke of Portland from Haverfordwest, where he has been anxiously awaiting tidings from the front :—

From Lord Milford.

"HAVERFORDWEST,
"*February 24th*, 1797, Six o'clock A.M.

"Since I had the honour of writing last to your Grace by express I received information of the French ships having sailed and left 300 men behind, who have surrendered themselves prisoners. The great spirit and

---

[1] Sir Michael Phillips, Bart., of Picton Castle, Cambridgeshire, was created Baron Milford in 1776; appointed Lord Lieutenant of Pembrokeshire in 1780, and held the post till his death at the age of eighty-five.

loyalty that the gentlemen and peasantry has shown on this .occasion exceeds description. Many thousands of the latter assembled, armed with pikes and scythes, and attacked the enemy previous to the arrival of troops that were sent against them."

"HAVERFORDWEST,

"*February* 24th, Nine o'clock P.M.

"I have the honour and pleasure to inform your Grace that the whole of the French troops, amounting to near fourteen hundred men, have surrendered, and are now on their march to Haverfordwest.

"I have taken first opportunity of announcing the good news to your Grace, and shall have the honour of writing again to your Grace by to-morrow's post."

On the following day (Saturday, February 25th) the Duke of Portland is able to reassure the Lord Mayor of London by the following official communication :—

"My Lord,

"I have the honour to acquaint your Lordship that intelligence has been received that two French frigates, a lugger, and a corvette appeared off the East of Pembroke-shire on the 22nd instant, and on the evening of that day disembarked some troops (reported by deserters to be about 1200 men, but without field pieces). Every exertion had been made by the Lord Lieutenant and gentlemen of that county and its neighbourhood, for taking the proper steps on this occasion ; and the greatest zeal and loyalty has been shown by all ranks of people. Immediately on account having been received at Plymouth of this force having appeared in the Bristol Channel, frigates were despatched from Plymouth in quest of them.

"I have the honor to be, etc.,

"PORTLAND."

The next letter from Lord Milford to the Duke of Portland has only lately been discovered, and for many reasons is exceedingly interesting :—

" HAVERFORDWEST,

"*February 26th, '97.*

" My Lord,

"In my last letter I informed your Grace that I had receiv'd an acc^t from Ld Cawdor, to whom I gave the command of the troops, that the French were inclined to surrender.   I have now the Pleasure of Informing your Grace that they have Capitulated, which, considering the very Inferior force that could be muster'd to send against them, I attribute to the very spirited answer his Lordship returned to the Proposals of Capitulation from the Commander of the French.   His attention has been unremitting and his exertions do him Infinite Credit.   I have seen the Commander, who from the description given of him by the first Prisoners that were taken I had reason to believe him to have been Col. Wall,[1] whose Person I well know. There has been firing at sea heard this day, and I am in hopes Admiral Kingsmill, to whom I despatched a fast sailing lugger, may have met with the squadron that sail'd from hence on disembarking the troops.

" I have the Honor

" to be your Grace's most

" Obedient and very Humble

" Servant, etc. etc.,

" MILFORD."

[1] Joseph Wall (1737-1802), Governor of Goree in 1782, where he caused Sergeant Benjamin Armstrong to be so severely flogged that he died from the effects of the injuries he received.   From 1784 to 1797, when he returned to England, Wall wandered over the Continent under an assumed name.   He was arrested in October, 1801, having offered to surrender ; was tried at the Old Bailey, convicted, and executed at Newgate on January 28th.   The public feeling against him was so strong that the efforts of the Duke of Norfolk, his wife's relative, to save him proved fruitless.   This fact throws light on the allusions to him in the letters of Lords Milford and Cawdor.

FACING the ENEMY not any by me ffli—

EARLY INVASION CARICATURE ETCHED BY ISAAC CRUIKSHANK. 1797-8

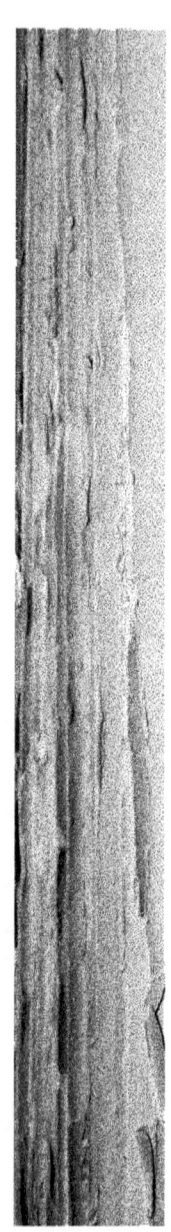

The state of public feeling in London hardly reflects that of Fishguard. News, even of an invasion, travelled slowly over the rut-riddled and almost impassable roads, but on the 25th February the Right Honourable W. W. Windham enters in his diary, "News of descent in Wales," while on the 4th March he notes[1] having gone "to the Admiralty to examine prisoners from Wales, viz. Tate and Le Brun, *alias* Baron de Rochemure." There is much interest felt in Le Brun. On the next day a M. de Williamson seeks for Pitt's War Secretary more information about the "M. Rochemure (le Baron de) who has been in the Cadres, and was second in command of the expedition to Wales."

On that very date Lord Cawdor, now at his lodgings in Oxford Street, writes an exhaustive report of all that happened to the Home Secretary :—

"OXFORD ST., *March 5th, '97.*

"Lord Cawdor to the Duke of Portland.

"My Lord,

"It being incumbent on me to explain to your Grace the situation in which I left the County of Pembroke, I shall recapitulate the outline of the late transaction, though not with sufficient Detail to do justice to the extraordinary and general spirit, zeal, and loyalty of individuals, which burst forth and co-operated with every wish I expressed during the short period of my Command. I received a messenger from a private friend at Haverford West on the 22nd of February at 11 at night with an account of the enemy being off Fishguard. I was collecting the troops when it was confirmed by the circular letter

---

[1] *The Diary of the Right Honourable W. W. Windham, 1784–1810,* edited by Mrs. Henry Baring, London, 1866.

from the Lord Lieutenant. As soon as the Troop of
Yeomanry, the Cardigan Militia and Pembroke Company,
commanded by Capt. Ackland, had passed Pembroke
Ferry, I proceeded to Haverford West and found it necessary after some conversation with Lord Milford to offer to
take the whole upon myself, if he engaged under his Hand
not to interpose his authority. It was not a moment for
compliments, and from the instant [he] transferred his
authority, I peremptorily required every person to put
himself under my Command. Lieut. Colby readily ac-
quiesced, and during the whole time gave me his utmost
assistance. I appointed Capt. Adams, Capt. Davis, the
Honb^le Mr Edwards, John Philipps, and Owen Philipps,
Esq^rs, my aides-de-camp; they were selected for their
activity and intelligence, and fully answered my sanguine
expectations. I sent to Mr Vaughan, the Ld Lieut.
for Carmarthenshire, on whose co-operation I could
depend, to order all the force of the County to support
me. I appointed Dr Francis Edwards, Mayor of H.
West, to be commissary, and many gentlemen co-operated
to avert confusion, and activity left no time for despondency.

" All the Force of the lower District being collected
as the enclosed return [shows] I proceeded to reconnoitre
the Enemy near Fishguard, and to animate the County.
On my return to hasten the Troops I overtook Lieut.
Col. Knox with his corps of Fishguard Volunteers retreating to H. West, and required him to put himself
under my orders and to return towards the Enemy. I had
found nothing to impede my making my own arrangements, and I derived very useful intelligence and information from Mr Nisbitt of Fishguard; it was obvious
that the Fishguard Battery was as useless for land operation as it had been to impede the disembarkation. The
position taken by the Enemy was upon the heights of
Pencaern, about 2^{mls} to the west of Fishguard. They

effected their landing on the night of the 22nd and morning of the 23rd, immediately under Pencaern rocks on a spot so unfavourable for de-barkation that 50 men instructed and prepared to avail themselves of the natural advantages would have rendered a landing impracticable. It was not impossible to dislodge them from their Position, but it was easy to hem them in and cut off supply. It required every union of regular and irregular forces to oppose the desperate effort to be expected from an Enemy in such a position. I had full confidence in my friends and in the County People.

"On the 24th the French laid down their arms on Good-ick Sands, and were on their march at 4 p.m. o'clock for H. West. The distribution of Provisions as they filed off and every direction to expedite their March had been executed to my Wishes, yet it was 1 o'clock in the morning of the 25th before they had marched the 17 miles and it was 4 o'clock before they were secured in the Churches and Prisons, etc. etc., a service I was obliged personally to attend from the want of interpreters. I did not think it safe to resign my Command, so once more in the town with the Lord Lieutenant and I took on myself to direct the necessary, measures. In the afternoon the officers were sent to Carmarthen under the escort of a De-tachment of the Cavalry, and orders were issued to pro-vide for the Prisoners afloat. The extra-ordinary efforts of the sea officers and sea men enabled me on the 27th in the morning to march 505 Prisoners from H. West to Milford, and in 20 minutes they were all on Board. On the 1st of March 200 more were embarked at the same place, and arrangements were taken for embark-ing the remainder together with 129 Prisoners from Pem-broke which I deem necessary for the security of the County, that small number, owing to the insecurity of the Prison, requiring 60 men of the supplementary Militia to guard them.

"I have expressed to Lord Spencer the obligation I owe to Capt. Longcroft, who put himself under my Command with officers and seamen who had marched to H. West with artillery and ammunition from Milford, Capt. Hopkins having left their revenue cutter under the charge of Capt. Shaw to act under the command of Capt. Longcroft. I have represented to his Royal Highness the Duke of York the merit of the officers on the half pay list who contributed to the service. Lieut. Gen^{rl} Rook[1] having approved the arrangements I had made, I left under his order the Persons in whom I had vested the responsibility of occasional services, and I judged it my duty to wait upon your Grace to give full information and to explain my late situation in the County, which I by your Grace [desire] to explain to his Majesty. I shall await your Grace's orders, and have left my Family in the Country until his Majesty's pleasure shall be known.

" I have the honor to be

" Your Grace's Obedt. Humble Servant,

" CAWDOR."

Just a week later, and Lord Cawdor finds time to let his wife at Stackpole have the latest news from London in a letter now in the possession of Mr. Laws :—

" OXFORD ST., *Monday Morn*,

" *March* 13, 1797.

" I have at length the satisfaction of an hour's time free from interruption to give you a short account of our employment etc. since I quitted you, but shall reserve much of the detail for your amusement when we meet, a moment I ardently long for. Near Tavern Spite I met a messenger with the D. of Portland's despatches to me signifying the King's approbation of my conduct, which probably General Rooke has shown you, accompanied also

---

[1] Rooke, *vide post*, p. 205.

by a handsome and flattering private letter from the Duke.

"Upon my arrival at Carmarthen I immediately sent off the messenger with my letter, and finding the impossibility of procuring horses until the following night, was in expectation of getting a quiet night, having procured a bed at a private house; but an alarm of fire in the town joined to confusion created by the report of a landing in great force in Glamorganshire, which I knew must have no foundation, prevented my obtaining sleep for one moment. Early in the morn we left Carmarthen, with three chaises; in the first, Joe Adams had charge of Tate and Captain Tyrell, the first alarmed and confused, the second a stupid Paddy. I had Le Brun with me, as dirty as a pig, but more intelligent and better manners; in the last, Lord E. Somerset had the care of Captain Norris and Lieutenant St. Leger, both greatly frightened, they had but little conversation. The whole road we passed through great crowds of people at all the places were [sic] we changed horses, and thro' Wales tho' the indignation of the people was great, I found my influence would protect them without difficulty. The women were more clamorous than the men, making signs to cut their throats, and desiring I would not take the trouble of carrying them further. All the military assistance I could get at Oxford as a guard for the night was a sergeant of your friend and landlord, and two recruits, but I had no apprehension of their escape as their remain [sic] with us was the only thing that assured their safety. At Uxbridge the rage of the mob was chiefly directed against Tate, who was supposed to be Wall, and he trembled almost to convulsions, by a little arrangement I contrived to bring them quiet through the parks, and lodged them in the Duke of Portland's before any crowd was assembled. My time since that moment has been taken up with attendance at the different offices, &c., and ministers are

I.—F

so bewildered by the difficulties at the Bank, &c., that it
is more than usually difficult to get access to them for any
time, but I have seen them all and stated to them plainly
and decidedly, the situation of Pembroke, &c., giving any
testimony in my power. The weather is extremely cold,
the town I hear dull and unpleasant, everybody I have
seen much interested about you. Mrs. Wodehouse . . .
and desires her love. Joe sends his respects."[1]

The more minute details of the days which immediately
followed the invasion of Fishguard have now lost all
interest, but the recollection of the event itself has been
kept green in Pembrokeshire by several ballads, of which
the following (kindly furnished to the writers by Mr. Laws)
are typical specimens :—

THE FRENCH INVASION

[Ballad transcribed from the dictation of an old man
who used to sing it, by the daughter of Mr. Olive, formerly
of the Pear Tree Inn, Jeffreston, near Tenby, who forwarded it to Mr. John Leach.]

> Ho, Britons, give attention
> To what I have to say,
> How Providence did favour us
> And mercy did display :
> How we were saved in Pembrokeshire
> From danger of the Gaul,
> When they attempted to land here
> With musket, sword, and ball.
>
> It was in February,
> The three-and-twentieth day,
> The French they came to Fishguard
> To take our lives away.

---

[1] *Fishguard in 1797*, pp. 23–24.

Full fourteen hundred of them bold
Did land on British shore,
Such dreadful sight was ne'er behold
In Pembrokeshire before.
Lord Cawdor and his loyal men
Rode bold to Fishguard town,
And Major Ackland likewise,
To keep the Frenchmen down.
Lieutenant-Colonel Colby
Rode like a valiant knight,
And for his king and country
Determined for to fight.
And worthy Captain Ackland,
To him praise is also due,
He and his men proved loyal,
Being willing and so true,
And Colonel Knox together,
In full career they went
To face the bloody Frenchmen,
Whose hearts did then relent.
Esquire Chiles of Begelly,
He mustered before day ;
And being a loyal subject,
He marched us all away.
He rode himself before us,
Upon his gallant steed,
And so to Fishguard town we went
To face the French with speed.

The country folks they gathered
To Fishguard from all parts,
And like loyal men were willing
To try their skill and hearts :
With hooks and knives and pitchforks
To oppose the enemy,
And for their king and country
Courageously would die.

The Frenchmen they desired
The British force to know ;
Before they did surrender,
They gave a fatal blow.

Two of our countrymen courageously did go.
They thought to meet them as their friends,
But met them as their foe.
In answer to the Frenchmen,
Lord Cawdor to them said, .
That they were four thousand—
On battle all were bent ;
And hundreds more were coming,
Increasing from all parts,
Who solemnly there did declare
To fight with all their hearts.

It was on Friday evening
That they gave up the field ;
It was a pleasant sight to see
So many forced to yield.
'Tis not our men, or strength of arms,
But Providence, we own,
Did fight the battle for us
And keep the Frenchmen down.
When they found out our forces,
They saw it was in vain
For them to stand engagement—
The case was made so plain.
Twelve hours they did desire,
And would surrender then.
Lord Cawdor he allowed it,
And so did all his men.

God bless our king and country
With plenty, joy, and peace,
And may all French and Spanish
From Britain ever cease.
Likewise all our noblemen—
Bless them with counsel wise
For to be loyal to their king
And face their enemies.

A new MACHINE (or RAFT) to cover (or protect) the Landing of the FRENCH on their intended

INVASION OF ENGLAND.

Engraved after an Original Drawing made by a FRENCH PRISONER of WAR.

This Machine is 600 / 2,100 Feet long, and 1,500 Feet broad : has 500 Cannon round it, of 36 and 48 Pounders ; at each end is two Wind Mills, which turn a Wheel in the Water at every port of the Wind to Navigate ; in the middle is a Fort enclosing Mortars, Furnaces, &c. It carries 60,000 Men, Cavalry, Infantry, and Artillery.

London, Published by W. HINTON, Engraver and Printer, 85½ Bishopsgate Street, Four Doors from Leadenhall Street, June 10, 1798.

PRICE ONE SHILLING.

1798

ANOTHER BALLAD ON THE FRENCH LANDING[1]

1st. Come all you loyal Welshmen,
And thank the Lord with speed,
It's late has been our Saviour
In a great time of need.
He saved us from invasion
That happened in this land,
His providence protected us
From their avenging hand.

2nd. 'Twas from fourteen hundred Frenchmen,
They landed in full view,
With arms and ammunitions
For this country to subdue.
If had not the great Almighty
Had pity on us all,
Before those cruel enemies
We should been forced to fall.

3rd. They landed at Llanwnda
In Pembrokeshire, I say,
And thought that in this country
They would make a desperate sway.
They came into this harbour
With glory and renown,
And said unto each other,
"We'll take the English crown."

4th. But thanks be to our Saviour
That saved us from all harm,
For certainly it was to us
A very great alarm.

[1] Sent by the present Earl Cawdor to Mr. Laws, with the following note:—

"STACKPOLE COURT, PEMBROKE,
"*December 17th*, '91.

"Dear Laws,

"I enclose a copy of an old *poem* which was recited by Lizzie Davies, the Corston (in Castlemartin parish) carpenter's daughter; it has been handed down by word of mouth from her grandfather.

"Yours sincerely,

"CAWDOR."

So the time when they came in
It's now I'll tell the year,
One thousand seven hundred
And ninety-seven is clear.

5th. In February month,
The twenty-second day,
Those villain murderers came
And did no time delay.
When the news went up to Fishguard,
'Twas with a dreadful sound,
That there were fourteen hundred
Upon Trehowel ground.

6th. For messengers so swift they sent
And fetch [*sic*] the very best,
To send the news directly
Straight on to Haverfordwest.
From Haverfordwest to Pembroke
In an instant without doubt,
To give the soldiers warning
They were to have a rout.

7th. The soldiers spoke together
And said, "We are but few,
But we'll appear before them
Like men of courage true";
Then on they went a-marching
Like men of fame and might,
And thought that with those Frenchmen
They should have been force to fight.

8th. Lord Cawdor's cavalry before,
A valiant troop indeed,
And the Cardigan Malitia [*sic*]
Did follow on with speed,
One hundred more from Pembroke
With Acklind[1] they did go,
And Colonel Knox's soldiers
Was ready for the foe.

[1] Ackland.

9th. The Volunteers from Haverford
Did quickly march along,
And all the jolly sailors
From Hackin in a throng,
So did the Tenby colliers,
They rose and took their flight
With hooks and scythes and pitchforks
Those ruffians for to fight.

10th. Then on they went a-marching,
Like men of valour true,
They did behold at Pencaer
A very dismal view—
Those ruffians were together
A marching all around,
It was a horrid sight to see
Upon the British ground.

11th. Lord Cawdor took his horse
And unto them did go,
The very foremost man of us
That face the daring foe.
He bid them to prepare,
They came at his command,
And put their swords and muskets
Down upon the Goodwick Sand.

12th. Then they were taken prisoners
And unto prison brought.
Oh ! when they were a-landing
Such thing they never thought.
The Lord had mercy on us
And saved us from their hand,
And never let such enemies
For to invade our land.

It is not astonishing to learn that while the ringleaders were *en route* for London, one of the subordinate officers was detected while on parole in the act of selling a silver chalice purloined from Llanwnda Church, and pleaded in

vain that the half-defaced word upon it really meant
" La Vendée." We will leave the filibuster Tate and his
comrade, Monsieur le Baron de Rochemure, *alias* Le Brun,
in London, and as " dirty as pigs." It is a fitting ending
to this " singular expedition," planned in malice and carried
out with folly. It is not surprising that a large-hearted
man and impartial writer like Captain Desbrière rejoices
to feel that its leader was not a Frenchman. In any case
Fishguard served as an appropriate text for one of the
countless patriotic broadsides issued during the second
period of the Great Terror, a facsimile of which is given
on the opposite page.

This day was published,

AN

ADDRESS to the PEOPLE

OF THE UNITED KINGDOM OF

Great Britain and Ireland,

ON THE THREATENED

INVASION.

EXTRACTS FROM THE ABOVE WORK.

AMONG the inexpressibly dreadful consequences which are sure to attend the conquest of your Island by the French, there is one of so horrible a nature, as to deserve distinct notice. This barbarous, but most artful people, when first they invade a country in the conquest of which they apprehend any difficulty, in order to obtain the confidence of the people, compel their troops to observe the strictest discipline, and often put a soldier to death for stealing the most trifling article. Like spiders they artfully weave a web round their victim, before they begin to prey upon it. But when their success is complete they then let loose their troops, with resistless fury, to commit the most horrible excesses, and to pillage, burn, and desolate, without mercy, and without distinction. But the practice to which I particularly allude will make your blood freeze in your veins. These wretches are accustomed, whenever they prevail, to subject the women to the most brutal violence, which they perpetrate with an insulting ferocity, of which the wildest savages would be incapable. To gratify their furious passions is not however their chief object in these atrocities. Their principal delight is to shock the feelings of fathers and brothers, and husbands! Will you, my Countrymen, while you can draw a trigger, or handle a pike, suffer your daughters, your sisters, and wives, to fall into the power of such monsters?

Specimens of French Ferocity and Brutality in Wales.

It is well known that in the last War some French troops succeeded in effecting a landing in Wales. They were greatly superior to the regular force which happened to be in the part of the country where they landed: but, upon seeing, at a distance, a number of Welsh women with red cloaks, whom they mistook for soldiers, they surrendered! The following proofs of their ferocity and brutality are well attested.

A peasant whom they had compelled to assist them in landing their stores, presumed to ask for some compensation, upon which the commanding Officer drew a pistol, and SHOT THE POOR FELLOW THROUGH THE HEART.

Two Officers went to a house, in which was a woman in child-bed, attended by her mother, who was upwards of Seventy Years old. The French brutes tied the husband with cords, and, in his presence, defiled both the wife and the mother!!!

LONDON
Printed by H. Bryer, Bridewell Hospital, Bridge Street.
The Address is sold by J. DOWNES, Temple Bar; J. SPRAGG, King Street Covent Garden; J. ASPERNE, Cornhill; and J. HATCHARD, Piccadilly.
Price Two-pence each, or Twelve Shillings the Hundred, and Eighteen-pence per Dozen.

CHAPTER III

"Crown so illustrious a life, by a conquest which the Great Nation owes to its outraged dignity."—BARRAS.

"CONQUEST has made me what I am, and conquest alone can maintain me." In this piquant sentence Napoleon Bonaparte summed up both his career and his aspirations. At twenty-eight years of age, having crossed swords with imperious Austria to her disadvantage, his name caused no little trepidation in the Courts of Europe, and politicians looked askance at each other when the latest tidings of the little man with the big brain came to hand. It was while the youthful General was at the head of the Army of Italy, almost before the ink had dried on the Treaty of Campo Formio,[1] which pacified the Continent for a time, that the Directory, "that ridiculous government of lawyers," appointed him Commander of the Army of England. The Land of the Free alone refused to come to terms with France; in the language of Pitt, its Government was at war in order to "provide for the security of our own country and the general security of Europe."[2]

[1] Signed on the 17th October, 1797.
[2] See Pitt's speech of February 12th, 1793.

74

In the summer of 1797, as has been already related, the Directory had formally agreed to an expedition against England, and now resolved to come to close quarters with as little delay as possible. Indeed, Monge gave it as his opinion that "the Government of England and the French Republic cannot both continue to exist," an axiom heartily endorsed by Bonaparte throughout his career. Probably English gold, rather than the subjugation of the country, was the object most desired in the present instance; the sacking of the Bank was infinitely more important than the capture of the kingdom.[1] The official order for giving actuality to the latest invasion scheme was issued on the 26th October, 1797:—

"The Executive Directory decrees what follows :

"Article 1.—There shall be assembled without delay, on the coasts of the ocean, an army which shall be called the Army of England.

"2.—Citizen General Bonaparte is named Commander-in-Chief of that army.

"LA RÉVEILLIÈRE-LÉPEAUX, *Pres.*
"LAGARDE, *Sec. Gen.*"

---

[1] "The whole army wants to go to England. It is there that is found the golden fleece which lures on these eager Argonauts."—Dumouriez MS., p. 276. In his pamphlet, *Tableau Spéculatif de l'Europe*, the General also remarks : "It is the interest of all the maritime Powers of Europe that the projected descent upon England should prove unsuccessful. The Continental Powers are actuated by the same motives. The universal bankruptcy that must follow the success of that measure, and the specie of Europe in the hands of a rapacious and unbridled nation, in possession also of every possible strength by land and sea, would leave no bounds to her ambition, which has always increased in proportion to her success. The subversion of every throne, and the annihilation of every political, civil, and religious Constitution, would be the fatal result. Democracy would devour Europe, and terminate by devouring itself."—*Gentleman's Magazine*, Vol. LXVIII, part i, 1798 ; p. 418.

General Desaix, an officer of great talent, for whom Bonaparte cherished a warm regard, was placed in temporary command of the troops. Fifty-six thousand men were already massed on the western coasts of France, and to them was assigned the double rôle of menacing England and keeping order, but it was only with difficulty that they maintained peace in that part of the Republic, which was in a lawless and troubled condition. They were to be further strengthened by a portion of the Army of Italy which Bonaparte was authorized to send back to France to " form the nucleus of the armament which your name and your activity would render formidable to the English." On the 12th November he writes to the Directory that he has " given all the necessary orders for moving our columns to the ocean," and that he is sending Citizen Andréossy to Paris the following day for the purpose of preparing artillery " of the same calibre as the English field-pieces, so that, once in the country, we may be able to use their cannon-balls," an idea eminently worthy of the young captain of the artillery train at the siege of Toulon. As the total number of men supplied by the Army of Italy to that of England amounted to some thirty-six thousand only, exclusive of troops drafted from the Army of the Rhine under the dashing Augereau, the force at Bonaparte's disposal was none too strong if a serious effort was intended. Masséna's division and several other regiments were to swell their ranks, but while on the march from Italy to the coasts they were suddenly diverted and sent to Switzerland, the independence of which had been violated by the Directory.

Bonaparte had already communicated to Talleyrand, the Minister for Foreign Affairs, the policy which he thought France ought to follow in her attitude towards England. "Our Government," he writes, "must destroy the English Monarchy, or expect itself to be destroyed by these intriguing and enterprising islanders. The present moment offers a capital opportunity. Let us concentrate all our efforts on the navy, and annihilate England. That done, Europe is at our feet."[1] This is exactly what the Conqueror of Italy did on his return to Paris, and for the nonce the army was put in the background, and the navy became first favourite. It is clear that he was under no delusion as to the supreme difficulty of the task before him. He informed the Directory that "for an expedition against England we require: 1st, good naval officers; 2nd, a great army, well commanded; 3rd, an intelligent and determined admiral—I think Truguet the best; 4th, thirty million francs in ready money." He discreetly adds : "Although I truly need repose, yet I shall not refuse, as far as possible, to sacrifice myself for my country."[2] To these general principles, which were only those of common sense, he remained faithful when he elaborated his later and more serious attempts at invasion. Although he endeavoured to foster his maritime resources in every direction when the reins of government were in his hands, lack of sea power was indirectly the cause of the decline and fall of the First Empire.

Leaving Rastadt, where a congress had been opened for the purpose of concluding the details of a *modus vivendi* between France and the Empire and the ratification of

---

[1] Bonaparte to Talleyrand, October 17th, 1797.
[2] *A Selection from the Letters and Dispatches of the First Napoleon,* Vol. I, p. 191, by Captain the Hon. D. A. Bingham.

peace between France and Austria, Bonaparte travelled
the many leagues which separated him from Paris with
all speed.   When the horses were changed he chafed and
fumed until the carriage was again careering over the
rut-wrinkled ground designated by courtesy a road.   He
arrived in the capital on the 5th December, 1797, after
a tedious but triumphant journey.   His welcome was
stupendous, but at the time he paid scant attention to the
acclamation of the multitude, and he distrusted the men
in authority, who envied him his rapid rise to fame, and
had actually gone so far as to send a man to Italy "to
keep an eye on Bonaparte."[1]   The stirring events of 1795,
when he had poured grape-shot into the unruly rabble,
had taught him that the mob is an uncertain quantity,
applauding one day and denouncing the next.   Always
a student of human nature, and none too great a believer
in its goodness, Bonaparte understood the *canaille* well
enough to know that unless he continually dazzled them
by brilliant exploits he could never hope to maintain his
present position, let alone put into operation the astounding ideas which were germinating in his fertile brain.   He
had endeavoured to become one of the Directors without
success, for his age was against him, and he was dubbed
"too ambitious"; but he knew that if triumph followed
triumph, and he made himself indispensable to his adopted
country, nothing could prevent him from gaining the
power he sought.   To use the apt phraseology of Barras,
the President of the Directory, who, it must be admitted,
was somewhat two-faced where the young General was
concerned, "Bonaparte was in quest of an outlet for his
ambition, and was going about seeking whom he might

[1] *Memoirs of Barras*, Vol. II, p. 513.

devour."[1] Never in the history of France had there been so many intellectual gladiators in the arena as at the end of the eighteenth century. A great mind-movement was in process of development, but it was too complex, too diffuse, to make its influence felt as a concrete whole. From the entangled threads of the Revolution was woven, not the sovereignty of the people, but the despotism of one man ; the very opposite effect the original cause was calculated to bring about.

At the fête given in the magnificent palace of the Luxembourg on the formal presentation by Bonaparte to the Directory of the ratification of the treaty of peace by the Emperor Francis II, Barras announced in pompous phrases the task which the popular hero had been called upon to undertake, declaring that " Nature had exhausted her energies in the production of a Bonaparte." Turning in the direction of the sallow-faced young soldier, who, garbed in the simple costume of a civilian, contrasted oddly with the elaborately decorated officials about him, he cried : " Crown so illustrious a life, by a conquest which the Great Nation owes to its outraged dignity. Go, and by the punishment of the Cabinet of London strike terror into the hearts of all who would miscalculate the powers of a free people. Let the conquerors of the Po, the Rhine, and the Tiber march under your banner. The ocean will be proud to bear you. It is a slave, still indignant, which blushes for its fetters. Hardly will the tricoloured standard wave on the blood-stained shores of the Thames ere an unanimous cry will bless your arrival, and that generous nation will receive you as its liberator."[2]

[1] Barras, Vol. III, p. 205.
[2] " Napoleon's Memoirs," quoted in Thiers' *History of the French Revolution* (1881 edition), Vol. V, p. 217, note.

Putting aside any ulterior object the Directory may have contemplated in urging Bonaparte to set sail for England, the last sentence in this farrago of fulsome flattery exactly conveyed the opinion of Frenchmen at the time. They firmly believed that the General would be received with open arms, that it only needed a spark to set England aflame with revolutionary principles.[1]   At St. Helena the Emperor stoutly maintained the same erroneous impression. Far from regarding Bonaparte as a saviour and an envoy of Utopia, many of the country folk firmly believed that he ground the bones of his own maimed soldiers in the dust beneath his chariot-wheels, and found his chief pleasure in listening to the groans of the dying; in a word, that he was the devil in sheep's clothing. The English press did its best to foster these beliefs; it represented him as a monster, an imbecile, a butcher, and a debauchee. It teemed with the most unsavoury libels about his person, his morals, and his methods. Stories about the " Corsican monster," especially those of an atrocious character, gained wide circulation. The whole country, individually and collectively, was led to believe that the idol of France was in very truth a fiend[2] in human shape. This phase of

---

[1] London was infested at this time with emissaries engaged in feeling the public pulse as to how a foreign invasion with universal liberty as its watchword would be received.   In a criminal trial arising out of these manœuvres Samuel Rogers, the banker poet, who had been approached by a person named Stone, gave evidence. See Rogers's *Table Talk*, edited by Rev. A. Dyce, pp. 146–51, also *post*, pp. 201, 202.

[2] Thackeray tells us in *The Four Georges* that when he was on his way to England to be educated the ship touched at St. Helena. Napoleon was pointed out to him by his Indian servant. " That's he," cried the dusky worthy, " that's Bonaparte. He eats three sheep a day, and all the children he can lay hands on."

The real View of the FRENCH RAFT as intended for the Invasion of ENGLAND Drawn from the Original at Brest.

the subject will be further dealt with in the chapters devoted to the humour, poetry, pathos, and satire of the Great Terror.

On the other hand, everything calculated to stir up hatred of John Bull in France was done. Talleyrand addressed a letter to all the diplomatic and consular agents directing them to foster this spirit of hatred and malevolence. "Your first and leading object," he averred, "must be to show everywhere how little the English Cabinet is worthy of confidence. Exert all your endeavours, citizens, in this main object of your labours. You must doubtless meet with great difficulties, but you will know how to surmount them. Be not disheartened—the Army of England will remove and smooth away the obstacles that oppose you."[1]

The gullible section of the French public was told that Monge was constructing a number of huge rafts, each of which was to be 700 yards long, 350 yards wide, and eight stories high. A contemporary publication, entitled *Recherche sur L'Usage des Radeaux pour une Descente*, by M——, Colonel in the Army of Condé, formerly member of the Royal Academy at Paris, deals fully with this chimerical means of transport, and gives elaborate statistics to prove the absurdity of the plan, which was not, of course, ever seriously intended by those in authority. "One of them," says the writer, "would require thirty fir trees in length, 900 in breadth and eight in height, in all 216,000 trees; each a foot square, each containing sixty cubic feet, each foot weighing from fifty-two to fifty-five pounds, would make 3120 to 3300 feet, or three horse loads; and the whole would require 618,000 horses or

[1] *Times*, January 8th, 1798.

I.—G

108,000 carriages and as many carters to bring them from
the forest to the sea. . . . The total weight of one raft
would be 44,550 tons . . . including the ramparts, the
citadel, and the masts or machinery substituted for them,
men, horses, cannon, and ammunition, provisions, draw-
bridges, and boats. . . . Four such rafts would carry 72,000
men and 8000 horses." [1]

French finances were now at a very low ebb, and two
schemes, widely differing in detail, were put forward by
the Council of Five Hundred for raising the necessary
funds for the expedition. The first was introduced by
Monnot, in the name of a committee, who proposed a
loan of 80,000,000 livres (francs) by the issue of 80,000
shares of 1000 livres each. Twenty dividends were to be
made, with an interest of twenty-five livres, payable every
six months, and one-tenth of the loan was to be repaid
yearly by a lottery, " the reimbursement of the capital of
the loan, and the payment of the interest, to be further
secured upon the produce of the Posts." The maritime
prizes taken from England were to repay one-twentieth
part of the sums advanced, and " the names of the lenders
shall be honourably inscribed in the archives of the Legislative body." Lamarck's proposition was on a philanthropic as well as a patriotic basis, and was much more
favourably received. Registers were opened all over the
country in which enthusiastic citizens could inscribe their
names and their contributions towards defraying the cost
of the proposed expedition. The merchants of Paris and
those who could afford to give did so generously, but the
total amount received was insignificant, and recourse was
had to plunder. Berthier was sent to Rome to fill the

[1] *Gentleman's Magazine*, Vol. LXVIII, part i, 1798, p. 315.

coffers of the Army of England, and after being appointed its treasurer was named as Chief of the Staff, although he was not expected to fill this position until he had pacified Italy.[1] It is evident, therefore, that either the office was a purely nominal one, that the invasion was not to take place for some considerable time, or that Bonaparte had some other object in view. In any case, he did not show his hand until later, and turned his attention to the naval resources at his disposal, leaving Desaix to enjoy the sweets of power as *ad interim* head of the Army of England.

At this juncture the Republic possessed fifty-seven sail-of-the-line in all, thirty-four of which were at Brest, two at Lorient, one at Rochefort, five at Toulon, six at Corfu, and nine remnants of the Venetian navy. To these must be added forty-six frigates and seventy-two smaller vessels—many of them privateers. Unfortunately, not a single ship at Brest was armed, and ten were undergoing repairs; but fourteen sail-of-the-line, seventeen frigates, and three cutters were building in Channel and Atlantic ports. Seven frigates were on colonial service, and therefore could not be taken into account. As Brest was to be the head-quarters of the naval forces of the expedition, Bonaparte and the Minister of Marine put their heads together and drew up a plan for the concentration of the scattered units of the navy at that port. The six ships at Corfu, which were under Brueys, with the same number of frigates, were to take four months' rations and then set out for Brest, taking care to avoid

---

[1] The cost of the Egyptian expedition was largely defrayed by plunder and forced contributions exacted from the Swiss. See Rose's *Life of Napoleon I*, Vol. I, p. 180.

Lord St. Vincent's squadron blockading Cadiz. The
Venetian ships were to be equipped and then proceed
to Toulon to replace the vessels at that port, which, after
being armed, were to unite with those at Brest. Spain
and Holland were also called upon to furnish both ships
and troops. There was still a show of spirit in their
fleets, but they were undermanned, and there was a
lamentable dearth of stores. Truguet, formerly Minister
of Marine, had been appointed ambassador at Madrid,
and worked with commendable assiduity to bring about
this international arrangement with the Spanish Court,
which was inclined to be favourable. The dogged blockade of Cadiz by the English was bitterly humiliating
to a country which still retained a shred of respect for her
past glories and a ray of hope for the future, as the port
in question held no less than twenty-two sail-of-the-line,
six frigates, and three or four smaller craft—all in a fair
state of repair—under Admiral Mazaredo. Two sail-of-
the-line, one frigate, and five brigantines were at Ferrol,
and seven frigates at Carthagena completed the available
Spanish naval forces.[1]

The Dutch General Daendels, whose invasion plans
have been noticed in the first chapter,[2] was still undaunted and sought to revive his pet idea, and proposed
that his squadron should make for the Forth and from
thence threaten the English while the French were either
invading Ireland or the south of England.[3] Wolfe Tone
was sent by Daendels to Desaix to arouse his practical
sympathy in the project, promising thirteen ships for

---

[1] Desbrière, Vol. I, pp. 286–8.   [2] See *ante*, p. 21.
[3] The most suitable places for landing will be found on the east or south-
east of England on the sandy or shingly beaches.—Dumouriez MS., p. 7.

the expedition, on board of which he hoped to embark 25,000 men for Scotland. Tone, with an axe to grind on behalf of the United Irishmen, who were still bent on the emancipation of Ireland and were prepared to accept the assistance of the Great Nation, provided she came as an ally only, received a favourable reception. It is apparent from his diary that he was more interested in the French diversion outlined by Daendels than in the programme to be carried out in Scotland, for he approached Desaix for an appointment in the *Armée d'Angleterre*. On receiving an assurance that he should not be overlooked, Tone went skilfully to work to secure an interview with Bonaparte. He accomplished his purpose in the middle of December, 1797, and in company with his colleague, Lewens, the unofficial "ambassador" from Ireland, discussed the situation with the Commander-in-Chief. Although they had three interviews with him, Bonaparte does not appear to have shown particular interest in the cause, and, according to Tone, betrayed lamentable ignorance in Irish affairs. Eventually Tone received his commission as Adjutant-General in the Army of England—a position which he had also held in Hoche's ill-fated expedition.

At first Bonaparte seems to have been taken with Daendels's idea of striking a blow at two vulnerable points of the enemy's territory. Orders were issued for the construction of 170 flat-bottomed boats in the ports of the Batavian Republic, to be ready by March 22nd, 1798, a month earlier than the date given for the completion of the Brest programme. Additional boats were put on the stocks in various French ports on the Channel and the Atlantic, and the means of transport were further augmented by the addition of many small trading vessels, either hired, purchased, or "bespoken." Great activity was apparent at Brest. Sané, Ordnance Commissary, and Vice-Admiral Lelarge, who were in charge of the arrangements, exerted themselves to the utmost, although the lamentable dearth of men and money retarded their efforts. On Desaix paying a personal visit to Brest to see how matters were progressing, he found things not at all to his liking. On the 23rd February, 1798, only ten ships were properly equipped, and all these lacked crews. Bonaparte also sent Forfait, then a rising Government engineer and later one of the most eminent naval constructors of France, to Havre invested with considerable authority. There Forfait found nine large gunboats, together with the disarmed flotilla of Muskeyn, and announced that he would shortly have sufficient vessels for the transport of 25,800 men. Not content with this vague promise, the Commander-in-Chief sent a peremptory letter to the effect that the whole force was to be in readiness by February 28th. Cherbourg, Granville, and St. Malo were all called into requisition, over sixty gunboats being in the various yards, and at St. Malo ten old ones were overhauled and refitted. Officers were enjoined to visit Boulogne and Dunkirk to report on the condition of the boats—relics of former invasion experiments—which still lay idle and unarmed at those places. Corsairs, with engineers on board, were ordered to reconnoitre the English coast from Folkestone to Rye, and to find out what batteries would have to be taken or silenced by a landing expedition.

Notwithstanding these preparations, we find Bonaparte writing to Berthier in the early days of the new year

ENGLAND INVADED OR FRENCHMEN NATURALIZED. BY ROWLANDSON [MARCH 1798]

(1798) thanking him for sending him observations on French naval establishments in the Ionian Sea. Bonaparte says : " I should much like to have you with me in England " ;[1] but the previous reference shows which way the wind of ambition was blowing, and that he only awaited a favourable opportunity to suggest the idea of an eastern and not a western expedition. He was now apparently more inclined to follow in the footsteps of Alexander than in those of Julius Cæsar, and told Talleyrand that the proper way to attack England was by seizing Malta, occupying Egypt, and afterwards invading India. "We may change the face of the world!" he said in a burst of enthusiasm over so dazzling a prospect. This did not, however, prevent Bonaparte from setting out on February 8th, 1798, to explore the coast, ostensibly to select the best points for embarking a force should the Directory turn a deaf ear to his plans for Oriental conquest. He was accompanied by Lannes, Sulkowsky, and Bourrienne, the latter having known Bonaparte since he was nine years of age, and eventually becoming one of his secretaries. It is significant that no sooner had the Commander-in-Chief left Paris than Talleyrand broached the question of an expedition to Egypt to the Directory, laying before them Bonaparte's own plans for such a design. However, the General gave his entire attention to the work on hand. Forfait and Andréossy were examined and cross-examined. Holland was told to supply twenty or thirty gunboats and from two hundred to two hundred and fifty fishing-smacks. Bonaparte sought information from all and sundry, and would discuss matters with

[1] To General Berthier, at Milan. Dated Paris, 6th January, 1798. Bingham, Vol. I, p. 198.

smugglers and other seafaring men long after his subordinates had retired to rest. He was in search of information, and neglected no possible source of obtaining it.

It was ever his policy to enter into minute details, and
it mattered little to him to what class a man belonged so
long as he could be utilized for this purpose. Plebeian
and aristocrat alike became his tools, and men of every
degree bent, often unwittingly, to his irresistible and
imperious will. The stirring up of dormant ambition in
others was also a characteristic trait in Napoleon's scheme
of leadership. He fostered their energy instead of curb-
ing it, but he trained the tender plant in the direction it
should grow, namely, around himself and his interests. An
aristocracy of brains was Bonaparte's ideal, and the Man
of Destiny acted up to it so far as circumstances allowed
him to do so. Even now he was gathering about him the
men who were to be his marshals and the future pillars
of his throne.

His restless activity in urging forward the necessary
preparations for the contemplated invasion of England
was apparent in all directions, and astonished everybody
with whom he came in contact. Forfait remarked on it
in one of his numerous reports. "General Bonaparte,"
he says, "reached Dunkirk on February 11th. He spent
the 12th there, and on the 13th left for Belgium. During
his short stay he investigated all our preparations and
works, and drew up a plan of armaments to be executed
by March 21st. He ordered the construction of fifty
large pinnaces, and I was enjoined to move heaven and
earth to get shipping accommodation for four to five
thousand horses, fifty thousand men and guns, and all
necessary supplies; to provide large and small gunboats

A VIEW of the FRENCH RAFT, as seen AFLOAT at St. MALOES, in February 1798.
This Machine is 600 Feet long and 300 broad, mounts 500 Pieces of Cannon, with all particulars, intended to convey 60000 Troops &c for the
INVASION of ENGLAND.

1798

to the greatest possible number; and so direct these operations that in fifteen to twenty days everything should be ready to move off."[1] Contracts for the building of these vessels were entered into by the Commission des Côtes de La Manche. The names of men who afterwards distinguished themselves in Napoleon's fight for the sovereignty of the sea are to be found in the list of commissioners. General Andréossy was director-general, M. Forfait was director, and Rear-Admiral Lacrosse was inspector - general, who had as assistants Captains Ganteaume, Decrès, Dumanoir Le Pelley, and de Casa Bianca.[2] That a serious effort was being made to meet Bonaparte's demands is shown in the interesting diary of an English spy.[3]

"On the road to Lisle," he notes, "every useful tree cut down, and sawyers at work, cutting plank and other scantling, and carts transporting it to the coast in great numbers." On the 13th February, 1798, he "met General Buonaparte between Furnes and Dunkirque, going to Ostend to inspect the port, and make contracts for building flat-bottom boats for the descent." The same informant gives twenty-one large boats, "made to row a number of oars, and a mast to strike or lay down when needful," as being on the stocks at Bergh,[4] "a small town on the side of the canal from Dunkirque to St. Omer"; eleven building at Rouen, at Havre "flat-bottom boats without number," sixty at Honfleur, and fifteen at Calais. Military measures were no less active. The same eyewitness states that on the 17th February 4000 troops

[1] Desbrière, Vol. I, p. 323.
[2] *The Royal Navy*, Vol. IV, p. 339, by W. Laird Clowes, etc.
[3] *Memoirs and Correspondence of Viscount Castlereagh*, Vol. I, pp. 165-8.
[4] Bergues.

arrived at Lisle from Holland; Douay, Cambray, and
Péronne were "all full of troops, horse and foot." In Paris,
"a guard at every corner of the street, but all quiet." In
Évreux there were 5000 troops "all ready for marching";
at or near Havre 21,000 troops were stationed, "ready
to embark at short notice." At Rouen, the head-quarters
of the Army of England, 25,000 men "are ready to
march at an hour's notice, mounted and dismounted
cavalry 3000, the rest are foot, but indifferent men, and
badly clothed." On the 8th March, 1798, the spy left the
capital for Calais. "On the road, troops and waggons
with arms, without number, moving in all directions."
The following day he arrived at Douay, where he found
ninety-one pieces of artillery in the churchyard, "getting
ready to set out next day for the coast, with a great
number of troops." At Gravelines "great preparations"
were also being made. He gives the total number of
troops ordered for the invasion as 275,000 men [sic],
"mounted and unmounted, cavalry battalion men, and
infantry, all to be within twenty-four hours' forced march
of the coast."

Having concluded his tour of inspection, Bonaparte
returned to his Paris residence in the Rue Chantereine,
and reported that the time had not yet arrived for a
western expedition. "Make what efforts we will," he
informed the Directory in an exceedingly lengthy report,
"we shall not for many years acquire the control of the
sea. To make a descent upon England, without being
master of the sea, is the boldest and most difficult operation ever attempted."[1] If it were possible at all, it would
be by giving the English blockading fleets the slip and

---

[1] Dated February 23rd, 1798. See *Correspondance de Napoléon I*, Letter
No. 2419.

crossing over by night to the coast of Kent or Sussex, therefore any month after April was unfavourable. In his later projects Bonaparte was of opinion that summer was the best time for crossing. He expressed himself as very dissatisfied with the condition of the navy, but he deemed the expedition still feasible if the following programme could be carried out :—

1. Equip and collect at Havre and Dunkirk all sloops and gunboats between Ostend and Bayonne. 2. Put an embargo upon, fit out, and charter all vessels destined to transport cavalry. 3. Charter and place an embargo upon the craft which Forfait and Andréossy had catalogued as existing between Cherbourg and Antwerp. 4. Enjoin the Batavian Republic to provide the vessels which Bonaparte had asked for. 5. Commandeer the best corsairs of less than 100 tons to be found between Bordeaux and Antwerp, and send them on to Havre or Dunkirk. If these demands could not be met speedily, or if the navy was not in a fit state, Bonaparte considered that the expedition had better be abandoned, but that appearances should be kept up, and the Rhine be made the objective as being near Hanover, which they should try to take from King George III. An expedition to threaten English trade in the Levant offered another alternative ; failing all these, the General suggested that France should make peace with her neighbour across the Channel.

By the end of March thirteen ships of the Brest fleet, after being repaired, were ready for sea, a result not at all propitious for the hoped-for completion of the thirty-four by the 20th April. The Directory accordingly issued a secret *arrêté* dated March 31st :—[1]

---

[1] *European Magazine*, 1798, Foreign Intelligence, p. 278.

"The Executive Directory, considering the accounts
which have been laid before it by the Minister of Marine
and the Colonies, during his late residence at Brest, and
reflecting that the want of concert between the operations
of the army and the fleet, intended to serve in the expedition against England, opposes obstacles to the necessary
despatch, and may retard the success of it, issues the following *arrêté* :—

> "Art. 1.—General Buonaparte shall repair to Brest
> in the course of the present decade,[1] to take the
> command of the Army of England.
>
> "2.—He is invested with the control and direction of
> all the land and naval stores that are to be used in
> the expedition against England.
>
> "3.—The present *arrêté* shall not be printed. The
> Ministers of War and of the Marine are charged
> in their respective departments with the execution
> of it.
>
> "MERLIN, President.
"LAGARDE, Secretary."

It is perfectly clear that Bonaparte then realized—and
it would have been well for him had he realized it in later
periods of his power—that the English navy was an
impassable barrier between the two countries. He was
also aware of the very considerable difference of opinion
existing among the Directors as to the practicability of
the plan of invasion then under consideration. The repeated failure of previous efforts in the same direction
certainly did not encourage too great a faith in the present
expedition, nor did the unhealthy condition of the Funds
favour the spending of "thirty million francs in ready
money," asked for so peremptorily by Bonaparte. It is

---

[1] The week of the Republican Calendar.

no cause for wonder that they hesitated between striking " perfidious Albion " *vià* the Channel, or effecting the same object *vià* Egypt, with an ultimate prospect of attacking her in India, where they believed wealth was to be had without running such obvious risks as the former plan entailed. Bonaparte's ardent temperament, tinged with the romance of the sunny South and intensified by the writings of Plutarch, lent itself readily to the glamour of the East. " Europe," he asserted, " is no field for glorious exploits; no great empires or revolutions are to be found but in the East, where there are six hundred millions of men." His brother Lucien is authority for the statement that Napoleon once spoke of endeavouring to enter the British army in order to take part in empire-making in India.[1] " If I ever choose that career," he remarked, with that wonderful self-reliance which was evident even before he entered his teens, " I hope you will hear of me. In a few years I shall return a rich nabob, and bring fine dowries for our sisters." [2] How humble an ambition this seems in the light of subsequent events! Yet at the time his family considered it to be but the day-dream of a high-strung and imaginative youth. Had the suggestion been acted upon, one wonders if the names of Wellington and Bonaparte would have both gone down to posterity as

---

[1] At St. Helena Admiral Sir Pulteney Malcolm, then in command of the Cape station, which included the island, had several conversations with the fallen Emperor, and asked him whether there was any truth in this statement. Napoleon replied that it was Paoli who had urged him to seek service in the English army, his reason for not following the advice being, besides the obvious difficulties of language and religion (perhaps not so great a barrier), that he " thought the beginning of a revolution a fine time for an enterprising young man."—See *A Diary of St. Helena: The Journal of Lady Malcolm*, p. 88.

[2] *Life of Napoleon Bonaparte*, Vol. I, p. 123, by Professor W. M. Sloane.

meritorious British generals instead of as lifelong antagonists?

Bonaparte soon flung himself into the scales for an Egyptian expedition, and after receiving the consent of the Directory, promptly but stealthily set about concealing the real object of his designs, continuing to sign himself "General-in-Chief of the Army in England," while preparations for the invasion were continued under General Hédouville. "The Directorate," says Barras, "believing that it should persist in its threatening attitude against England, decided that the fitting out of the expedition should be so hurried forward as to enable an army to land in that island in the following month of October."[1] A month before he set sail from Toulon Bonaparte outlined a plan which not only reveals his increasing aggressiveness and an astounding want of principle, but also his belief in the practicability of placing an army on English soil.

"In our position," he says, writing on the 13th April, 1798, "we ought to fight England with success, and we can do so. Whether we have peace or war, we ought to spend forty or fifty millions in reorganizing our navy. Our land army will be neither more nor less powerful in consequence; but, on the other hand, war will force England to make immense preparations which will ruin her finances, destroy her commercial spirit, and completely change the constitution and manners of her people. We ought to spend the whole summer in getting ready our Brest fleet, in exercising our seamen in the roadstead, and in finishing the vessels which are under construction at

---

[1] *Memoirs of Barras*, Vol. III, p. 208. This expedition was undertaken, but the objective was altered to Ireland. See chap. iii.

Perspective representation of a RAFT, and its APPARATUS as intended by the FRENCH for their proposed
INVASION OF ENGLAND.
(from a french drawing)

This Machine, which extends 2,100 feet in length, by 1,500 feet in breadth, is to be navigated by four wheels, (x) turned in the water by the action of the wind, and moving it equal on the defence of the troops, in their disembarkation: the Raft is intended on the centre is a Fort; (b) this encloses quarters and a battery, or the defence of the troops, in their disembarkation: the Raft is intended on the centre the whole constitutes a battery of 5,00 pieces, and is intended to carry 60,000 Men, &c.

PRICE ONE SHILLING

1798

Rochefort, Lorient, and Brest. If we put some energy into the business, we may hope to have, in September, thirty-five [ships-of-the-line] at Brest, including the four or five which can be built at Lorient and Rochefort.

"Towards the end of this month we shall have in the various ports of the Channel nearly two hundred gunboats. These should be stationed at Cherbourg, Havre, Boulogne, Dunkirk, and Ostend, and should be utilized throughout the summer for training our soldiers. If we continue to grant to the Commission des Côtes de la Manche 300,000 francs every ten days, we can effect the construction of two hundred other boats, larger in size, and fit for the transport of horses. Thus we should have in September four hundred gunboats at Boulogne and thirty-five ships of war at Brest. By that time the Dutch should also have twelve ships of war in the Texel. In the Mediterranean we have ships of two kinds : twelve ships of French build which, between now and September, can be supplemented by two new ones, and nine of Venetian construction. It would be possible, after the return of the expedition which the Government is projecting in the Mediterranean, to send round the fourteen to Brest, and to retain in the Mediterranean only the nine Venetian ships ; and thus, in the course of October or November, we should have at Brest fifty men-of-war and nearly as many frigates.

"It would then be possible to transport to any desired spot in England 40,000 men, without even fighting a naval action if the enemy should be in stronger force ; for while 40,000 men would threaten to cross in the 400 gunboats and in as many Boulogne fishing-boats, the Dutch Squadron, with 10,000 men on board, would threaten to land in Scotland. An invasion of England, carried out in that way, and in the month of November or December, would be almost certainly successful. England would exhaust herself by an effort which, though immense, would not protect her against an invasion. The truth is that the expedition to the East will oblige the enemy to send six additional ships of war to India, and perhaps twice as many frigates to the mouth of the Red Sea. She would be forced to have from twenty-two to twenty-five ships at the entrance to the Mediterranean; sixty before Brest; and twelve off the Texel; and these would make a total of a hundred and three ships of war, besides those already in America and India, and besides the ten or twelve 50-gun ships and the score of frigates which she would have to keep ready to oppose the invasion from Boulogne. In the meantime we should always be masters of the Mediterranean, seeing that we should have there nine ships of Venetian build.

"There would be yet another way of augmenting our forces in that sea; that is, by making Spain cede three vessels of war and three frigates to the Ligurian Republic. That Republic can no longer be anything more than a French department; it possesses more than twenty thousand excellent seamen. It is excellent policy on the part of France to favour the Ligurian Republic, and even to see to it that she shall possess a few ships of war. Should difficulties be foreseen in inducing Spain to hand over to us or to the Ligurian Republic three vessels of war, I think that we ourselves might usefully sell to the Ligurian Republic the nine ships which we have taken from the Venetians, insisting that the Republic shall construct three more for itself. We should find that we had thus gained a good squadron manned by good seamen. With money which we should have from the Ligurians we might cause three good vessels of our own construction to be built at Toulon ; for the ships of Venetian build require as many sailors as a fine 74 ; and sailors are our weak point. In future events which may occur, it will be much to our advantage that the three Italian Republics, which should balance the forces of the King of Naples and the Grand Duke of Tuscany, shall have a stronger navy than that of the King of Naples." [1]

By the 9th May, 1798, the Army of England totalled 56,424 men, but it had lost its chief, and also its *raison d'être*, and detachments were sent back to the Army of the Rhine at Mayence, whence they had partly come ; others to Namur, Liège, and Belgium generally ; and a further large contingent to the Upper Rhine and across it into Switzerland. The whole affair was carried out very quietly, so as not to attract undue attention. Thus Bonaparte's first Army of England was gradually disbanded. Masséna's division, which had been sent to Switzerland, and consisted of the veterans of Italy, was now at Toulon, and a part of the ill-fated General Joubert's division joined them. At the end of the same month the muster roll of the *Armée d'Angleterre* had sunk to 47,330 men, dispersed along an immense stretch of Channel seaboard, and the invasion was indefinitely " postponed." The ships in the various ports were held ready in case of emergencies, but armaments were not proceeded with, and expenses were reduced all round. Many vessels and crews were taken out of commission, and orders countermanded.[2]

---

[1] *Victoires et Conquêtes*, Vol. X, p. 375. It is significant that on Bonaparte's return from Egypt he began the reorganizing of the navy.

[2] Desbrière, Vol. I, p. 334.

Early in 1798 Bonaparte had turned his attention to the two small islands of St. Marcouf, in the Channel,[1] whose possession by the English was a constant source of irritation to France. Andréossy was commissioned to make full inquiries as to the possibility of recapture, and outlined three plans for that purpose. At the moment nothing was done, although General Kléber was entrusted with the project, which he did not think would be successful. After-events proved the truth of his adverse report. On the night of May 7th, Captain Muskeyn, having under him a number of gunboats and smaller vessels, mostly manned by deficient crews, set out on this hazardous undertaking. He met with defeat, for the English offered a stubborn resistance, and the French were obliged to retreat under a hail of fire, with five men killed and fourteen wounded. The ubiquitous Wolfe Tone is constrained to note in his diary : "'What!' may the English well say, 'you are going to conquer England, and you cannot conquer the Isles Marcouf!' It is a bad business, take it any way. I wonder will the Directory examine into it? If they do not seriously establish a rigid responsibility in the Marine, it is in vain to think of opposing England by sea. There is a bad spirit existing in that corps, and I neither see nor hear of any means taken to correct it."[2]

Although Pitt and the English Cabinet knew of the hasty preparations now being made at Toulon, no definite information as to the ultimate destination of the French fleet could be obtained. One day the Prime Minister and his colleagues were informed that the troops now assem-

---

. [1] These islands are off the north coast of France, in the department of Manche, some six miles east of the coast of Cotentin.
[2] *Autobiography of Theobald Wolfe Tone*, Vol. II, p. 314.

REHEARSAL OF A FRENCH INVASION AT THE ISLAND OF MARCOUF, MAY 7, 1798.
BY THOMAS ROWLANDSON

bling at that port, as well as at Genoa, Ajaccio, and Civita Vecchia, were to be landed on the south coast of England; twenty-four hours later rumour whispered that ships and men were bound for Ireland, or to cut a canal through the Isthmus of Suez, which indeed was more than half a truth, and was one of three secret articles included in Bonaparte's instructions.

England had a floating armament which, from a mere numerical point of view, was more than sufficient to cope with France and her allies. The sea must ever be the life-blood which nourishes the British Empire, and the moral force which recent successes had given to her was an added fighting weight in the tremendous struggle for supremacy which, begun in a half-hearted way, was to be carried on in real earnest under Bonaparte as First Consul and Emperor. Watching the ports of France in which there was any semblance of a fleet, as well as guarding the seas which beat against the white cliffs of the Motherland, were men of whom England had every right to be proud.[1] Admiral Lord Bridport commanded a squadron in the Channel[2] and often appeared off Brest; in the North Sea was Admiral Lord Duncan; and Portsmouth, Plymouth, the Downs, and the Nore were all strongly guarded. Vice-Admiral Robert Kingsmill commanded at Cork, while divisions cruised in the Bay of Biscay, off the Irish coast, and elsewhere. As we have already noted, Lord St. Vincent was blockading Cadiz with the only

---

[1] In the year under review the British navy consisted of 120 sail-of-the-line, and over 500 smaller vessels, requiring the services of 120,000 seamen and marines. Supplies amounting to £13,449,388 were granted.

[2] "The Channel is the key of the position, the vital spot to secure against surprise, and it must ever be the base of our naval operations throughout the world."—Colomb's *Essays on Naval Defence*, p. 7.

squadron we had in the Mediterranean at the time, and on hearing that preparations were going on at Toulon, he immediately detached Nelson to find out the true condition of things at that port.

The capture on the 21st April, 1798, of the new French 74-gun ship *Hercule* by the *Mars* (74-guns), under Captain Alexander Hood, who lost his life, and the abortive attempt made in May on the part of Captain Home Riggs Popham to blow up the lock-gates and sluices of the canal at Ostend—which, although partially successful, did little to prevent the small craft from making their way from Holland to France for the purpose of concentration, and lost the British 163 men in addition to 1100 taken prisoners—were the only naval measures of importance in the early months of this eventful year.

"Time is everything" was a precept followed by Napoleon throughout his meteoric career, and on the 19th May, 1798, his fleet weighed anchor. Brueys was in naval command, with Ganteaume, Villeneuve, and Decrès as his subordinates, while Kléber, Desaix, Marmont, Dumas, Leclerc, Murat, Davoust, and Lannes— military men who had already distinguished themselves or were soon to write their names in the annals of France— held responsible positions in the Army of the East, which, to use Bonaparte's own words, was also "one of the wings of the Army of England."[1]

Rear-Admiral Nelson had been detached by Lord St. Vincent to reconnoitre at Toulon, as noted above, but a gale seriously disabled the *Vanguard*, his flagship, and to a great extent dispersed his fleet, reducing him to "such distress that the meanest frigate out of France

---

[1] Thiers' *French Revolution*, Vol. V, p. 265.

would have been an unwelcome guest." The severe weather served Bonaparte in good stead, for he and his host were now on their way to the land of the Pharaohs. Thus began the long series of games of hide-and-seek which the fleets of the two nations were to play for some years. The island of Malta, which had been for centuries in the possession of the Knights of St. John, and was to play so prominent a part in the diplomatic history of 1803, was "reduced" during Bonaparte's outward voyage, and £200,000 found its way into the French coffers, every coin of which was sorely needed. The knights were expelled, with the exception of fourteen who had either furnished Bonaparte with information or offered subscriptions for the invasion of England.[1] It is not within the province of this work to enter into particulars of the Egyptian expedition, but had not Nelson succeeded in destroying the greater part of the French fleet in Aboukir Bay,[2] Bonaparte might possibly have founded the great Eastern empire which so much appealed to him. In his own words, "If it had not been for you English, I should have been Emperor of the East; but wherever there is water to float a ship, we are sure to find you in our way."

From the evidence we have examined, there can be little doubt that Bonaparte believed the invasion of England to be perfectly feasible, but not with the slender means then at his command—in other words, the psychological moment had not yet arrived. The army assigned to him for the purpose was a mere handful of men compared with the vast force he congregated with a similar object in 1803-5. The navy was in a pitiable condition; the ships

[1] Bingham, Vol. I, p. 210.
[2] Battle of the Nile, 1st August, 1798.

undermanned, and what crews there were at the lowest ebb of efficiency. As he told Lewens, England "was a Power of the first rank, and the Republic must never threaten in vain." Money was scarce, and the Directory only supported him in a half-hearted way. That so ambitious a man as Bonaparte should hesitate to place himself at the head of an expedition having but a slight chance of success and practically no opportunities for self-aggrandizement calls for little comment. Miot de Melito tells us that during a conversation with the young General at the close of 1797, the latter said : " They were in a great hurry to make me General of the Army of England so that they might get me out of Italy, where I am the master, and am more of a sovereign than commander of an army. They will see how things go on when I am not there. I am leaving Berthier, but he is not fit for the chief command, and, I predict, will only make blunders. As for myself, my dear Miot, I may inform you, I can no longer obey ; I have tasted command, and I cannot give it up. I have made up my mind, if I cannot be master I shall leave France ; I do not choose to have done so much for her and then hand her over to lawyers."[1] This does not seem to accord with Miot's remark that after Bonaparte's return to Paris from Rastadt he was "entirely absorbed in the idea of a descent upon England. The survey which we made of the Channel and Atlantic coasts, and the remarks of some able men whom he met on his way, induced him to abandon his project, the execution of which seemed to him, at any rate for the time, impossible."[2] That Miot should believe in the genuineness of this projected invasion of England, as is

---

[1] *Memoirs of Miot de Melito*, Vol. I, p. 226.   [2] *Ibid.*, p. 265.

clearly shown in the above quotation, is worthy of note, for he saw nothing but a pretext in the elaborate arrangements of 1803–5, which ended in the annihilation of the allied fleets at Trafalgar. We shall have occasion to refer to this part of the question in a later chapter.

To sum up the whole matter, a consensus of authority goes to prove that at this time in Bonaparte's mind Egypt opened a vista of glorious possibilities not to be found in a descent on the British coasts. If Las Cases is to be trusted, he afterwards bitterly repented of the decision he arrived at. " If instead of the expedition to Egypt," he exclaimed, " I had undertaken that against Ireland, what could England have done now ? On such chances do the destinies of empires depend ! " [1]

[1] *Memoirs of Las Cases.*

CHAPTER IV

ENGLAND ON GUARD—PLANS FOR THE NATIONAL DEFENCE IN 1798 AND 1799

"The spirit and courage of the country has risen so as to be fairly equal to the crisis."—PITT.

ALTHOUGH the national anxiety of England concerning the projected invasion was soon, for a time at least, laid to rest by Bonaparte's departure for Egypt and the consequent gradual dispersal of the armaments on the northern coast of France, for many months the designs of the Directory occasioned serious perturbation to the British Government, awakening the fear of the country at large. There can be no doubt that the existing means of defence was totally inadequate to meet the approaching storm; but from a military point of view the figures on paper look brave enough. From the statistics published in January, 1798,[1] the second year of the crisis which we venture to term the Great Terror, it would appear that the regulars numbered 31,824, in addition to which there were sixty-nine regiments of militia totalling 45,000; 13,104 fencible cavalry; 11,042 fencible infantry; 252 troops of gentlemen and yeomanry cavalry, numbering 15,120; 856 companies of volunteers, 51,360 strong; and a supplementary militia of 60,000: making a total force of 227,450 men,

[1] *The Times*, January 15th, 1798.

exclusive of 117 companies of artillery; ten companies of invalids; fifty-nine independent companies of invalids; and the marines in garrison.

The correspondence of eminent experts of the period make it perfectly clear that England was on guard—theoretically at any rate. That is to say, although there were plenty of volunteers, the methods of organization were faulty, and the issue of weapons slow and inadequate. The Hon J. W. Fortescue, the greatest living authority on the British army, says: "Setting aside coloured levies, I think it extremely doubtful whether in any one year from 1793 to 1802 the effective strength of the regular army and auxiliary forces exceeded, even if it attained, the figure of 200,000 men."[1] The voluminous documents relating to internal defence at this period help us but little, and a lengthy search at the Record Office only confirms the opinion already voiced by Mr. Fortescue, that Henry Dundas, the Secretary of State for War, and Pitt's pet minister, was not only quite unfit to cope with the difficulties of the military situation in general, but was also "the very worst man that could possibly have been chosen to found the traditions of such an office."[2] Truth to tell, it was a case of too many cooks spoiling the broth, and the offices of the Secretary of State, the Under Secretary of State, and the Secretary at War continually clashed. The arrangements for internal defence were under the immediate supervision of the Deputy Secretary at War, and as no statistics apparently exist amongst the Home Office and War Office records respecting the number of men employed in this important

---

[1] Fortescue's *History of the British Army*, Vol. IV, part ii, p. 894.
[2] *Ibid.*, Vol IV, part i, p. 208.

service from 1793 to 1801, it is clear that there was a lamentable lack of system. It should be mentioned, however, that previous to July, 1794, the Home Office controlled all such matters. The most able administrator was the Duke of York, who was appointed Commander-in-Chief in Great Britain on the 3rd April, 1798. He proved himself worthy of the responsible post to which he was called, and the numerous circulars he issued to those in authority when invasion threatened is sufficient evidence of his keen interest in everything connected with the protection of the realm.

The King's message to Parliament, read in both Houses on January 11th, 1798, sounded a shrill note of alarm, and ten thousand men belonging to the Supplementary Militia were authorized by Parliament to volunteer into the regular army to the extent of not more than one-fifth of that force in any given county. No liability was attached to them to serve out of Europe. Half of this force was to be embodied before the 10th March, and the remainder whenever necessary. Following quickly on this an Act was passed, on the 5th April, "to enable His Majesty more effectively to provide for the Defence and Security of the Realm during the present War, and for indemnifying persons who may suffer in their property, by such measures as may be necessary for that purpose."[1] The scheme was pioneered by Dundas, who admitted that "it is not in our regular forces alone that we rest with security. Never could this country boast such a force as it now has to look up to, resting on the basis of voluntary exertions. Not less than fifty or sixty thousand men are ready to be brought into the field, in support of the

[1] 38 Geo. III, c. 27.

AN OFFICER OF THE HIGHLAND ASSOCIATION.

ONE OF OUR **VOLUNTEER DEFENDERS OF 1798**

106
1

country against the enemy, upon the principle of voluntary service, actuated by zeal for the cause in which the country is engaged. . . . The purport of the Bill is confined to two or three objects. It does not go further than what has already been adopted in many of the larger counties. In the county of Dorset, in particular, individuals have come forward in a manner similar to what it is proposed they should by this Bill. Many means of defence against the enemy have been taken. The Sheriff of the county has come forward at the head of the *Posse Comitatûs*."[1]

As Dundas frankly stated, this latest plan was based upon Mr. Clavell's admirable methods,[2] which were fully described in a little work published at the time by William Morton Pitt,[3] M.P. for Dorset, entitled *Thoughts on the Defence of these Kingdoms, and the raising of the Posse Comitatûs*, which proved invaluable to those upon whom the important duty of forming armed associations devolved. These were brought into being by the Act of the 5th April, 1798, and their members were to carry on a sort

---

[1] Speech in the House of Commons, 27th March, 1798.

[2] See *ante*, p. 27.

[3] William Morton Pitt, of Kingston Maurward, son of John Pitt, of Encombe, Dorset, M.P. for Wareham and Dorchester, by Marcia, daughter of Mark Anthony Morgan, of Ireland (cousin of the first Lord Rivers). Born the 16th May, 1754; M.P. for Dorset; married (first) Margaret, daughter of John Gambier, (second) Grace Amelia, daughter of Henry Seymer, of Hanford. He died the 29th February, 1836. He was in advance of his age in his philanthropic efforts to improve the condition of the poor on his estates in Purbeck and Kingston. He established manufactories for spinning twine and making sail-cloth at Corfe Castle, with a view to detaching the Purbeck coasters from their smuggling habits. Also on his estate at Fordington he began a bleaching, spinning, and weaving industry in 1795. Nor was Pitt unmindful of the religious condition of his tenants, for both in Wareham and Corfe Castle he established Sunday-schools, managed by a local committee and organized by a regular system of parochial visitors. In literary tastes he was not deficient. The second edition of Hutchins' *History of Dorset*—to which he was a valued contributor—was dedicated to him.

of guerilla warfare, and to make themselves useful in the way outlined by the High Sheriff of Dorset. The remuneration of the men was one shilling a week if requested ; but they were obliged to provide their own uniforms unless the parish did so. The following letter, hitherto unpublished, from the Marquis of Buckingham to John Penn of Portland, is specially interesting because it shows how Clavell's methods and Morton Pitt's book influenced the history of the time :—

"Dear Sir,   "STOWE *Feby.* 9 1798.

"A work having been transmitted to me entitled Thoughts on the Defence of these Kingdoms by Mr. Wm Morton Pitt, containing Precepts Warrants & Schedules under which a plan was digested a few months since for raising the Posse Comitatus of the County of Dorset by their very active & excellent H Sheriff Mr Clavell: I communicated it yesterday to an Adjourned Q^r Sessions & Gnrl meeting of the Lieut^{cy}, who all agreed with me wishing for a full discussion of a measure so interesting so feasible & so essential at this period, & for this purpose I have summoned the Magistrates & Dep^y Lieut^{ts} to meet me at Aylesbury on Friday the 16th ; to consider of a plan for obtaining such returns & information as may enable the H Sheriff to call out by his writ, & under his command the Civil force of the County as a Posse Comitatus, in case of riot insurrection & invasion. I have directed Mr Chaplin to send you a copy of these papers, & I trust that (as your official appointment will have taken place) you will honour us with your attendance, & assistance in digesting measures which in your hands will I am persuaded be of the utmost advantage to the country in any of the unfortunate cases to which these precautions look. I well know how warmly your constitutional zeal and loyalty will induce you to give your most serious

JOHN BULL ARMING

ARMING FOR THE FRAY. 1798-99

consideration to this subject, & I am anxious that you should be possessed as soon as may be of the several data necessary for you to obtain before you can exert (in the manner you would wish) the constitutional powers which will be vested in you; & if any deviations from the plan pursued in the Cʸ of Dorset should appear to you necessary, I am persuaded that every attention will be given to your wishes by the Lieutᶜʸ & magistracy. I have written to our friend Mr Sullivan to request him to favour us with his assistance, as I know he has turned his mind very much to this subject.

> " I am Dear Sir with the truest regards & esteem
> " Your very faithful & obedᵗ Servant
> " BUCKINGHAM."[1]

Three armies and a corps of reserve were formed for the defence of the capital—two of 15,000 men, and one of 30,000 men stationed at Colchester, the low-lying Essex coast offering many advantages to an invading host.[2] That gallant old soldier Marquis Cornwallis, then Master-General of the Ordnance, saw that there were many weak spots in the plan of defence. " I have no doubt of the courage or fidelity of our militia," he writes, " but the system of David Dundas,[3] and the total want of light

[1] Mr. Broadley's collection of Dorset MSS. Mr. Penn was the lineal descendant of the founder and first Lord Proprietor of the State of Pennsylvania. George III gave him the site on which he built Pennsylvania Castle, Portland, and there, while residing at Weymouth, the King more than once reviewed the corps of Dorset Yeomanry raised by Mr. Penn's exertions.

[2] *Gentleman's Magazine*, Vol. LXVIII, part i, 1798, p. 76.

[3] Sir David Dundas (1735–1820) was probably the best tactician in England at the time. He drew up the "Rules and Regulations for the Formation, Field Exercises, and Movements of His Majesty's Forces," which were issued to the army in June, 1792. After seeing much active service he was made Lieutenant-General and Governor of Landguard Fort in 1797. Dundas was made a K.B. in 1804, and five years afterwards he became Commander-in-Chief.

infantry, set heavy on my mind, and point out the advantages which the activity of the French will have in the country, which is for the most part inclosed."[1]   Neither was Cornwallis blind to the defects of the corps stationed in Essex, which he avers is "a most difficult county to defend with inexperienced troops, unaccustomed to move against a most active enemy, who have derived confidence from their extraordinary success against the most powerful and warlike countries of Europe."[2]   Things were in no way improved in May, when the preparations at Toulon were in an advanced state, and invasion seemed imminent. Cornwallis thought either Portugal or Ireland was the destination of the expedition, "I should rather think the latter."   The supply of arms was deficient, a serious failing duplicated in 1803, and, as the Marquis says, "the only means by which the innumerable local corps in all parts of the country can be armed is by providing balls for fowling-pieces."[3]

Brigadier-General John Moore, of Peninsular fame, and then but recently returned from the West Indies, who made a tour of the east coast in company with an officer of the Engineers acting under the orders of Sir William Howe, commanding the district including Essex, Suffolk, and Norfolk, has left on record that "the coast from the Thames to Harwich is the most vulnerable," but that the fourteen miles of coast known generally as Clacton Beach

---

[1] To the Hon. Col. Wesley.   Dated from Whitehall, February 23rd, 1798. *Correspondence of Charles, 1st Marquis Cornwallis*, Vol. II, p. 333, edited, with notes, by C. Ross.   Cornwallis uses the original spelling of the name. The connection between the Wellesleys and the Dorset Wesleys, the ancestors of John Wesley, is now generally admitted.

[2] To Sir William Howe, March 26th, 1798.   *Ibid.*, Vol. II, p. 334.

[3] To Major-General Ross.   Dated from Whitehall, May 19th, 1798.   *Ibid.*, Vol. II, p. 337.

affords good anchorage and an opening to Colchester. Hollesley Bay, below Woodbridge, Aldborough, Southwold, Lowestoft, and Yarmouth are the most important points from Harwich to Yarmouth for this purpose. "Encampments have been little used in England during this war," he notes. "Barracks have been substituted, and are erected wherever it has been thought proper to station troops. These stations in the Essex and Suffolk districts are upon the great road leading from London to Yarmouth; it runs parallel to the coast, and is nowhere more than thirteen or fourteen miles from it. Stations— Chelmsford, Romford, Colchester (head-quarters), and Ipswich. There is a small supply of provisions at each of these stations, but the depôts are in a rear line of Braintree, Indbury, and Thetford." The batteries at the entrance of the Yare "are completely inadequate," and can only "protect the town and shipping from the insults of privateers." Yarmouth he regards as "a desirable possession." At Cromer, "a little fishing town," a battery was erected on the cliff "for the protection of trading vessels. Thirty of the inhabitants, formed into a company of artillery, man the battery." Of places below Harwich chosen as suitable for the erection of batteries he mentions "Walton Gap, Holland Marsh, and Clacton Wick."[1]

Mention has been made that the Isle of Wight had been looked upon with envious eyes by the French in 1777.[2] The following semi-official communication with reference to its defenceless state twenty years after the note of warning had been sounded shows that England, then as now, was slow to move in putting her own house in order.

[1] *Diary of Sir John Moore*, Vol. I, pp. 261–7, edited by Major-General Sir J. F. Maurice.   [2] See *ante*, p. 3, note.

"*Private.*   "CARISBROOKE CASTLE,

"My Dear Sir,   "*6th March*, 1797.

"I trouble you with the charge of the enclosed to the D. of Portland and I am well persuaded, that you will kindly give y^r aid to our sollicitations from hence for a little more attention than has been paid to us.—When I was last here—about Xtmas—(since which my ill health has obliged me to be absent) I have succeeded in obtaining general resolutions for exertion in aid of Government, and at that time Mr Wm Pitt helped us materially by his assurance of recommendation, that we might be protected by a respectable regular force and a support of Artillery. Our Militia had been instructed in the use of Cannon & it was proposed, that two or more Field Pieces sh^d be supplied for the Corps. They are still without any, & indeed there are none of that description in the Island nor of any other, except those which are mounted in one or two of the Old Forts, and which w^d afford a very limited protection.—You will see what I have said upon this head in my letter to the D. of Portland; & I earnestly hope that this serious deficiency may be soon remedied. Mr Wm Pitt thinks that we sh^d immediately have some twelve pounders and indeed we are dreadfully exposed without them. Can you tell when?

"It is wonderful with what reluctance the People here are induced to be enrolled under the Cavalry and supplementary Militia Acts because of the little attention paid to us. But I have ventured to encourage better hopes and notions, and all things at present promise well. I have engaged proper persons in separate districts throughout the Island to make returns of the stock &c.—and we shall forthwith fix upon a proper place to which it may in case of necessity be removed. Associations are forming rapidly and of a real usefull kind, but we shall be able to do nothing without arms. I sh^d hope that we may form

Companies to the amount of fifteen hundred or two thousand men, who will really give up a suff^t portion of time for necessary exercise. Major Cooper, who is employed here under Col. Nesbit in attention to the Foreign Corps, and is a very active, intelligent officer, has hinted to me, that there are always a great many light Artillery Carbines at the Ordnance, which might suit some of these Companies and might well be spared.—He has here upon the spot a few hundreds of heavier Musquets, which are not wanted for any partic^r purpose and w^d answer well for other Companies, if we may obtain an order for them. But indeed we must have the number required from some quarter. We must not suffer again this spirit to cool.—

"In regard to the Cavalry and supplementary Militia, we shall be complete, I trust, on Sat^y next, and I shall then make my report according to directions, that we may be furnished with Cloaths and Arms.—I have just rec^d the patterns, which you was so good as to send, and We shall adopt them.—

"Excuse the intrusion of this scrawl, I thought it might be desirable for you to know how matters go in various quarters, and I therefore give you a sketch of ours. I hope, that the Enemy will not be in a condition to attack us, till we have obtained our Cannon &c. &c.

"I congratulate you upon the glorious exploits of my friend Sr J. Jervis.[1] The consequence must be admirable. Rule Britannia! Huzza!

"Ever, my dear Sir, most truly

"Y^r faithfull humble Ser^t

"Thos. Orde-Powlett."[2]

[1] Battle of Cape St. Vincent, fought on February 14th, 1797.

[2] Thomas Orde-Powlett was Secretary to the Treasury in 1782, and Secretary to the Duke of Rutland when the latter was Lord Lieutenant of Ireland. Through his wife Powlett inherited the estates of the Duke of Bolton and assumed the name of Powlett and was raised to the peerage. The above letter is from Mr. Broadley's collection of MSS.

I.—I

The diary of "Weathercock" Windham, the Secretary-at-War, contains many references to the subject which was then the chief topic of conversation in palace and cottage, and fully corroborates the criticisms passed by Cornwallis on the subject of defence. The following may be cited as examples :—

"11th (January, 1798). Saw Sir W. Howe. Much impressed with danger, he thought force insufficient in '95' when North threatened, by 12,000 men ; said so, and got rebuked for it. Could not, in his present district, viz. Essex, bring against an enemy who should land at Clayton, or Clacton (near Ipswich river as it would seem), more than 6000. River Lea ought to be provided with sluices. Thinks there should be much light infantry : present arms as good as any ; much endeavour to teach use of bayonet. Great difficulty with light infantry to teach them to disperse. Only three positions—Colchester, Chelmsford, and Brentwood—Lord Petre's, not Warley. Two former would require 25,000 men. . . .[1]

"25th. Promised by Huskisson a sight of the plan prepared by the Adjutant-General for police of London, in case of invasion; also copy of the paper of stations, prepared by Sir Charles Grey. Nepean[2] showed me scheme of distribution of gunboats ; three divisions, viz. Downs, Portsmouth, Plymouth."[3]

"30th (March). Saw Duke of York. Talk about

---

[1] *The Diary of the Right Hon. William Windham,* 1784-1810, p. 383, edited by Mrs. Henry Baring.

[2] Sir Evan Nepean (1751-1822). In 1794 he was made Under Secretary for War, and in the following year he became Secretary of the Admiralty. Created a baronet, 16th July, 1802; Chief Secretary for Ireland, 20th January, 1804. In September of the same year Nepean was appointed one of the Lords Commissioners of the Admiralty. He purchased Loder's Court, Dorset, in 1799.

[3] *The Diary of the Right Hon. William Windham,* 1784-1810, p. 389, edited by Mrs. Henry Baring.

defence of country. Stated my plan of opening the country for cavalry. Duke rather seemed to like it. Recommended also the abolition of drafting. Duke agreed about danger of landing in Cawsand Bay. Had seen Delancey on same subject in morning. House: Committee on Mr. Dundas's Bill for Driving Country. Conversation with Rose, jun., who is full of apprehensions about the Isle of Wight and the Needles. . . ."[1]

"4th (April). . . . Colonel R. assured me that six days before, when he left the Isle of Wight, the 10th Regiment had not arrived there, nor, as I understood him, was there any other regular regiment but one of about two or three hundred men; no guns but about four, nor any measure of defence taken.

"8th. Information by Hammond confirming immediate intentions of a descent."

Windham also alludes frequently to the persistence with which the Cabinet evaded a definite settlement of the mode of defence. From November, 1797, to May, 1798, his diary abounds with such references as the following:—[2]

"Council. . . . Much talk afterwards about measures of war." "Cabinet at Duke of Portland's. Understood question to be brought forward of measures of defence. . . . Nothing said at Council about defence, as I learnt afterwards from Lord Spencer." ". . . Met Clinton, sen.; talked about the state of defence of the country; full of apprehensions; deeply impressed with the deficiency of our force in every respect, particularly in the total want of Light Infantry. Duke of York was to settle next day at the city about the regulations of London, so that hitherto, nothing seems to have been done but to prepare loose plan that is at the reading-room." "Council at eleven. . . . Made attempt to bring on question about

[1] *Ibid.*, p. 390.　　　　[2] *Ibid.*, pp. 382-95.

state of country, but could not succeed.   Have seen since and with some vexation, that I might and ought to have succeeded, so far, at least, as to have made several of the observations that I wished.   Dinner at Pitt's."   "Council. . . . Again brought up question about defence : begged off for the moment, but promise that it should be taken up soon."   "11th (May).   Clear now that there is no general plan settled ; the whole idea, the bringing round all the troops possible.   Notion that we did not want light troops, because our troops upon the Continent had been victorious whenever they had been tried against the enemy by themselves."

Many wealthy men came forward and organized their tenantry and others dependent upon them into volunteer corps.   The Prince of Wales set an excellent example by enrolling his servants in the corps attached to the parish of St. James's, and among others the Duke of Northum-. berland furnished clothing and other accoutrements to those of his tenants and labourers who cared to volunteer, paying them one shilling per day for each time of exercise. Both infantry and cavalry were included in this corps, which the Duke commanded in person.   The firemen of the Phœnix Fire Office were trained as artillerymen at the expense of the proprietors, and the Governors of the Bank of England raised a corps of employés to defend the building from the hands of potential French despoilers.   The men were divided into six battalion companies and two flank companies, one of grenadiers and one of light infantry ; quite a formidable little force.

All contributions for the defence of the country were as "thankfully received" in England as they were for its invasion in France.[1]   To this end a fund was opened at

[1] See *ante*, p. 82.

of *Stafford* ——

—— —— affociated

ferve without Pay, for the Protection thereof,
in Cafe of any Emergency, at the Requifition of
the Civil Power; but not to take Rank in Our
Army, nor the faid *Affociation* to be fubject
of the faid
iven at Our
at St. James's the *fifteenth* Day *of June*
in the *Thirty Eighth* Year of Our Reign.

By His Majefty's Command,

Portland

Thomas Clifford Efq: Captain
a Company of Infantry of
affociation of the Town of
Stafford) ——

FACSIMILE OF A VOLUNTEER OFFICER'S COMMISSION. JUNE 15, 1798

the Bank in January, and although both cash and promises were slow in coming in at first, when once the ball was rolling it did not stop until the very respectable sum of £2,500,000 had been secured. On the 9th February an influential meeting was held in "the square at the Royal Exchange," and £46,534. 3s. 6d. was raised by 218 sub-scribers, and at a previous gathering at the Mansion House the donations amounted to £20,000. During the early months of the fund the King contributed £20,000; the Queen £5000; the Duke of York £5000; the Cabinet Ministers £2000 each; the five Princesses £100 a year each during the war; the Bank of England £200,000; the Marquis of Buckingham "all fees and profits received in his office of Teller of the Exchequer, during the war; after reserving the sum of £2700 and the allowances to the clerks," in other words, about £10,000 per annum; the Bishops gave £1000 each at least, some of them more; the Duke of Marlborough £5000; the University of Cambridge £1000, that of Oxford £500, to which must be added the donations of several individual Colleges. In Edinburgh a subscription of £19,000 was raised in two hours; the boys of the Merchant Taylors School avoided the "tuck" shop and sent a cheque for £105, while practically every city voted £500 or more. The various city companies, never backward in supporting a good cause, subscribed liberally. Nor were the contributions confined to. the private citizen or public body, for many regiments gave up a day's pay to help swell the fund, and Jack Tar was no less patriotic. The seamen and marines of H.M.S. *Argonaut* gave ten shillings each out of their wages "to drive before us into the sea all French scoundrels, and other blackguards that would take their parts." Many of the corporations throughout the country agreed to abolish all feasts and to send the money that would have been spent on them to the fund. Patriotic munificence was very much the order of the day, once the initial difficulty of overcoming public inertia had been surmounted.

The corporation and citizens of Liverpool sought and obtained powers from Parliament for the purpose of erecting batteries and taking other measures of precaution against an invading force, half of the expense to be met by the corporation, and the remainder by means of a general rate. Pitt seized eagerly upon this commendable display of public and private spirit, and called it "a most useful suggestion, and might be made the groundwork of a most excellent general defence." The shipowners of Campbeltown, in Argyllshire, placed their vessels, aggregating some three thousand tons in all, at the disposal of Government. The male inhabitants of the various City wards were called upon to form themselves into armed associations, the able-bodied to learn the use of arms, the remainder to procure constables' staves and be sworn in as supernumerary constables. Each ward was commanded by its own alderman. The rallying point was to be the Mansion House on the appearance of Bonaparte's troops, and all the associations were to be united in one band, if necessary, under the direction of the Lord Mayor and the Court of Aldermen. It should be noted, however, that some corps were raised on the distinct understanding that they should not be required to leave their own parish unless by individual consent. Within a few months there were forty thousand members of the various associations of London and Westminster,

PREPARATIONS *(in the* SPRING CAMPAIGN)

THE LIFE OF A VOLUNTEER IN 1798-9 AS PORTRAYED IN A CONTEMPORARY CARICATURE

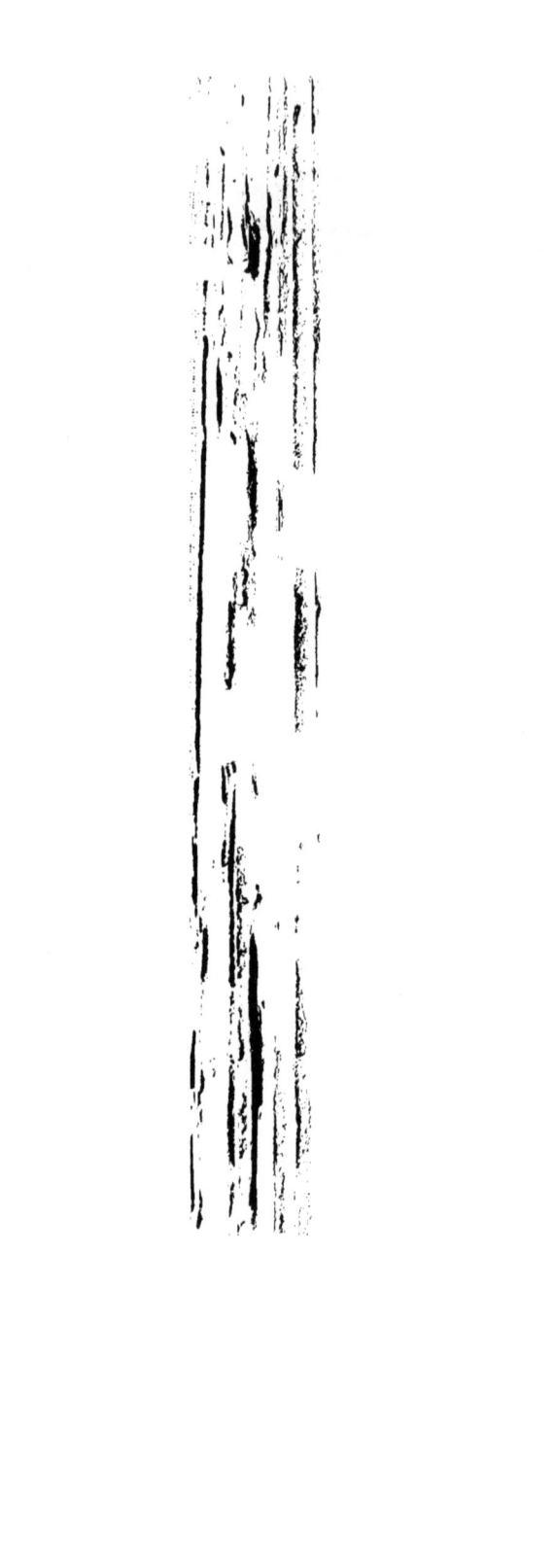

proof positive of the splendid spirit which animated the nation. With few exceptions, such as the Christ Church Association; the St. Pancras Volunteers; the St. George's, Hanover Square, Armed Association; the Marylebone Volunteers; and the Hans Town Association, who chose blue as the colour of their uniforms, red was the prevailing note, with blue, yellow, black, or white facings. Almost every conceivable design of head-dress was represented, including "helmet hats" with regulation feathers; black bearskins, with red feather tipped white, and small hair cockade; and hats closely resembling those worn by the C.I.V. in the late South African campaign. White pantaloons, with whole or half gaiters, usually completed a picturesque uniform which would contrast oddly with the more sombre ones of the present day. On a small breast-plate was inscribed the name or initials of the corps.

Not the least interesting body of citizen soldiers was Sadler's Sharpshooters, who were armed with a patent gun and long cutting bayonet invented by the man who did so much to bring the force into being, and whose name it bore. Sadler lived in Pimlico, and was "a very ingenious machinist, inventor of the celebrated war chariot, in which two persons, advancing or retreating, can manage two pieces of ordnance (three-pounders) with alacrity and in safety, so as to do execution at the distance of two furlongs."[1]

In a letter to Lord Mornington, Pitt admirably sums up the situation: "The two great objects of our attention and exertion now are," he says, "to endeavour to raise spirit enough in the country to contribute voluntarily

[1] Description of plate in *Loyal Volunteers of London and Environs.*

to the expense of the war, such a sum as in addition
to the assessed taxes may bring our loan within a
moderate shape, and next, to be prepared both by sea
and land for the invasion which I have little doubt will
be attempted in the course of the year, though the latter
is much the easier work of the two.   And I hope we shall
have to make the option between burning their ships
before they set out, or sinking them either on their
passage or before their troops can land, or destroying
them as soon as they have landed, or starving them and
taking them prisoners afterwards.   Indeed the scheme
seems so romantic (without the prospect of any naval
force to support it) that at any other moment it would
not be credible; and it can hardly be attempted on any
other notion but that it may be worth the enemy's while
to devote two-thirds of an immense army to immediate
destruction, for the sake of the mischief which the
remainder may effect before they share the same fate.   In
the meantime, however (though on the whole I think the
attempt will be made), there are two possible events which
may prevent it.   One is if there should be fresh confusion
in France, which seems not distant, and of which the issue
cannot be even conjectured.   The other is, if the new
King of Prussia and the powers of the North should at
last awaken, of which there is just now some appearance,
but it is not yet decided enough to rely upon.   The new
decree aimed at our commerce,[1] but tending to annihilate
a large part of the profit of neutral nations, may perhaps

---

[1] By a law passed on the 8th January, 1798, the French Government
decreed that all vessels that had touched at an English port should not be
allowed to enter any French port.   Ships with British goods on board were
also declared to be lawful prize.

(added to the danger of Hamburg and the North of Europe) bring Denmark at least, if not Sweden or Russia, to be ready to enter into an effectual concert with Prussia. And this prospect may tempt Prussia to take a decided part, which if it does, Europe will at last be saved." The Prime Minister adds, with reference to the voluntary contribution, that "tho' it has begun but languidly, I have now good hopes of success; as I have been enabled today to announce to the Bank, the King's intention of giving one-third of his privy purse. . . . We in office have thought it right to give an ample *fifth* of our income."[1]

Writing to the same friend three months later, Pitt is more optimistic than ever. "The voluntary contribution has succeeded to a great extent. The spirit and courage of the country has risen so as to be fairly equal to the crisis. . . . The French go on, I believe in earnest, with plans and demonstrations of invasion; but the effect here is only to produce all the efforts, and all the spirit we can wish."[2] On the last day of May he forecasts to Lord Mornington another attempt on Ireland, in which matter he was correct, as subsequent events proved, although neither the port mentioned nor the anticipated surprise was a successful prophecy. "The French," he says, "will probably try a magnificent project of invading Ireland from Toulon; but will be surprised at meeting Lord St. Vincent in the Mediterranean, where they least expect him. . . ."[3]

Bonaparte's movements at Toulon were duly recorded

[1] *Pitt*, p. 205, by Lord Rosebery. This letter is dated from Wimbledon, January 26th, 1798.

[2] *Ibid.*, p. 208. This letter is dated from Wimbledon, April 22nd, 1798, 9 p.m.

[3] *Ibid.*, p. 210. Dated from Downing Street, Thursday, May 31st, 1798.

in the British newspapers. It was believed at first that he contemplated invading Portugal by sea, but on April 24th *The Times* printed details of the expedition, followed three days later by the intelligence that in all probability the fleet was destined for Portugal or Ireland. The publication of the following " Hints to assist in the General Defence of London, etc.," on the 25th shows that the fear of an immediate invasion of England was by no means over :—

" 1st.   Block Houses to be built in each square for the *Corps-de-Garde*.

" 2nd.   Horse to Patrole the streets.

" 3rd.   Barricadoes for each street, to be defended by the inhabitants of the street ; the corner houses to be supplied with hand-grenades, and for the more easy communication, passages should be made from house to house on the roofs.

" 4th.   A bell in the centre of each street, to summon the inhabitants to their posts.

" 5th.   Corner houses and barricadoes to be the general rendezvous in case of an alarm.

" 6th.   Artillery parks to be in the squares, and as many artillery as possible to be placed at the barricadoes of the main streets.

" 7th.   Night cellars in the city and St. Giles's, etc., to be examined, and every precaution to be taken, that they should not harbour improper persons.

" 8th.   All communications to be cut off from house to house underground.

" 9th.   All obnoxious foreigners to be sent out of the country.

" 10th.   No foreign servants, male or female, to be allowed.

" 11th.   Prisoners to be put into prison ships, in the most secure situations ; so that they may be destroyed instantly, in cases necessary for the defence of the country.

" 12th. No quarter to be given the enemy when found in the actual attempt of invading the country, whether in transports, gun-boats, or otherwise.

"'13th. No Dutch boats to be allowed to supply the country with fish, as they carry back much useful information to the enemy.

" 14th. Every company of watermen, lightermen, lamp-lighters, coalheavers, hackney-coachmen, etc. etc., to be formed into corps for the defence of London—they are to be called out, in case of actual danger to the town, and magazines of arms to be placed in the Companies' Halls for their use.

" 15th. Fire-engines to be placed in proper stations.

" 16th. A large *Corps-de-Garde* to be placed to defend the water-works and pipes which supply the town.

" 17th. *Têtes-de-Pont* to be erected for the Defence of the Bridges on the Thames, and *casson* works for the southern slope of the bridges.

" 18th. All barges, vessels, and boats, to be taken from the Surrey-side of the Thames, in case of the enemy making good their landing.'

Towards the end of February, 1798, something like consternation reigned in London and several of the southern counties. A number of ships had been seen off the isle of Portland, and not having replied to the signals from the shore, were taken to be the enemy's fleet. The intelligence was telegraphed to Weymouth, to the dismay of the inhabitants and visitors, and the Prince of Wales, who was at his seat at Crichel,[1] immediately sent off a messenger with letters to the King, and to Commander-in-Chief the

---

[1] The Dorset seat of the Sturts, now occupied by Humphrey Napier Sturt, Lord Alington. Mr. Charles Sturt of Crichel, M.P. for Bridport (1763–1812), was detained for many years as a prisoner by Napoleon, and subsequently published his adventures in France. His widow, a daughter of the fourth Lord Shaftesbury, survived till 1854.

Duke of York, telling them of the rumour. On the latter receiving the intelligence, which had been expected daily, and looked for with enthusiasm in some quarters and dismay in others, he sent to Nepean and Dundas, and then made his way post-haste to the War Office. There the report was corroborated by an express from Dorchester. A meeting was hastily summoned, and the Duke of York, Pitt, Lord Grenville, Earl Spencer, Dundas, and Nepean met at the Admiralty to consider what steps should be taken to resist the invaders. While they were discussing the matter a despatch was received stating that the enemy's fleet had resolved itself into a number of homeward-bound West Indiamen, to the intense relief of all concerned.

By the middle of April, 1798, the beacon-masts, watch-houses, and semaphore telegraphs which had been in course of erection on the east coast were completed, and it was said that the approach of an enemy's fleet could be announced from Yarmouth to the Nore in less than five minutes. There was a telegraph station at the Admiralty, and a similar apparatus was placed on one of the towers of Westminster Abbey.

In his speech of May 6th, which received applause from both sides of the House, Mr. Secretary Dundas again voiced the fears, not only of the Government, but of the whole country, as to the outcome of Bonaparte's preparations, and outlined a still greater movement on the part of the people. "The truth," said he, "is undeniable, that the crisis which is approaching must determine whether we are any longer to be ranked as an independent nation. We must take the steps which are best calculated to meet it ; let us provide for the safety of the infirm, the aged, the women, the children, and put arms into the hands of

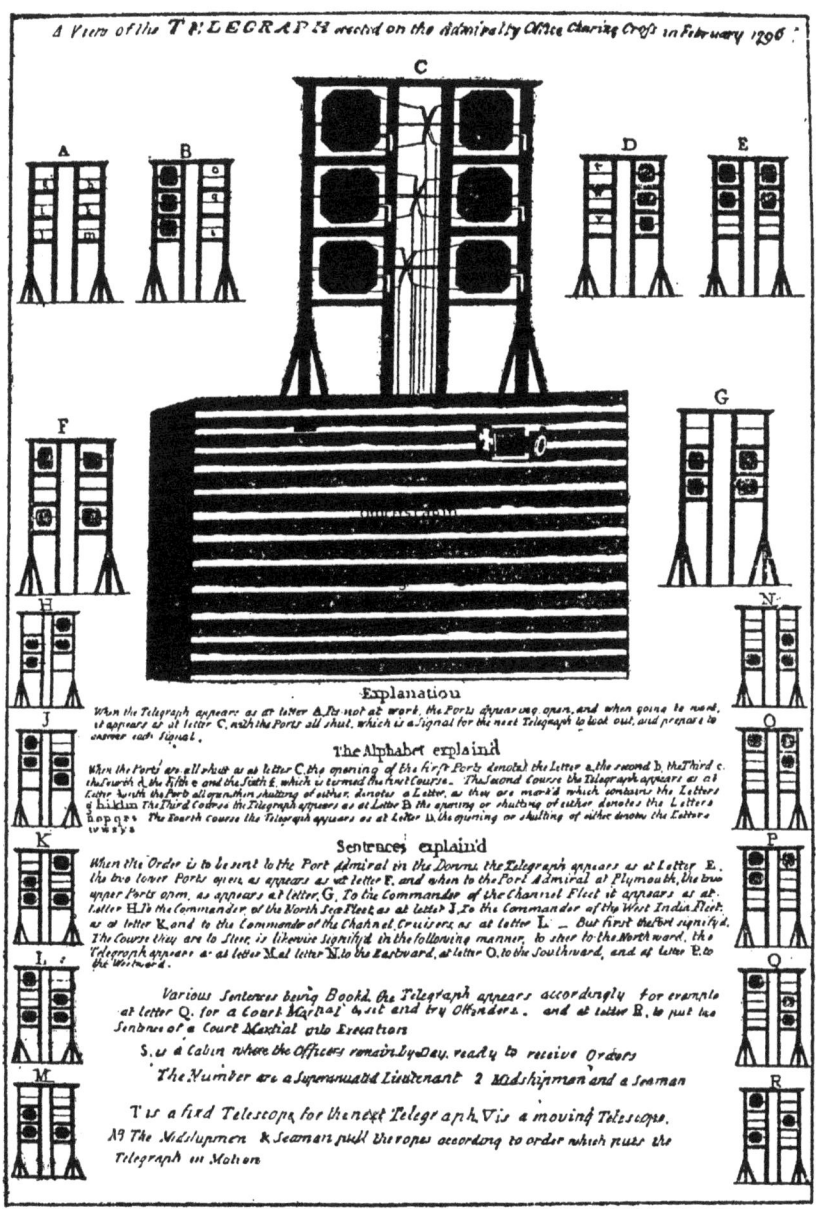

The semaphore telegraph erected on the Admiralty Office in 1796. Duplicates of this ingenious apparatus were placed on the east coast in 1798.

the people. We must fortify the menaced points, accumulate forces round the capital, affix on the church doors the names of those who have come forward as volunteers, and authorise members of Parliament to hold commissions in the army without vacating their seats. I am well aware of the danger of intrusting arms to the whole people without distinction. I am no stranger to the disaffection, albeit much diminished, which still lingers amongst us; I know well that, under the mask of pursuing only salutary reforms, many are still intent of bringing about a revolution, and for that purpose are willing to enter into closest correspondence with the avowed enemies of their country. But, serious as is the danger of intrusting arms to a people embracing a considerable portion of such characters, it is nothing to the risk which we should run if, when invaded by the enemy, we were unprepared with any adequate means of defence. I trust to the good sense of the great body of the people to resist the factious designs of such enemies to their country. I trust that the patriotism by which the immense majority of them are animated will preclude them from ever using their arms but for worthy purposes: I trust to the melancholy example which has been afforded in a neighbouring kingdom of the consequences of engaging in popular insurrection, for a warning to all Britons who shall take up arms, never to use them but in defence of their country, or the support of our venerable constitution."

On the same day General Sir Charles Grey,[1] who was in command of the Southern District, in which were so many "danger zones," issued his General Orders :—[2]

[1] Afterwards first Earl Grey.
[2] *Annual Register*, 1728, p. 189 of Appendix to the Chronicle.

"BARHAM COURT,
"*May 6th.*

"General Sir Charles Grey, judging it necessary to announce to the troops he has the honour to command in the southern district, that, from the vicinity of the coasts of Essex, Kent, and Sussex, to that of France, and the very great preparations the enemy are said to be making to carry their long threatened invasion of this kingdom into execution, which though he cannot bring himself to believe, from the impossibility of its success, yet it is not impossible but they may be mad and desperate enough to try the experiment, to make a little confusion without a hope : he is therefore persuaded of being more successful, should the daring attempt be made on the coasts of the districts, namely, Essex, Kent, and Sussex, in which he is most immediately concerned ; and he does not hesitate to say, that it is an event more desirable than not, from the reception he is convinced they will meet from the troops under his command, seconded by the loyalty, zeal, and spirit of all ranks of the community in defence of their king and country, their lives and properties, dearest interests and attachments ; and, whom he doubts not, will, with the usual spirit of Britons, unite hand and heart in repelling, and severely chastising the insolent foe, who come for the declared purpose of striking at their dearest rights and privileges, by the overthrow of their happy constitution.

"And although General Sir Charles Grey will pledge himself for the result being most brilliant, honourable and glorious, for England, yet it would be unwise not to be prepared at all points, as we are ; but, nevertheless, and to guard against accidents, the general apprizes the troops, that, in case a landing should be made by the enemy, and escaping the vigilance of our well-conducted and numerous navy, to the eastward in Essex, or to the westward in Kent or Sussex, and which are certainly more immediately threatened, it may be necessary to embark a part of the troops, to make a successful landing behind the enemy, whilst an army is acting on their front, in which situation their communication would be cut off; and their flanks and rear being acted upon, it would not be a contest of many hours' duration, before the invaders would feel the fatal effects of their temerity, by being ignominiously driven back into the water, killed, or made prisoners.

"In case of this event happening, and sudden orders given for embarkation, General Sir Charles Grey positively orders, that every regiment and corps of all descriptions, included in the orders for embarkation, leave the whole of their heavy baggage behind, under a proper guard, composed of the worst and the weakest men, commanded by an officer, the soldiers carrying only a change in necessaries, their blankets, haversacks, and canteens; and not one woman, on this occasion, must accompany the soldiers. The officers commanding regiments and corps will see them [the orders], and be responsible for their being strictly complied with.

"General Sir Charles Grey pledges himself that every attention shall be paid by him to the care of the soldiers' wives, and having them conveyed to their respective regiments should their absence be of any length, and they not return to the quarters from whence they embarked, which is by no means likely to happen, but, on the contrary, they will quickly return.

"The general is sure that every thinking good soldier will readily see the convenience to themselves, and propriety, of this order, and cheerfully submit to a short separation.

"(Signed)

"JOHN VISCHER, A.D.C."

If additional proof were necessary to show that Pitt and his colleagues felt the grave responsibility resting upon them, even if their plans were not as efficient as they might have been, it is furnished by an official book of some three hundred pages which they caused to be privately compiled and printed for their own use.[1] It is a " Report on the Arrangements which were made, for the internal Defence of these Kingdoms, when Spain, by its Armada, projected the Invasion and Conquest of England; and Application of the wise Proceedings of our Ancestors, to the Present Crisis of public Safety." John Bruce, to whom the task of obtaining the information from the musty tomes in the State Paper Office was entrusted, evidently did his work conscientiously and well, for minute details are entered into regarding the military and naval arrangements made in the days of good Queen Bess. Not the least instructive feature of the book is a chart of the Thames, reproduced from " Expeditionis Hispanoram in Angliam vera descriptio, A.D. 1588, Roberto Adams Authore," and according to the inscription said to have first suggested the designs of the tapestry in the House of Lords. Chains and forts protected the river at various points, and batteries were erected for the defence of many of the creeks.

It is evident that certain plans outlined in the Report were incorporated in later Acts of George III, and it would almost appear as if High Sheriff Clavell had adapted some of them. Dorsetshire seems ever to have been a county looked upon with favour by an enemy, and

---

[1] The copy in Mr. Broadley's collection belonged to Mr. Secretary Dundas. It has autograph corrections throughout by the author, together with inscription and signature. The appendixes number sixty-nine.

I.—K

its inhabitants equally ready to defend every inch of their territory, for "every measure of precaution was taken" when Philip of Spain threatened. Pioneers, artificers, carpenters, smiths, and wheelwrights all had their part to play in its defence.[1]

The Report contrasts the forces disposable in 1588 and 1798 as follows: "The army of Elizabeth consisted only of a few regiments, or such bands, as the nobility, counties, and towns could summon together, to support the Crown; and yet these, almost irregulars, had not only to guard the coasts against the Armada, but to watch over the northern frontier of its temporary ally, the Scots.[2] The army of Britain, at this time [1798], besides a large body of regulars, consists of numerous and disciplined militia and fencibles, and of a great part of its respectable yeomanry and inhabitants, in array, voluntarily embodied, and zealous to defend their lives, their families, their property, and their envied constitution."

The only portion of the Report which concerns us is

---

[1] In General Dumouriez's elaborate MS. volume on the defence of the British Isles (see Introduction, p. xxiv) he says: "Dorset is the pivot on which the defence of the west of England turns, and it should be strongly guarded according to the rules of the art. A descent in Dorset threatens Portsmouth and Plymouth equally, but it would be by way of a diversion and its temerity would meet with its due punishment. The coast abounds with stations and harbours of considerable strength, as Poole, Weymouth, and Lyme, etc. The hilly nature of the county gives it great strategical advantages, and the Stour, Puddle, and Frome, backed as they are by heights in amphitheatre, are excellent lines of defence."—MS., p. 174.

[2] According to the Report, "the total of the foot and horse, to be furnished by England, were 87,281; and by Wales, North and South, 45,408, making together, 132,689." As in 1798, the City of London acquitted itself with honour, and provided 20,696 men, not included in the above figures. Although no voluntary contributions were sought, a loan was asked from the Queen's "loving subjects," which amounted to the substantial sum of £74,462.

that dealing with the arrangements made to organize and arm the people. These are summed up by the author when dealing with the measures as "applied to the present Crisis of public Safety." He draws attention to the fact that the Crown, "by its Lord Lieutenant, exercised, during the reign of Queen Elizabeth, the power of calling on Counties, Towns, Bodies corporate, beneficed Ecclesiastics and others, to furnish, in cases of menaced invasion, quotas of arms, ammunition, military stores, pioneers, artificers, &c., necessary for the army; and armed vessels, mariners, and a proportion of victuals, for them, to assist in repelling the common enemy; making the Lord Lieutenant, his Deputies, and the Justices, judges of such exemptions, as might be pleaded, from any of these services. That the Crown, by the like power delegated to the Lord Lieutenants, could call on all landowners, farmers, &c., to furnish carriages, posts to convey information of the approach, or actual landing of the enemy; and by himself, or by his Deputies, to issue orders, for driving away the cattle and horses from the coasts, inland; for burning and destroying the corn, or whatever might be of use to the enemy; for breaking down bridges, cutting up roads, and, in general, for doing everything which might prevent, or might check, if he actually landed, his progress in conquest; measures which the recited acts of the legislature have in part adopted, and in which the general loyalty of the subject in the present crisis has happily co-operated."

Bruce then refers to the oath of supremacy administered to all the forces in Queen Elizabeth's service owing to her having received information that "Philip, and the Catholic party, had sent emissaries into her Kingdom, to undermine the allegiance of her subjects." He adds: "As the law authorizes a similar measure, or the taking and renewing the oath of allegiance to the Sovereign, would it not, in the present crisis, be a test, which would detect those *reformers* who seek for *revolution*, or those rebels who have entered into a foul conspiracy to assist the enemy in bringing humiliation and ruin on their country? Should fear, or should hypocrisy, induce men of either of these descriptions, to take, or to renew the oath of allegiance to their lawful Sovereign, such men must forfeit the confidence of those associates of sedition, or rebellion, and render themselves publicly infamous and criminal."

Steps were certainly taken by Parliament to prevent foreign emissaries from spreading revolutionary notions in the British Isles. The Alien Bill was revived and amended. Those letting lodgings were obliged to send returns to Government of all foreigners living in their houses, and no aliens were allowed to set foot in England until the master of the vessel had received permits authorizing them to land. "The secret encouragement held out (to the French) by a considerable number of domestic enemies" led to the suspension of the Habeas Corpus Act for a time.

The number of armed citizens was growing daily. We are told by the *Bath Chronicle* of May 3rd, 1798, that "the first Company of the Bath Volunteers met this day and elected for their Captain, Mr. Bossier; first Lieutenant, Captain Young; Second Lieutenant, Mr. Redwood. They likewise chose at the same time for their uniform, a scarlet jacket with black collar and lappels, white waistcoat, and blue pantaloons edged with red." Such items were of frequent occurrence in the contemporary Press, and the advertisements of enterprising tradesmen who sought the

ORDER ARMS 2ᵈ Motion

A MEMBER OF THE HONOURABLE ARTILLERY COMPANY IN 1798.
AFTER ROWLANDSON

patronage of volunteers were no less evident, of which the following is a specimen :—[1]

BATH

THE MEMBERS of the *BATH ARMED ASSOCIATION* may be supplied with *WARRANTED FIRELOCKS* at 2£ each at *STOTHERT* & Co's warehouse, No. 15 Northgate Street.
Likewise *PISTOLS* and *SWORDS* from the first manufactory *BELTS* and *CARTOUCH BOXES*.

On June the 4th, 1799, the anniversary of the King's birthday, a grand review of over eight thousand London and Westminster volunteers was held in Hyde Park. The corps were headed by General Dundas, and His Majesty was attended by the Prince of Wales and the Dukes of York and Cumberland. The scene was witnessed by the Queen and the Princesses from a house in Park Lane, and although the weather was unfavourable, no fewer than 150,000 spectators assembled, many of whom took up positions of vantage on roofs, walls, and trees, to watch the corps manœuvre. " The firing was, with some few exceptions, executed with great regularity. The exceptions apply to a few of the newly-formed corps and to others, which, originally small in numbers, had been incorporated with each a small time previously to the review."[2] Among the associations present were the Hon. Artillery Corps, St. George's Regiment, Loyal Hackney, Royal Westminster, Loyal Islington, Bloomsbury, St. James's, North-East London Volunteers, Loyal Hampstead, Temple, Loyal Pimlico, Finsbury Square, Somerset Place, Knight Marshall, the Ward Associations of Farringdon Without

---

[1] *Bath Chronicle*, May 17th, 1798.
[2] *Gentleman's Magazine*, Vol. LXIX, part i, p. 519.

and Within, Castle Baynard, Stoke Newington, Totten-
ham, Enfield, Edmonton, St. Andrew and St. George,
St. Clement Danes, Clerkenwell, St. Sepulchre, St. George
(Bloomsbury), Loyal London Volunteers, St. Luke's
(Chelsea), Brentford, St. Margaret and St. John, St. Mary-
le-bone, St. Martin's, Union, Chiswick, St. Paul's (Covent
Garden), Fulham, St. George (Hanover Square), South-
East London Volunteers, Streatham, Limehouse, Ratcliffe,
Clapham, Battersea, St. Catherine's, Poplar and Blackwall,
Whitechapel, Highgate, Lambeth, St. Pancras, Wapping,
Hendon, St. Olave, eight Ward Associations, and Shore-
ditch. The cavalry corps of Islington, Clerkenwell, Batter-
sea, Clapham, Wimbledon, Lambeth, and Deptford were
also present. A return of the London volunteers at this
time gives their strength as 12,208.[1]

"After the firing," we are told, "the whole line waved
their caps in the air, and gave three hearty huzzas; which,
joined to the sound of military music striking up at the
same moment, and the various expressions of joy from
the spectators, even the female part of them joining by
waving of handkerchiefs, is said to have drawn tears of joy
from their gracious Sovereign. An aide-de-camp from
the Commander-in-Chief, by his special command, went
round to the commanding officers of corps, to say that
His Majesty's sentiments of the general appearance and
military proficiency of the Volunteers assembled should be
more fully expressed hereafter."[2]

After the review the Queen held a Drawing Room at
St. James's. "Hitherto," continues the chronicler, "the war
has certainly not diminished the spirits nor the wealth of

---

[1] *Loyal Volunteers of London and Environs*, Introduction, p. vi.
[2] *Ibid.*, p. 519. The King expressed his thanks in the *London Gazette*
of June 4th, 1799.

LORD RODNEY FEASTS OVER 5000 KENTISH VOLUNTEERS AT HIS SEAT NEAR MAIDSTONE
IN THE PRESENCE OF THE KING AND ROYAL FAMILY. AUGUST 1, 1799

the country, which are no more than fairly represented by the gaiety and magnificence of the first Drawing Room in Europe. About half past two the Ode was performed in the anti-chamber leading to the Drawing-room ; and his Grace the Archbishop of Canterbury delivered a congratulatory oration on the happy event. The noble personages present, exclusive of their Majesties and the Princesses, were the Prince and Princess of Wales, Duke and Duchess of York, Dukes of Clarence, Kent, Cumberland, and Gloucester, Princess Sophia, the Prince and Princess of Orange, the Imperial, Hanoverian, Danish, Neapolitan, Portuguese, Turkish, Russian, and American Ministers ; the Archbishops of Canterbury and York ; Bishops of Norwich, Lichfield, Salisbury, Winchester, London, Durham, Chichester, and Meath, and the Dean of Wells ; the Lord Chancellor, Chancellor of the Exchequer, Speaker of the House of Commons, Master of the Rolls, Attorney and Solicitor General, Lord Chief Justice Eyre, and Baron Macdonald, Sir William Scott, the Lord Mayor and Sheriffs of London, a number of officers present at the review, and an amazing show of nobility and gentry. The Court did not close till six o'clock, and it was past seven before the company had left the palace. The Royal family went to the apartments to see the procession of the mail-coaches. The Prince of Wales appeared at one of the windows with the young Princess, his daughter, in his arms, and afterwards handed her to the King, amidst the applauding shouts of the populace. The Royal family then sat down to dinner."[1] The Great Review is immortalized in Sir Robert Ker Porter's picture representing George III raising his hat to a corps in the act of saluting.

---

[1] *Loyal Volunteers of London and Environs*, pp. 520-1.

On the 21st of the same month the volunteer corps "in and about the Metropolis" were inspected by His Majesty. Practically the whole of the circuitous route from Westminster Bridge to Islington was lined by armed citizens, and the scene in Finsbury Square was particularly brilliant. After dining with the Lord Chancellor at Islington, the monarch rode to the Foundling Hospital, where he walked through the children's apartments, and then proceeded to Hyde Park. He seemingly never wearied of encouraging the martial spirit of the nation, for the Surrey Volunteers were reviewed on the 4th July, 1799, and those of Kent on August 1st, the former on Wimbledon Common, and the latter in the lovely grounds of Lord Romney's seat near Maidstone, where a wonderful dinner was given to the 5319 men thus brought together. Every point of vantage was taken up by the large concourse of people which gathered together to show their respect for the gallant sovereign and his citizen army. Fortunately the fever which had coursed so madly through the veins of every Frenchman since the beginning of the Great War was stayed, only to break out afresh under the consulate of Napoleon Bonaparte. The supplementary militia was disbanded, and the number of the militia, including the volunteers raised under the Act of 1794, was fixed at 76,566 men for England and Wales.[1]

Two important contemporary works on the volunteers by T. Rowlandson warrant special mention here. Both of them were issued in 1799. *Loyal Volunteers of London and Environs* was dedicated to the Duke of Gloucester, and numbered amongst its many subscribers the King, and several other members of the Royal Family, the Emperor

[1] Clode, Vol. I, p. 285.

FRONTISPIECE OF THE RARE VOLUME OF COLOUR-PLATES DESIGNED AND ETCHED
BY ROWLANDSON, AND PUBLISHED BY THE ANGELOS IN 1799

of Germany, the King of Prussia, and the Archduke
Charles of Austria. In his preface, which is dated
August 12th, 1799, R. Ackermann, the publisher, states
that his "primary object is to raise a lasting monument to
the credit of those Volunteer Corps, who, in the moments
of alarm and of imminent dangers, so readily and honourably stood forward, at their own expense, to assist the
Civil Magistrates, and to preserve the tranquility of this
GREAT and COMMERCIAL EMPORIUM; and to defend the
PROPERTY of their less qualified neighbours from the
ruffian hands of interested depredators, and from the
malicious schemes of disloyalty." Rowlandson very
clearly depicted the costumes of the various corps in his
coloured plates, and made them of practical value by
showing each representative in the act of performing a
manual, platoon, or funeral exercise. For instance, beneath
the figure of a clean-shaven son of Mars belonging to the
Bethnal Green Volunteer Light Infantry is the following :
"Support Arms, 1st Motion. At the word Arms, the
right hand seizes the Firelock at the small of the Butt,
leaving room between it and the lock for the left Arm,
which is at the same time brought across the Body holding
the Firelock tight, with the cock resting on the Arm."

A second book, "designed and etched by T. Rowlandson," was also published in 1799. The title, *Hungarian
and Highland Broad Sword*, sufficiently indicates the nature
of its contents. Some of the pictures are highly theatrical,
and the colours have been laid on with charming inexactness and an utter disregard for detail. The artist evidently
believed in picturing the worst side of war ; the dead and
dying—chiefly Frenchmen—are much in evidence, and in
one plate a stately cathedral is in flames.

CHAPTER V

THE FRUSTRATED ATTEMPTS ON IRELAND, 1798

Great warriors all, obey the glad call,
　To welcome brave Humbert who's just come to land ;
With pike, scythe, and hedge-stake, now let us the field take,
　And prove to the world we can yet make a stand.

TOPICAL SONG.

ON the 23rd May, 1798, four days after Bonaparte had sailed for Egypt, the Irish Rebellion broke out. It was the far-off echo of the first phase of the French Revolution. The inhabitants of the Emerald Isle now determined to make a supreme effort to shake off the yoke of Saxon supremacy. The spirit of revolt had possibly been fostered by the harsh acts of men in authority, who hoped by this means to nip the insurrection in the bud before French help was forthcoming. The momentary success achieved in County Wexford was sufficient excuse for the Irish exiles in France to again approach the Directory with a demand for immediate assistance.[1] As usual, they were met with vague promises, much goodwill and graciousness on the surface, and the inevitable delays. Eventually a start was made, and the French Government expressed its willingness to send over one thousand men and four thousand

---

[1] "Ireland is not difficult to invade, the points of landing being many. But an invader can hardly hold out more than three months, even with the help of the natives."—Dumouriez MS., p. 276.

muskets to augment the resources of the insurgents, offering at the same time five frigates for the purpose of transport. This force, of course, was so hopelessly inadequate as to be of little practical value. But the Directory had been bitten and, with its greatest military commander on the high seas, was shy. Had it been seriously interested in the welfare of Ireland, it would have been quite possible to send over a formidable detachment of the Army of England, now doing nothing in particular, and this in the Brest squadron, which was in a sufficiently advanced state of readiness to allow of its being utilized. Tone begged and prayed with all his native eloquence and aggressiveness for a measure more worthy of the Great Nation, but to no purpose. The Directory preferred puny efforts, and was not at all disposed to generosity. Bruix, the Minister of Marine, determined to send over a number of French troops in vessels belonging to the Batavian Republic, but the Dutch threw cold water on the idea, protested that it was next to impossible to elude the vigilance of the British blockading force off the Texel, and prophesied nothing but failure. After much trouble, however, General Daendels again championed the cause, and two small vessels and three hundred men were granted.

Bruix, not satisfied with what savoured of a practical joke more than of anything else, busied himself with the French expedition, perhaps for no better reason than that his non-success with the Dutch might cast a reflection on his ability as an organizer. He managed to secure an addition of one ship-of-the-line and a sixth frigate. Divisional-Commander Bompard was put at the head of the venture, and over two thousand soldiers were ordered to march to Brest for embarkation. Then followed a long pause, and it was not until the beginning of July that General Chérin was appointed Commander-in-Chief. The total strength of the force at his disposal was now increased to eight thousand men, including those stationed at Rochefort under General Humbert, who, it will be remembered, had taken part in Hoche's attempt, and those at Brest under General Hardy. They were to sail in two divisions from these ports simultaneously and effect a junction off the coast of Ireland if possible. The main body under Chérin was to have its head-quarters at Brest and to follow as quickly as possible.

Humbert was given the frigates *Concorde* (44), *Médée* (38), and *Franchise* (44), on board of which had been stowed 3000 muskets and bayonets, 3000 pouches, 400 swords, 200,000 cartridges, and 1000 French uniforms, in addition to three field-guns and the necessary ammunition.[1] He was ordered to use the utmost caution and to attempt nothing big until he had been joined by Hardy's division. Moderation was to be the golden key with which they hoped to unlock the gate which kept Ireland from despoilers. There were to be no harsh measures, no pillage, no breach of morals. By preserving strict discipline in his own ranks Humbert hoped to set a good example to the Irish insurrectionists. Special care was to be taken that national customs and religious observances were respected. This expedition, with its noble ideals, was to receive a further check before starting. General Chérin, the nominal Commander-in-Chief, fell ill, and was on bad terms with Schérer, the Minister of War, as Bonaparte had been before him. He complained that the main force was

[1] Desbrière, Vol. II, p. 70.

THE FRENCH INVADER IN IRELAND. CARICATURE BY GILLRAY AFTER A DESIGN
BY SIR JOHN DALRYMPLE. MARCH, 1798

not sufficiently armed. Schérer turned a deaf ear to his entreaties and hardened his heart, giving Hardy and Humbert more than their proportionate share of the 200,000 livres (francs) which had been voted for the whole force. Chérin retaliated by appointing subordinates at variance with those of the Minister. Such petty spite and bickerings only served to pour contempt on the persons most concerned. Schérer held the trump card in his hand, and Chérin was ordered to Italy.

Humbert, an enterprising individual with a keen eye to the main chance, had been pushing forward his preparations at Rochefort, while his superior officers had been merely wasting time. Captain Savary had been put in command of the naval part of Humbert's division, and he hoisted his 'pennant on the *Concorde* on July 12th, his secret instructions being to sail at night in the hope that the British fleet might not observe his movements. He was to steer for Achill Head, the Mullet, or Cape Teelin, whichever circumstances favoured. After landing the troops he was to return to France; but should the enemy make a " successful attack during the landing,"[1] he was to reinforce the soldiers by the crews of the frigates, and burn the latter, thereby cutting off all hope of retreat —surely a quixotic way of waging warfare. These orders presumed that the junction with Hardy's division of one sail-of-the-line and six frigates had not been found possible. Should they join forces, as it was hoped, Bompard was to take charge of the combined fleet, being the superior officer in rank.

At last Humbert's three frigates set sail on August 6th, 1798, with 1019 troops on board. There had been much `

---

[1] Desbrière, Vol. II, p. 78.

trouble about the pay of the men, but funds having arrived, the question of wages ceased to trouble them. The sheer audacity of so hazardous an exploit was fully worthy of Humbert, who cared nothing for his skin and little for his life. On the 20th land was sighted, and hoisting the British flag two days later, he stopped a brig, secured her pilot, and received on board a captain of the Prince of Wales's Fencible Infantry, who had been sent out with despatches, the port surveyor, and two sons of the Bishop of Killala, all of whom had rowed out to meet him and fell into the trap. Anchoring in Killala Bay, in the county of Mayo, the troops were disembarked, and by the following day everything in the way of arms, ammunition, and stores necessary for the desperate campaign was on shore. Three companies of grenadiers under Adjutant-General Sarrazin marched on Killala, where a tiny garrison, variously esti-mated at from fifty to two hundred fencibles and yeomen, was routed, with a loss to the French of three wounded. Twenty-three prisoners were made, in addition to several prominent clerics, and two killed. Some of the prisoners were let out on parole or kept in the Bishop's house; others were taken on board the frigates, which shortly afterwards made all sail for France.

Dr. Joseph Stock, the Bishop of Killala, has left a descrip-tion of Humbert's men, whom he found very good fellows. He tells us that "intelligence, activity, temperance, patience, to a surprising degree, appeared to be combined in the soldiery that came over with Humbert, together with the exactest obedience to discipline. Yet, if you except the grenadiers, they had nothing to catch the eye. Their stature for the most part was low, their complexions pale and sallow, their clothes much the worse for wear: to a superficial observer they would have appeared incapable of enduring almost any hardship. These were the men, however, of whom it was presently observed, that they could be well content to live on bread or potatoes, to drink water, to make the stones of the street their bed, and to sleep in their clothes, with no covering but the canopy of heaven. . . .

" Humbert, the leader of this singular body of men, was himself as extraordinary a personage as any in his army. Of a good height and shape, in the full vigour of life, prompt to act, quick in execution, apparently master of his art, you could not refuse him the praise of a good officer, while his physiognomy forbad you to like him as a man. His eye, which was small and sleepy (the effect, probably, of much watching), cast a sidelong glance of insidiousness, and even of cruelty : it was the eye of a cat, preparing to spring on her prey. His education and manners were indicative of a person sprung from the lowest orders of society, though he knew how (as most of his countrymen do) to assume, when it was convenient, the deportment of a gentleman. For learning, he scarcely had enough to enable him to write his name. His passions were furious, and all his behaviour seemed marked with the characters of roughness and violence. A narrower observation of him, however, served to discover that much of this roughness was the result of art, being assumed with the view of extorting by terror a ready compliance with his commands. Of this truth the Bishop himself was one of the first who had occasion to be made sensible."[1]

---

[1] *A Narrative of what passed at Killalla, in the County of Mayo, and the Parts Adjacent, during the French Invasion in the Summer of 1798*, p. 34, by an Eye Witness [the Bishop], 1800. Dr. Stock afterwards became Bishop of Waterford.

On the 12th September the Directory was informed by Savary, who had arrived safely at Royan, at the mouth of the Gironde, on the 7th, of the joyful news of Humbert's landing. Its attitude towards invasion was now a little more kind, and orders were given to the captain to fit out a relief expedition—a small one it is true—but made more formidable by the addition of a frigate, the *Charente*, and the lugger *Renard*, to his existing force. The two vessels which the parsimonious Batavian Republic had grudgingly contributed were now ready, and the soldiers on board, but they seemed as securely held in check by the enemy as ever. However, the *Anacréon*, a fast-sailing brig, managed to slip out of Dunkirk with a number of refugee United Irishmen on board, the chief of whom was Napper Tandy, who had " boasted that thirty thousand would rise in arms on his appearance."[1]

Meanwhile the response of the Irish in rallying round Humbert was anything but encouraging, although the General was joined by a few hundred sons of the soil, and proceeded to Ballina, eight miles from Killala. There good fortune again attended them ; some yeomanry were worsted, and the place fell. On the 25th August the little army marched in the direction of Castlebar, where it was met by some seventeen hundred men[2] under General Lake, a name calculated to inspire fear by the sternness of his previous measures, and the victor of Vinegar Hill. His men held the most advantageous positions of the town, and it should be remarked in passing that a numerous force had been set in motion by Lord

---

[1] *Autobiography of Wolfe Tone*, Vol. II, p. 346.
[2] *History of the British Army*, Vol. IV, p. 592, by the Hon. J. W. Fortescue. In his report Humbert stated that 6000 men were opposed to him.

Cornwallis, Viceroy and Commander-in-Chief in Ireland,[1] and hurriedly marched to every point of importance. Humbert must have realized before a single shot was fired that nothing short of a miracle could wrest victory from the troops drawn up on the heights. It was not a question of fools rushing in where angels feared to tread when the French General gave the order to attack, but the determination of a brave man to inflict some kind of punishment on his enemy, no matter at what cost to himself. Had he failed, the verdict of history would have been that it was a mad freak to attempt an issue; but the miracle happened, and Humbert is deservedly praised. The Irishmen who had rallied round him certainly did not show their native valour to advantage, for they beat an ignoble retreat almost as soon as the English opened fire, and apparently dispersed into thin air, for they made no further appearance that day. The French troops fought with superb daring, but Sarrazin with his handful of soldiers, numbering some 480 in all, who had been held in reserve, decided the fortunes of the day. One of Humbert's battalions was holding out behind a stone wall, and another behind a ditch; both were sorely pressed. Sarrazin led the whole force up the heights, carried the trenches, captured the town and many guns, pursued the Royal troops for some distance, and thus turned what seemed inevitable defeat into certain victory, although the French lost more than the vanquished. The garrison of two hundred men which had been left at Killala also acquitted itself with honour by frustrating an attempt at landing on the part of the crews of two small English vessels.

---

[1] Lord Cornwallis held this post from June 13th, 1798, to March 17th, 1801.

I.—L

During his stay at Castlebar Humbert issued the following Proclamation calling upon the Irish to rally round him, but the measure was not attended with the success he anticipated :

"Liberty.   Equality.
    "Army of Ireland.

"At the Head-Quarters at Castlebar, the 14th Fructidor, in the 6th Year of the French Republic,[1] one and indivisible.

"General Humbert, Commander-in-Chief of the Army of Ireland, wishing to organise, as soon as possible, an administrative power for the province of Connaught, orders as follows :

"1.—The Government of the Province of Connaught shall reside at Castlebar till further orders.

"2.—The Government shall be composed of twelve members, who will be nominated by the Commander-in-Chief of the French army.

"3.—Citizen John Moore is appointed President of the Province of Connaught. He is particularly charged with the nomination and union of the members of the Government.

"4.—The Government shall immediately direct its attention to the organisation of the militia of the Province of Connaught, and to securing the provisions necessary for the French and Irish armies.

"5.—There shall be formed eight regiments of infantry, each of twelve hundred men ; and four of cavalry, each of six hundred men.

"6.—The Government will declare rebels and traitors to their country, all those who, having received arms and clothing, shall not join the army within twenty-four hours.

[1] 31st August, 1798.

" 7.—Every individual, from sixteen to forty, inclusively, is called upon, in the name of the Irish republic, to repair immediately to the French camp, to march in a mass against the common enemy, the Government of Ireland— the English; whose destruction alone can secure the independence and happiness of ancient Hibernia.

" The General Commanding in Chief,

"(Signed)   HUMBERT."[1]

The document in question was seized upon with avidity by a rhymester whose name does not transpire, and made the subject of a witty little song entitled " Humbert's Mistake," the first three verses of which are reprinted below.   It was sung to the tune " Moggy Lawder."[2]

From Castlebar, the French declare,
    It is their sole intention,
On Connaught forthwith to confer
    Freedom of their invention;
        What freedom this
        You soon may guess
    By Humbert's proclamation;
        "You dogs," said he,
        "You shall with me
    Go plunder your own nation."

As Cooke, when on a savage shore
    He friends would make of boobies,
So beads and trinkets they brought o'er,
    As presents for cropt boobies;
        Of green surtouts,
        Three thousand suits,
    They gave the rabble round them,
        Who on that night
        Played least in sight,
    Nor have the Gauls since found them.

---

[1] *Annual Register,* 1798; *State Papers,* p. 235.
[2] *A Collection of Constitutional Songs,* p. 118, Cork, A. Edwards, 1799.

This novel "freedom" next "commands"
  "That all men under forty
Shall in a mass, with pikes in hands,
  Go fight the Orange-party";
    But when they hear
    Cornwallis near,
  These mighty boasters scamper;
    And as they run
    From town to town
  Their front and rear we hamper.

Humbert was now in a quandary, for he had no definite information as to the movements of the United Irishmen, upon whose help he was so largely relying. Of one thing only was he certain : that Sligo and Leitrim were but ill defended, and he therefore determined on marching to Dublin. Fortune again favoured him, but at the same time drew him nearer to his doom. He evaded meeting the main body of Cornwallis's and Lake's troops ; and although he had several successful brushes with detachments of the enemy, Lake's cavalry harassed his rear-guard and disarmed two hundred of them. At Ballinamuck he found his retreat cut off by a body of regular troops under Cornwallis, and he was forced to surrender on September 8th. The French entered Dublin, not as conquerors, but as prisoners. They were sent to Liverpool shortly after, and the officers to Lichfield. A better fate awaited General Humbert, and he was allowed to return to *la belle France*, where he planned yet another attempt to snap the link which bound Ireland to England. Of the Irish fugitives who had given Humbert the benefit of their support, Matthew Tone[1] and Teeling[2]—the latter had

[1] Matthew Tone had almost as chequered a career as his brother. After having travelled in America and the West Indies, he crossed to France in 1794, and was arrested as an English spy. On being liberated from prison

acted as his aide-de-camp—were court-martialled and executed, while Sullivan [3] was fortunate enough to make good his escape. It was not until the 23rd September that the rebel garrison at Killala, which numbered some 4000 men, was defeated by 1200 fencibles, yeomanry, and militia, under General Trench. All the French soldiers, with the exception of an officer named Charost and two subordinates, had joined their comrades at Castlebar. The defence of Killala was well maintained, but the town was retaken by the loyalists after some hundreds of the recalcitrants had been killed.

Had the Directory supported Humbert's attempt by sending over Hardy's division, the rebels might have co-operated in sufficiently large numbers to offer a serious resistance to the Royal troops. Considering that the rebellion was no longer a flame, but smouldering ashes, that the French General's resources were hopelessly inadequate, and that he did not receive the assistance from the native Irish that he had been led to expect, the result is astonishing. Well may Lecky ask what would have happened " if during the previous year or two 14,000 or 15,000 men had landed of the same stamp as Humbert ? "[4] " It was not merely vainglory," says a more modern authority,

in the following year he again went to America, returning to France at the end of 1797, and becoming a captain in the army. He was executed on September 29th, 1798.

[2] Bartholomew Teeling was born in 1774. He became a United Irishman and later a captain in the French army under the name of Beron. Humbert wrote personally to Lord Cornwallis, praying for clemency on behalf of his young comrade (see *Ireland in '98*, p. 398) ; but although the jury commended him to mercy, he was executed.

[3] Sullivan was the nephew of Madgett, Secretary at the French Foreign Office.

[4] *A History of England in the Eighteenth Century*, Vol. VIII, p. 212, by W. E. H. Lecky.

"when he wrote after his landing to the Directory that, if he were reinforced by two thousand men, Ireland would be free."[1] As it was, Napper Tandy's miniature army reached the coast of Donegal after Humbert had surrendered. Hearing that their comrades had met with disaster, the *Anacréon* was headed for the Shetlands. After having made a desperate fight with an English naval brig and captured a merchant ship, the refugees steered for Norway, being closely followed by a British man-of-war. Tandy was arrested at Hamburg, and after having been handed over to the British authorities, was tried and acquitted on a point of law.[2]

General (afterwards Sir) John Moore's diary shows that the means placed at his disposal during his term of service in Ireland (December, 1797–June, 1799) were quite inadequate. "Should an invasion be attempted," he notes on the 16th April, 1798, "there will be no head to direct, and no previous arrangements made; the scene will be disgraceful, and I wish to retire from it."[3] "The batteries erected at Bantry since the French were there would throw some impediments in the way of an enemy, but nothing but a considerable corps of troops could possibly prevent his landing. The way is too extensive to be defended by batteries."[4] Again, writing after Humbert had landed, "General Lake was particularly warned not to risk an action until a sufficient force had been assembled to ensure

---

[1] Fortescue, *History of the British Army*, Vol. IV, p. 594.

[2] A second trial took place in 1801, and he was condemned to death; but both Bonaparte and Cornwallis exerted themselves on his behalf, and he was released. He died in 1803.—See *Autobiography of Theobald Wolfe Tone*, Vol. I, p. 54, note.

[3] *The Diary of Sir John Moore*, Vol. I, p. 288, edited by Major-General Sir J. F. Maurice, K.C.B.   [4] *Ibid.*, p. 272.

success, as in the state of Ireland any check in the beginning might prove fatal in its consequences." [1] After the
little French army had been defeated, he acknowledges
that Cornwallis's troops were "bad and undisciplined,
and if he had met with the least check the country was
gone." [2]

It now remains to follow the operations of the second
division of the French expeditionary force. The hesita-
tion and indecision of the Directory in sending aid was
largely a question of funds, one of the causes of the
delay in sending off Humbert. The crews refused to
work the ships until they had been paid their wages,
which were not forthcoming, and the troops were equally
clamorous. So early as July 21st the one sail-of-the-line
and six frigates at Brest were waiting for their comple-
ments, and General Hardy had received his instructions,
which were almost identical with those of his colleague,
before Humbert had sailed. The course Commander
Bompard was to steer and the precautions to be taken
were similar to those enjoined upon Savary.

If there was not actual mutiny there was seething discontent, much growling, and little done, although the men
were full of enthusiasm as to the ultimate success of the
expedition. Not until some 70,000 francs had been
received and distributed did serious work begin, although
the six field guns they were to take were already on
board. Six thousand muskets and bayonets, 1,000,000
cartridges, 6000 pouches, 1200 swords, 2000 French
uniforms, and equipment for 150 dragoons were hastily
stowed away. On the evening of the 20th August, the
day on which Humbert sighted the Irish coast, Bompard

[1] *Ibid.*, p. 312.   [2] *Ibid.*, p. 324.

slipped his cables, his naval force having been augmented, and was composed of the *Hoche*, a 74-gun sail-of-the-line, and the frigates *Immortalité* (40), *Coquille* (36), *Embuscade* (36), *Sémillante* (36), *Résolu* (36), *Romaine* (40), *Bellone* (36), *Loire* (40), *Biche* (36), and *Fraternité*, having on board some 3000 men, including Wolfe Tone, who sailed in the flagship *Hoche*. Ill fate dogged Bompard from the very start, for on his trying to pass Ushant he found a British squadron on guard, and two of his frigates collided. There was nothing for him to do but anchor in the roads until an opportunity should come to elude the enemy, which was not until September 16th, almost a month after his first start. Two frigates and a brig of the Brest blockading squadron pursued him from the following day until October 3rd, when Bompard shook them off. They therefore made for the North of Ireland, and on the 11th joined Commodore Sir John Borlase Warren's fleet, which had been sent to intercept Bompard's ships. Off Tory Island the Frenchman found three sail-of-the-line and six frigates, including the two which had given chase, quietly awaiting his coming.[1] The reports of the contestants do not agree in several particulars. Bompard makes the battle begin at 7.30 a.m. on October 11th,[2] while James gives the date as the 12th, and the time of opening 8.30 a.m.[3] The British frigate *Magnanime* (44 guns) and the sail-of-the-line *Robust* (74 guns) closed with the *Hoche*, which was supported by the *Embuscade*, *Coquille*, and *Bellone*. The *Amelia* (38 guns) also attacked the French

---

[1] *Epitome of James's Naval History*, p. 141.

[2] Desbrière, Vol. II, p. 169.

[3] There is a curious mistake in the epitomized edition of James's *Naval History*, edited by Robert O'Byrne (1888): on p. 140 the date of the battle is given as October 12th, and on the following page as the 13th.

SIR JOHN BORLASE WARREN DEFEATS THE FRENCH INVADERS
OFF THE IRISH COAST, 1798

flagship, and inflicted considerable damage on her as she passed under her stern, and the *Canada* "took a distant part in the action."[1] The French vessels offered a gallant resistance, although the crowded state of their decks impeded the efficient working of the guns. In two hours the *Hoche* was little more than a hulk, with five feet of water in her hold. Tone's son says that she was surrounded by four British sail-of-the-line and one frigate, which is misleading, seeing that the *Robust* and the *Magnanime* really bore the brunt of the fight, the other vessels being engaged with the French frigates. For instance, the *Melampus*, after opening fire on the *Hoche*, turned her attention to the *Embuscade*, which she handled severely, and, the *Foudroyant* coming up, she was forced to surrender. The *Coquille* attempted to escape with the remaining frigates, but was overtaken and captured. Not until the next day did the *Bellone* strike her flag to the *Ethalion*, which carried a heavier armament and sustained severe damage. The remaining ships of Bompard's division, with the exceptions of the *Romaine*, *Sémillante*, and *Biche*, which escaped to French ports, were captured.

The honours at sea on the French side were well won by the *Immortalité*, which managed to get away, and was making for Brest when she was sighted on the 20th by the British *Fisgard*[2] (38 guns). From 11 a.m. till 3 p.m. a fearful struggle ensued, and at first the *Immortalité* had the advantage, the *Fisgard* being rendered almost unworkable. It was a sorry ship that towed a sorry prize into Plymouth harbour, and the most famous contemporary naval historian admits that the action was

---

[1] *Epitome of James's Naval History*, p. 142.　　[2] See *ante*, p. 52.

"ably contested on both sides, doing credit to the vanquished as well as to the victor. No obtrusive vessel became a spectator of, much less a participator in, the long and arduous struggle. Considering the numerous cruisers, British in particular, that are usually roaming about the chops of the Channel, a fair single combat, from first to last, is rare, and, therefore, deserves to be prized."[1] The total British casualties are returned at 24 killed and 100 wounded, and those of the French at over 350 killed and wounded, although no official records of the latter seem to be extant. Wolfe Tone, who had fought for his mistaken cause like a hero, was arrested and tried, but escaped execution by committing suicide.

Whatever else might be forgotten, it would seem as if the French never by any chance left their native land without taking a generous supply of more or less flamboyant Proclamations with them. Copies of the following address were found on board the *Hoche* by her captors, and incidentally shows that Hardy thought the illustrious name borne by his flagship one to conjure with.

"LIBERTY! EQUALITY! FRATERNITY! UNION!

"(*Device.*—A cap of liberty. Two hands united, and the rising-sun.)

"THE GENERAL COMMANDING THE FRENCH ARMY IN IRELAND, TO THE UNITED IRISHMEN.

"United Irishmen,—The persecution which you experience on the part of a Government atrociously perfidious, has excited sentiments of indignation and horror in the breast of every friend of humanity. The lovers of liberty, while they admire your fortitude, deplore the situation to

---

[1] *Epitome of James's Naval History*, p. 147.

which you are reduced. The complaints of your suffering country are heard in all parts of the world, but your cause has become more particularly that of the French people. It is to give you new proofs of their affection, it is to second your generous efforts, that the Executive Directory of the French Republic has sent me among you. I do not enter your country with hostile views, to spread terror or desolation around me. I come not to dictate the law. Companion and friend of the gallant Hoche, I follow scrupulously the line of conduct which he marked out. I come to fulfil his engagements ; to offer you friendship and assistance ; to bring you arms, ammunition, and all the means necessary to break the barbarous yoke under which you groan ; I present to you my brave companions ; they know no other road but that of honour and victory. Long trained in the art of humbling tyrants, under whatever form they may present themselves, they will join their courage with yours ; they will mix their bayonets with your pikes, and Ireland shall be free for ever !

" Unhappy victims of the most execrable despotism, you who groan in hideous dungeons, where at every moment you are plunged by the ferocious cruelty of your English tyrants, let hope once more revisit your hearts ; your chains shall be broken. Unfortunate inhabitants, who have seen your houses, your property, wrapped in flames by your pitiless enemies, your losses shall be repaired.

" Rest in peace, gallant and unspotted spirits of Fitz-Gerald, of Crosbie, of Coigley,[1] of Orr, of Harvey ;[2] your blood, shed for the sacred cause of liberty, shall cement the independence of Ireland ; it circulates in the veins of all your countrymen, and the United Republicans swear to punish your assassins.

" (Signed)   HARDY."[3]

[1] Or Quigley.

[2] Rebels who had been hanged, with the exception of Lord Edward FitzGerald, who died in prison on the 19th May, 1798.

[3] *Popular Songs,* etc., part iii, pp. 109-11.

Shortly after the return of Savary with the frigates which
had conveyed Humbert and his men, and before it was
known that they had sustained defeat, General Kilmaine,
who was still in command of the so-called "Army of
England," expressed his willingness to go to the relief of
the rebels. Being of Irish extraction, he flattered himself
that he knew how to handle the men he felt would rally
round his standard once he had set foot on Hibernian soil.
He was not content with a fugitive experiment such as had
characterized the policy of the Directory since Hoche's
disaster, but boldly asked for seven thousand men. Nor
was he satisfied with mere frigates; he wished to use seven
of the ships-of-the-line lying idle at Brest, as well as eight
frigates, and to take over with him twenty-five thousand
muskets, so that he could make sure of having a present-
able force when the peasants were armed, for four or five
thousand of whom he intended to take over French uniforms. He also realized that the possession of a plentiful
supply of ready money was necessary to successful warfare, and asked for a million francs. Contrary to what one
might expect in the light of past events, the Directory entertained the proposal, and the resourceful Bruix heartily
concurred. The list of "wants" for the expedition drawn
up by the Minister of Marine not only shows the practical
side of the Admiral's character, but also his regard for details which, at first sight, might be thought of little consequence. He included 150,000 ells of green and white
ribbon to make cockades for the Irish, but reduced the
number of sail-of-the-line asked for by Kilmaine to six,
the money to 700,000 francs, the guns to twelve, the
soldiers to 5000, and the muskets to 15,000.[1] The decrease

---

[1] Desbrière, Vol. II, p. 192.

in the armament was probably not from reasons of economy alone, but because supplies were running low. Everything was approved of; the Directory was in an optimistic mood. Bruix was not daunted even when he heard that Humbert had surrendered, but went on steadily with the preparations. He urged upon the Dutch the necessity for energetic co-operation, asking shipping accommodation for 1200 troops. At the end of October things were in a forward state, for Kilmaine had busied himself in gathering together his soldiers. But the inevitable happened : funds were not forthcoming, and before the Commander-in-Chief had got the members of the Directory to fulfil their financial obligations the disaster that had overtaken Bompard and Hardy crushed out all faith in the success of another attempt. Operations were suspended, and Kilmaine, disappointed of his hopes, went back to his old command of the Army of England. To complete the discomfiture of all concerned, the two Dutch frigates managed to leave the Texel on October 24th, having on board some three hundred troops, with the intention of reaching Galway Bay by sailing round the northern coast of Scotland. The British frigate *Sirius* coming up with them, they were compelled to offer battle ; and although the former fought under great disadvantages, the Dutchmen were forced to surrender.

Savary, apparently unaware of the non-success of Bompard and Hardy, had set sail with six vessels for their relief on October 12th. He had strict orders to return with his 1090 men if bad news awaited him in Ireland. Two of his frigates left the main body, but the remainder reached Killala Bay. By a strange coincidence Savary was met by several British officers and men, whom he made prisoners, following the precedent set by Humbert. The captain then heard of the unhappy fate of his comrades, but Adjutant-General Cortez, who was in command of the troops, showed some spirit and endeavoured to win over Savary to land the troops. Although the latter was inflexible as to obeying his orders to the letter, he decided to anchor for a few hours, and barely managed to escape an encounter with four British ships the following day. He was chased for seventy-two hours, keeping up a running fight with two of them, but escaping by taking the desperate measure of throwing everything overboard except the specie, so as to lighten the frigates.

Further attempts against the British Isles were mooted by General Andréossy, the still undaunted Humbert, and others, but the Directory wisely left them alone. Its members had by this time become convinced that the road to London, for the French invader, at any rate, was not practicable "by way of Ireland."

CHAPTER VI

INVASION PROJECTS OF 1801—PLANS OF ATTACK
AND DEFENCE

"In war men are nothing; it is a man who is everything."—NAPOLEON

ALL practical thoughts of an invasion were put aside until 1801, when Bonaparte, now First Consul, and but recently returned from the brilliant campaign which had culminated in Marengo, again meditated a hand-to-hand grapple with England. A letter written by him to Talleyrand, the Minister of Foreign Affairs, shows how ambitious were his naval as well as his military designs.[1] This communication, an unusually elaborate one, states that the writer had received a very friendly communication from Paul, the half-witted Czar, who was destined two months after to be the victim of a dastardly conspiracy. An alliance between Russia and France is not at all so peculiar to our own time as many people believe. Bonaparte said that " Russia ought always to make common cause with France."[2] Such an *entente* was evidently a favourite scheme with Napoleon at one point of his career, indeed this letter sketches a vast programme of naval expeditions to be undertaken by the allied fleets of France,

[1] *Correspondance de Napoléon I*, Vol. VI, p. 746. Letter No. 5327, dated from Paris, January 27th, 1801.
[2] *Talks of Napoleon at St. Helena*, p. 157.

159

Spain, and Holland, supported by the Northern Powers of Russia and Denmark. Powerful armaments were to be organized for the following purposes: (1) An expedition against Ireland; (2) Against Brazil and India; (3) Against Surinam, Trinidad, and the West Indies; (4) Hostile operations with similar objects in the Mediterranean. The First Consul proceeds to unfold minute details of these comprehensive schemes. Everything was to be organized on the principle of first decoying the main naval force of Great Britain to Egypt. It is remarkable, however, that while he apparently designed to conquer England's sovereign possessions and to annex the most commanding strategic positions both East and West, no mention is made of invading the Motherland. Ireland entered into his calculations, although no attempt was made to put the matter into execution until 1803, and then it was dismissed; while the crossing of the Channel was certainly contemplated in 1801, but without the aid of sail-of-the-line. The flat-bottomed boats built during the *régime* of the now defunct Directory, with new additions, were to be used for this purpose. The idea of treating some of the European nations as his feudatory vassals and making Russia his tool *par excellence* is quite worthy of this phase of Napoleonic statesmanship.

The human dynamo soon set the wheels of his mighty machine going; and the ports were busy fitting out expeditions to Egypt and India. Not until March 7th, 1801, did Bonaparte betray the fact that he entertained any notion of crossing the Channel, and then it was only by inference. Writing to Forfait, now Minister of Marine, he requests him to say how long it would take to collect at Boulogne one hundred gunboats, and also to state where

these craft are at present situated and in what condition
they are in. The despatch is interrogative almost throughout. " How many men would they accommodate? How
many could leave Boulogne at a single tide? And how
many at a time could the harbour contain?" A fortnight
afterwards Bonaparte writes impatiently to the same
official respecting his report of the condition of things on
the coasts. The Minister had failed to render anything
like the good account which his exacting master had expected, although of gunboats proper, large and small, and
pinnaces, there were 276 in the ports of St. Malo, Cherbourg,
Havre, Dunkirk, Ostend, Flushing, Brest, and Lorient.

The First Consul determined that this scattered fleet,
which was sadly lacking in organization and served no
useful purpose, should be placed under the charge of an
efficient commander. La Touche Tréville, the only French
admiral approaching Nelson in genius, and certainly the
best naval officer Bonaparte ever had, was chosen for the
task. A man of less abundant energy or unfailing optimism would have declined the post as offering the maximum
of work with the minimum of reward, for the repeated
failure of previous attempts to use the vessels augured ill
for the future. In Bonaparte's decree of March 13th,
1801, instituting a flotilla of gunboats, its possible objective
is only remotely hinted at, but the officers were advised to
keep their crews efficient by constant exercise at sea. The
Admiral himself was told that the flotilla was for the protection of the coasts and coasting trade, and the addition
of another powerful means of offence when opportunity
presented itself. The crews were always to be on board
and ready—a sufficient indication that there was a probability of an expedition being undertaken in the future,

I.—M

although at the moment the sea-board departments were
denuded of troops.

La Touche Tréville's innate hatred of the English
prompted unremitting labour on his part, and it is clear
that he had great faith in the utility of the means which
he hoped to have at his disposal before many months had
passed.   New boats were put on the stocks and old ones
placed in dry-dock for repairs.   In April he was able to
report that good progress was being made, although the
First Consul's ambitious naval plans received a serious
check.   The previous year (1800) he had entered into
a close alliance with Russia, Prussia, Denmark, and
Sweden, with the avowed object of resisting British
supremacy at sea.   This was practically a revival of the
Armed Neutrality of 1780; but the battle of Copenhagen,
fought on the 2nd April, 1801, brought the power of the
Maritime Confederacy to an untimely end, and showed
that Nelson was more than a match for his foreign rivals.
This set-back was not at all encouraging for an attempt to
cross the Channel, and Bonaparte certainly did not give
much attention to the flotilla.   On the other hand, La
Touche Tréville visited the maritime ports, took stock of
resources, and was satisfied with their general fitness for
his own special purpose, with the noteworthy exception of
Boulogne, which was in a destitute state, with no defences,
no soldiers, and a single weak battery.   These numerous
disadvantages did not deter him from deciding upon it as
the best place for collecting the vessels.   The Admiral was
already anxious to head an expedition, and told Bonaparte
that from Calais alone he could embark twenty-five thousand troops, who would form the right wing of an army,
the centre being at Boulogne and the left at Étaples.   The

First Consul's reply was not favourable, and discountenanced the idea of concentration. Not in the least disconcerted by this ill-concealed rebuff, La Touche Tréville frankly disobeyed orders and began to collect as many boats at Boulogne as possible. Eventually he succeeded in winning over Bonaparte to his own opinion, and on the 1st June, 1801, an order was issued for an extraordinary fund of 305,000 francs to be applied to the repair and reconstruction of the jetties and quays of the port, which were to be adapted to the accommodation of vessels drawing more water than could hitherto be admitted into the harbour. This, of course, presaged the deepening of the harbour at some future time, which was done.[1]

La Touche Tréville was anxious to have fifty gunboats built after the Spanish model, which he purposed to use as the vanguard of the invasion flotilla, the vessels being larger and more heavily armed than the French type. He had early recognized that the light-draught boats of the Dutch would be of great service for the transport of cavalry horses, and would make a valuable addition to the fleet of fishing-smacks which had been fitted up for that purpose. The Admiral made repeated experiments with the various kinds of vessels, and his men were frequently manœuvring within gunshot of the English cruisers. He exacted a high standard of efficiency in the comparatively few sailors he had at his disposal, and even went so far as to offer to molest the Kent and Sussex coasts "every night, with a thousand or twelve hundred braves,"[2] his retreat being assured by the Boulogne flotilla. For a really serious attempt on England he estimated that seventy-five thousand men would be required. It is evident from

---

[1] See *post*, Vol. II, p. 20.   [2] Desbrière, Vol. II, p. 316.

Bonaparte's note of June 23rd, 1801, to Augereau, in command of the Army of Batavia, that whatever the First Consul's initial ideas may have been concerning the Channel armaments, he had again abandoned the thought of striking a blow in England herself. " You will receive instructions," he writes, "for the formation at Flushing of five divisions of gunboats, which, added to the sixteen divisions in Channel ports, will impose on England."[1] La Touche Tréville probably surmised from the fact that there was no artillery at Boulogne, and no soldiers at Dunkirk, that the project had been postponed, but that did not prevent him from announcing in July that he had sufficient transports for thirty thousand troops, should they be forthcoming. In the middle of the same month Bonaparte gave a tardy order for a reinforcement of 3870 soldiers to help man the boats, so great was the dearth of sailors. Time showed that the plan, paradoxical as it seemed, was a sound one.

The utmost difficulty was experienced by divisions of the flotilla making their way to the port of concentration, for the British cruisers continually harassed their movements. This trouble was partly overcome by the erection of a powerful battery near Cape Gris-Nez. Repeated applications for the Spanish gunboats failed to meet with any response, and as La Touche Tréville believed them to be the key of the situation, this is additional evidence against the reality of Bonaparte's intentions. Eventually 150 boats had been gathered together at Boulogne, Calais, and Dunkirk before the belligerents decided to lay down their arms for a season. The number of craft actually built totalled 250, which would have accommodated about 25,000 of the 75,000 troops available for the expedition.[2]

---

[1] Desbrière, Vol. II, p. 314.   [2] *Ibid.*, p. 411.

The cry of "Wolf! wolf!" had been heard so often that at first British statesmen showed a disposition to wait and see, rather than to go and prepare. In January, 1801, there were not more than 198,000 armed men in the British Isles, including volunteers, and although their ranks were augmented from time to time, England was ill prepared for a really serious attack. It is true that her squadrons still kept the French fleets in their harbours, with one or two exceptions, but previous expeditions had effected an escape, and it will be remembered that the flotilla was to be protected in crossing by its own gunboats, not by men-of-war. The British ships in actual commission included no fewer than 127 sail-of-the-line; France had only forty-nine, and many of these were in a bad state of repair. The following circular reveals the mode of internal defence for the United Kingdom so clearly that it is given *in extenso* :—

February, 1801.

Information and Instructions
FOR
COMMANDING GENERALS
AND OTHERS.

"HIS Royal Highness the Commander-in-Chief thinks it necessary on the present occasion to point out the following circumstances and instructions for the guidance of the commanding generals and others, that they may be acquainted with the leading principles of defence of the country, and be the better enabled to apply them to the peculiar situation of their district.

"We must naturally suppose, from the host of foes that surround us, and from the advantages our insular situation gives us while they can be kept at a distance, that their great object must be an invasion of these countries. The consequences of success would be to them so great, that they may be led to attempt it, notwithstanding the superiority and exertions of our navy, and the vigilance and gallantry of our seamen, who have hitherto ensured our safety; and from circumstances of wind and weather it is not impossible for them to accomplish on some one or more points of our very extensive coasts, a partial but considerable landing. Under this idea and expectation we must therefore be prepared, and in readiness to repel such an attempt, whether proceeding from the coasts of our inveterate and implacable enemy which more immediately threaten the capital and centre of the country; or from those of our more distant ones, who have such great preparations to make, such probable difficulties to encounter, and so many perils to escape, that invasion from that quarter, though not beyond the chance of possibility, may be considered as less imminent than the former.

"Before the descent of the enemy is undoubtedly expected, or the particular object of it is known, the troops will be cantoned or encamped in the manner that appears the most advantageous. The various lines of defence will in general have been ascertained. The combinations of the troops and their marches upon their several points of rendezvous, in consequence of the part of the country the enemy shall attempt, will be well understood and known to such as have an active part depending on them. The troops will be in a state of field preparation, and apprized of the general nature of the service that is to take place. Their subsistence will have been arranged and secured on their lines of march and probable operation. All the civil arrangements of Government will have been made and ready to carry into execution. Measures for reinforcing the army, for internal security, and for forming strong reserves will have been taken. Dispositions will have been made for breaking up roads, driving and abandoning the country on the enemy's route, &c. Though our stake would be great, our advantages in defending it would be many, our principal ones ought to arise from our supplies, our certainty of subsistence, and our constant increasing force.

"When an enemy lands, all the difficulties of civil Government and the restraint of forms cease, everything must give way to the supplying and strengthening the army, repelling the enemy, and preserving as much as possible the quiet of the country; the strongest and most effectual measures are necessary for these indispensable purposes.

"On the first landing of an enemy, if he cannot be prevented in the attempt, not a moment must be lost in assembling the troops, and pushing on the most advanced, however few in number, till more can be collected. The great object must be constantly to harass, alarm, and tire an enemy, and to impede his progress, till a sufficient force assembles to attack him; the nature of the country affords every advantage for that purpose; intricate and inclosed, it is exceeding difficult for an enemy to advance, he is never to be lost sight of by the light troops, every inch of ground, every field may to a degree be disputed, even by inferior numbers.

"As soon as ever he has quitted the coast, he must be surrounded in front, flank, and rear; a knowledge of the country, and a superiority of cavalry gives that advantage. He must be obliged to fight for every article of sustenance. The country must be driven, and everything useful within his reach destroyed without mercy; this the necessity of the case, and the infinite consequence of giving him an immediate check demand; cattle and horses must at all events be removed.

"On the side of the enemy, the difficulties of advancing through an inclosed country where there is an active opponent in front, flank, and rear, seem almost insurmountable; such as routes to be opened for the columns under an adversary's fire, unless the march is made along the high road, on a narrow front, and therefore the easier opposed. The means of connecting these columns and making them act and move in concert; the disability of protecting and communicating with the flank ones, which are always exposed, and liable to an attack; the uncertainty of where is the principal danger, and from what quarter to expect the greatest effort of his adversary, the want of every comfort, of every necessary but what the individual can himself carry.

" The combination of these circumstances when opposed with vigour, seem to render it impossible for an enemy to make much progress forward; for as he must have landed with a very moderate proportion of artillery, ammunition, and provisions, or at least without the effectual means of transporting them, fatigue, and the want of nourishment will soon exhaust him, despondency will begin to take place, and despair will soon follow, if unable to advance in front, a retreat must be resolved on, or a desperate and unequal action hazarded. No such retreat can be made in a very regular manner; confusion will arise, a re-embarkation with great loss will be attempted if there is any possibility of getting off, perhaps the scene may terminate in a total surrender.

" All this supposes in the defendant the most indefatigable and unremitting activity and valour, every circumstance should induce him to this conduct, to allow time for putting in motion each spring, and applying every resource. Each day decreases the ardour, spirit, and numbers of the attacker, and increases in a much greater proportion the confidence and strength of the attacked, not only of the soldier and the militia-man, but of the very peasant; a sure retreat is always open; plenty, and refreshment of every kind await them, and the support of increasing numbers.

"If, notwithstanding every effort, the enemy should advance within reach of the capital, a great action must take place, but at such a distance as to allow of the prospect of rallying and making a second stand in case of a repulse. In this situation, the advantage of artillery, cavalry, and in some degree the choice of the ground ought to decide against an enemy who would want these, and who would be encompassed on every side by superior numbers, though perhaps not of regular troops: when things are brought to this point, determined valour, with these advantages must ensure success.

"After taking possession of one of the coast towns, and of a certain district of country, should he not advance towards the capital, or towards some other material point, but endeavour to establish himself and protract the war, a new scene would arise; these previous arrangements would enable us to act with advantage, and the sequel would depend on the circumstances of the moment.

"From the moment that an enemy is discovered from the coast and pointing to a place of landing, the driving of the country must begin, be strongly enforced, and made if possible by other routes than those of probable operation of the troops, whose movements must not be interrupted, and when the acting direction of the enemy is sufficiently ascertained, nothing within the probability of his reach should be suffered to remain; nor would this incommode the advanced troops, for their supplies would readily come up from their rear, and above all the removal of horses of every description must be accomplished, if this is rigidly executed, his future movements will become exceedingly slow and fatiguing, perhaps impossible. The mode of doing all this is prescribed, and will be arranged in every county and district of the exposed coast, the execution allotted to the yeomen cavalry, and every reasonable hope may be entertained of its being carried into effect.

"Nothing will more effectually disappoint and disconcert the project of an invading enemy than the driving and abandonment of the country, and the total destruction of the roads for miles round whatever point he made his landing at, or at least for several miles on each side of the route he meant to pursue. Could this be accomplished as easily as imagined, he would find himself in a desert, unable to advance, or to give the time necessary to free himself from the first embarrassments thrown in his way, and which would only be a prelude to more considerable opposition. This alone persevered in, would stop all progress, his distresses and wants would increase in proportion to his numbers, and if his communication was interrupted by a superior naval force, he must soon be reduced to the greatest difficulties. But as this cannot be expected to the desired amount, it may be essential to point out how far the roads of the country should be destroyed, so as to be disadvantageous to the army, and advantageous to ourselves.

"It is desirable to reduce the enemy to advance on a small front, to prevent him from extending his flanks, and to throw as many obstacles in the way of his progress to the front as can be devised; but to do this, it is necessary to reserve access to his flanks, to be able to follow his rear, and in opposing him in front, to have our own rear open for a speedy retreat, or for receiving supplies and reinforcements. The reconciling all these circumstances is no easy matter, and different opinions may be formed on the subject; it is thought however that the destroying the communications between the various routes that lead to the capital, must be to our advantage, for it will not prevent light troops from harassing the flanks of the enemy's march, and it will reduce his progress to be made on one great route, including such collateral ones, as with much labour and delay he may be induced or attempt to open, and which in some parts of the country is no easy matter; for if under such circumstances he pressed forward on two great routes that cannot communicate or support each other, he gives us the opportunity of attacking him with an united force. From the time we take a position in front of the enemy we can only destroy direct roads in proportion as we retire, side ones we can prepare and shut up, to prevent the enemy's altering his position, but with our permission, for it is one of the great advantages which our inclosed and intricate country affords us, and from the instant an enemy has landed, we must endeavour by our various operations to determine his advance on such lines as we deem most advantageous to ourselves.

"The great extent of our coast makes it difficult to guard it everywhere, and from the nature of an invasion, an enemy if he escapes our navy and all the perils of the sea, generally arrives with a force much superior to what can be assembled to oppose him; still he should be resisted as much as possible in the moment of descent, for it is to him a moment of weakness and may be of great loss and discouragement, but this should not be persevered in, beyond the instant of landing, if the enemy's superiority is evident and decided; the troops that immediately oppose him, should therefore be prepared on a signal, to quit the ground in the quickest manner (always supposing the rear and flanks sufficiently open) and to assemble again, at perhaps the distance of half a mile; everything must be methodized and in due preparation for destroying and spiking the guns and carriages on the shore batteries, before the enemy can reach them, and it is believed the ordnance have provided and furnished for each gun the means of so doing, and if any neglect should therein arise, the perpetrators should be punished in the most exemplary manner.

"Therefore when the enemy shall be master of the shore, the troops are never to lose sight of him, they are to fall back to such a moderate distance as circumstances seem to require ; they are to extend and in arriving from all quarters to endeavour to encompass him, for their general intention and application must be to draw as much advantage from attacks on his flanks and rear as they can propose to do from opposition in front. These attacks should be kept up incessantly, made by bodies both of small and large numbers, and every encouragement given to such enterprizes. And in acting in this manner the troops are thoroughly to understand, that though our object or situation does induce us at first to fall back gradually till our force can be collected on a given point, and enabled to advance upon and attack the enemy, yet that we are always to hold that event in view, and to conduct ourselves accordingly, and that it becomes us to know, and to profit from the many and singular advantages we possess.

" Nothing can be so frequently and strongly inculcated into our infantry of every description, as the advantages they possess in attacking the enemy, who has few or no cavalry to offend them, while on all occasions, they enjoy the fullest support from our own ; for active individuals and light infantry may remain in perfect safety within the smallest distance of such an enemy, watching every opportunity of distressing him, and larger bodies of infantry can never be pressed or overtaken, if their rear is clear, and their cavalry bold and active. By dint of repetition, every soldier should be brought to understand, that even if he is worsted in action, and compelled to fall back, that his duty and honour require him to stop and rally, as soon as possible, that he need never hurry, and that he is perfectly safe at a quarter of a mile distance from an enemy, who has no cavalry to make a quick pursuit, therefore that he ought to face about, form, and again advance or retire in a cool soldier-like manner, and in doing this, from his peculiar advantage, he is always protected by his own cavalry. But above all it must be impressed upon him, that although retiring and falling back gradually before the enemy, may at first be ordered and necessary, to allow the force of the country to collect ; yet our great object is to attack him on every favourable opportunity, and that not so much by fire, which is merely defensive, as by the bayonet, and by that bold, manly and vigorous exertion, which must inspire soldiers fighting for their religion, liberty and constitution—For however successful the enemy may seem to be at first, and however long it may be necessary to postpone our general attack upon him, the moment will arrive, when by our accumulated numbers and united efforts, we shall overwhelm, and may extirpate an army of unprincipled and merciless invaders.

" There cannot be too many light infantry established, either in companies or battalions. They are essential in the country we are to preserve, and when intelligent and well led, they will by their spirit, perseverance and exertion soon attain an ascendant over those of the enemy, who have so many difficulties to encounter, and who unprotected by cavalry of their own, will not be so forward when exposed to the rapid and decided attacks of ours. To this service the small corps of militia and the unregimental companies of volunteers are peculiarly applicable, and in no other can they distinguish themselves in a manner more honourable to themselves, or more beneficial to their country.

" Although the face of the country does not in general allow us to draw to its fullest extent from our numerous and formidable cavalry all those advantages we should otherwise possess, yet against an enemy destitute of that arm, and endeavouring to advance into the country, we seem to be placed in a most favourable and decisive situation. Many parts will allow of the action of cavalry in considerable bodies, and other parts will soon be made so, inclosures are in general slight, and could be opened round interesting positions. But as our cavalry have no enemy of the same kind to encounter, they need not be too circumspect in their movements, and there are few impediments their horses would not surmount, great boldness and activity would give them every advantage of attack, and free them from every danger of retreat. They should never hesitate with impetuosity to attack infantry wherever they can get at them on tolerable terms, particularly light infantry, whose loose order makes no great resistance when assailed with vigour. They would be ordered to move and act more in small bodies than in line, in support of infantry and of each other. They would harass and interrupt every communication of an advancing enemy. They would give confidence and support to our volunteers and more inexperienced troops, and in any great and combined attack, they might arrive and act from so many points with an energy peculiar to themselves that must prove decisive. The advantage they would possess is of so singular a nature that unless they forgot their inherent vigour and activity, and that the existence of their country was at stake, nothing could resist their efforts.

" The excellence of our field artillery, and its capability of increase to any extent, must give us the most decided advantage against an enemy, who will be exceedingly inferior in that arm. Well horsed and under the protection of our superior cavalry, it may be moved with the greatest rapidity to the most favourable and decisive situations, at the same time that we are enabled to take care that by no sudden effort, there is any danger of its being lost or destroyed.

" The enemy has elsewhere gained so many advantages, from the rapidity of his movements, and disencumbering himself from baggage, that he would certainly persevere in the same course, and seek for no more horses than would transport his moderate share of artillery and ammunition, and if possible mount part of the cavalry men he might bring with him ; he has been accustomed to find provisions in the countries he quickly passed through, and occasionally shelter in close cantonments, as he frequently had not with him the means of encampment.

"We must therefore be prepared to move in the lightest manner. Start without baggage of any kind, expect to hut, not to encamp, and for this the country furnishes abundant and advantageous materials, and every fifth soldier should be provided with a bill-hook for cutting wood. The soldiers should carry their own kettles as formerly, and not of too great a size. From our rear we will be certain of plentiful supplies.

"Circumstanced as we are, with our honour and existence at stake, against the mere persons of an insolent and unrelenting enemy, whom we and our ancestors have so often encountered, and who spurning at those generous modes of warfare so long established between civilized and rival countries, openly declares his aim to be our utter destruction as a nation.—Against such an enemy we must employ his own weapons, for a time be as ferocious as himself, raise the indignation of the country to the highest pitch, and hurl back upon him that terror which he has so successfully struck into others, who had not the same liberty, renown, and constitution to contend for. In this manner will he be successfully opposed; and if we profit from the many and singular advantages we possess, and exert that spirit and vigour which becomes a great and free people, fighting for their laws, their religion, and everything that can be dear to them against an implacable enemy, there can be no doubt of an honourable and glorious termination of the contest.

"In conformity to the before-mentioned circumstances, the commanding generals being thoroughly acquainted with the local situation of their districts, must have already, or will frame a regular system of defence and operation, which they will communicate in its various degrees, and with full explanation to each person materially concerned in its execution.

" They will point out the most probable places of descent from an enemy, the works that now exist for their defence, and the arrangements to be made at each for opposing him. Supposing the enemy, notwithstanding every effort to prevent him, to have made good his landing at any one place, they will point out where the troops shall reassemble, and keep firm to hold the enemy in check, and in case of being farther pressed they will show the line of falling back, and the measures they order for throwing troops on his flanks and rear, and arresting his progress till assistance arrives.

" The generals commanding are also farther instructed to cause the greatest alertness to be observed in the execution of all duties, and that every one is ready in the instant to repair to the point of rendezvous assigned him. If the necessary horses for the artillery are not provided, to keep a sufficient look-out that they may be immediately procured on any emergency, and for the regiments to furnish such men and to train them, as are wanted for the artillery service.

" That the orders and instructions, as published concerning the Baggage and Marches of the Army in case of assembly, are strictly observed, and to take the first opportunity of punishing offenders and destroying improper baggage on the spot. Of using every means of circulating intelligence, and orders quickly, but without harassing the cavalry. Of attacking the enemy in the critical instant of landing, if there is the least chance of success; and if obliged to recede, to fall back as short a space as possible, and never to lose sight of him in front. Of detaching bodies, though ever so small, to confine him on his flanks, and of increasing those in proportion as he advances. Of exerting every means to create delay, and give time for assistance to come in. Of hastening the inhabitants in the neighbourhood of the enemy to withdraw with their cattle and horses, to enforce this by every means, and to destroy without compunction whatever provision is tardy in its removal, or can be of use to him; such removals will be made to a sufficient distance, according to the district plan ascertained, and the routes in it ordered and pointed out. Such arrangements in consequence of the general plan laid down must be made with the Lord-Lieutenants and Magistrates of the different counties, as may ensure the punctual execution of these most essential services.

" To take particular care that horses do not fall into the hands of the enemy, and also that no loss of artillery is endangered. Wherever he makes good a landing, such adjoining batteries as can no longer be preserved must be relinquished in time, the guns damaged, and ammunition and carriages destroyed. This requires discretion and no hurry, for in many situations they may still afford support to the flank corps.

" To provide for the removal of such sick, horses and baggage as may be near to, or in the probable route of the enemy. To keep an especial look-out to the providing his own troops with bread and forage, with as much regularity as possible, if no perfect and undoubted mode of supplying them is then established.

" The farther the enemy gets from the coast, the more must the cavalry be ordered to get on his flanks and rear; to give night-alarms to the enemy, however small the parties may be that do so. To destroy roads on his flanks the more to circumscribe him in an inclosed and difficult country, and at whatever point he lands, to have such a disposition ready for breaking up roads, and to be immediately executed, as will tend to prevent his extending, and force him to move in a particular line and on a small front of operation. Wherever the enemy enters the strong woodland counties, if trees are felled on all the roads for miles around him, he will find it very difficult to advance.

"During all this possible service, small corps cannot depend on encamping. On the contrary they must trust to their own ingenuity for hutting and covering themselves, and will be provided with axes, hatchets, and billhooks accordingly.

"The general officers will see, and are instructed, that the infantry of all kinds in their exercises practise more than has been usual the use of their bayonets, and charge frequently with them in different situations, and under various circumstances: also that not only the light companies are adroit at their peculiar exercise, but that individuals, and divisions of other companies are occasionally detached, and understand how to act as flankers and as skirmishers, in attacking or repelling those of the enemy; also to be provident of their ammunition, and that they ought never to fire but when they have a good mark, and a good aim. All these are points and objects that should be strongly recommended to, and form the principal part of the exercise of small corps and volunteer companies, to enable them to perform the most effectual service that can possibly arise.

"A part of the force of each district, as shall be particularly named, will be established as a district reserve, and being provided with camp equipage, &c. will be held as the first to be called upon, ready to move at a moment's warning, and to unite as a body on the point attached, whether of their own, or of any adjoining district. The whole will form the general reserve; and orders will be in readiness for the march of the distant parts of it, on whatever point the enemy may land. The commanding generals of districts will be acquainted before-hand with such dispositions, and know when and from whence they may expect assistance. They are also empowered, on the appearance of an enemy, to call out the yeomen and volunteer corps of their respective districts, with whom (having obtained a previous knowledge of their numbers, state of discipline, limitation of service and other essential circumstances) they will have made such arrangements as may ensure their speedy assembly, and the due performance of the duties allotted to them. They will also be empowered to call upon certain specified corps (according to situation) of the reserve, and of the adjoining districts.

" In consequence of all these circumstances, and of such other local ones as present themselves; the commanding generals of districts will take their measures, give their orders, make the previous preparations, and communicate such material matters as they have not already done to his Royal Highness the Commander in Chief.

" *By Command of His Royal Highness,*

" *The* COMMANDER-*in*-CHIEF,

" HARRY CALVERT,[1] Adjutant-General."

The outlook was not improved by Pitt's resignation in February, 1801, but the news that the army which he had sent to Egypt under Sir Ralph Abercromby in the previous January had routed the French was at once a tonic and a sedative to the nation. Some people thought it should be an incentive to further effort to crush the man who was rapidly becoming the military dictator of Europe; others saw in it a prospect of peace. The following

[1] Sir Harry Calvert succeeded Sir W. Fawcett as Adjutant-General of the forces in 1799, after an active military career, in which he had been frequently on active service. He eventually became Lieutenant-Governor of Chelsea Hospital, and died in 1826, by which time he had been promoted to the rank of General. The above instructions were first issued in 1800, and again in 1801 and 1803.

hitherto unpublished letter[1] from Charles James Fox to his brother, General Fox, shows the uncertain state of affairs at the time :—

" My dear Brother,

" I have written seldomer than I should have done from doubting whether you ever received my letters, but from yours of the 6th of last month I find that you had received one, and so, of course, I suppose the others. I am much obliged to you for enquiring about the language. I guessed, of course, that there was Greek, Latin, Spanish, Italian and probably some Moorish, but I still doubt about the Irish very much. You don't say anything of Mrs. Fox and the children, so I conclude they are well. Indeed I hear with great pleasure from Caroline that Mrs. Fox was remarkably so and much better than when in England. You have probably long before this heard the fate of Egypt. Here we are all in a state of uncertainty about it and unfortunately all we know about it is that our killed and wounded amounted to near 2000 before the famous action of the 21st, 22nd and 23rd,[2] over all these three days which is given by various reports. Every report is in itself unauthentic, but yet there have been so many reports of an action and a victory of the English about that time makes one think something has happened, which is at least called a victory. Why Egypt should be of such importance to either the French or to us I never could discover, and I have always thought the expedition there the foolishest part—perhaps the only foolish part, of Napoleon's conduct, unless he had some views connected with it in connection with the internal politics of France of which we are not informed, or (which I have always suspected) that he had a desire to be out of the way of

---

[1] Mr. Broadley's collection of MSS. Purchased at the Bunbury Sale.
[2] Battle of Alexandria, March, 1801. Sir Ralph Abercromby was mortally wounded, and died on the 28th inst.

accepting or refusing the command of an army destined to invade England. I hope we shall soon hear that it is over, and with as little slaughter as possible whichever way it ends. Both armies have what we used to call at Newmarket 'a good hedge,' since the vanquished will probably be able to return to their own country while the conquerors must remain in Egypt.

"As to the state of things here I believe almost everybody is as much in the dark as I am. The K[ing] is certainly not quite well, nor do I believe he ever will be. When I was in Town last week he was not allowed to see any of his family. I now read in the newspaper that he walked in Kew Garden with the Queen and Princesses and that he is going very soon to Weymouth. If they allow him to go there where he is in public all day it seems very inconsistent with what has generally been given out, that he is indeed well, but that great quiet and retirement are necessary to his perfect re-establishment. In short I cannot believe that he will go, but how long things are to go on in this state nobody knowing in fact whether we have a K. or not I have no guess. The exact state of out situation as regards the Baltic is as little known as anything else, and if you ask me as to peace the same answer must be given. Nobody knows what steps have been taken towards negociations, nor even what degree of hope is entertained of success. In short I have nothing to tell you of public affairs.

"With regard to myself I am here well and happy and should be truly sorry if anything should make it necessary for me to enter again into public business. The P[rince] and D[uke] of Y[ork] are supposed to be ill together. The Dukes of Clarence and Kent are supposed to side with the former. The D[uke] of Cumberland with the latter. I have not heard which way the other two Princes are. The best news here is that wheat has fallen, and is falling, in price, for the misery endured by the poor, and indeed by those a little above the poor and who are obliged to give charity when they are in a position rather to ask it themselves has for the last twelve months been dreadful. Your mare is very well, but as I ride her so little I have had her used in the cart and at plough, which I should not have done if I had thought there was any chance of her lasting as a riding horse till Mrs. Fox returned. I have also had her covered, and I expect a fine foal from her. I hope this is not wrong. Mrs. A. desires to be kindly remembered to you. Pray give my love to Mrs. F. and the children. You say nothing of William Dixon, who has, I fear, behaved very improperly. His father is, as you may suppose, very anxious about him.

" Yours affectionately,

" C. J. Fox.

"St. Anne's Hill, 15 *May*, 1801."

Addington, the new Prime Minister, while determined upon peace at any price, discreetly made some show of continuing the preparations made by Pitt. He largely relied upon the genius of Nelson, who was appointed to a command extending from Orfordness, in Suffolk, to Beachy Head, in Sussex, to circumvent Bonaparte's plans should his hopes of a cessation of hostilities be dashed to the ground. At first Nelson was not inclined to take the First Consul's preparations at all seriously, but when he had seen with his own eye the preparations being made by La Touche Tréville, his views changed. He gave it as his opinion that the French had determined upon putting their threat into execution, but was convinced that the flotilla was not the only force he would have to contend with. " This boat business," he says, " may be a part of a great plan of invasion; it can never be the only one."[1]   The Admiral felt sure that the wily ruler of France would play him a trick, and came to the conclusion that the French navy would be utilized to put him off the proper scent.   "Although I feel confident that the fleets of the enemy will meet the same fate which has always attended them, yet their sailing will facilitate the coming over of the flotilla, as they will naturally suppose our attention will be called on to the fleets."   On the 25th July, 1801, Nelson addressed an important Memorandum to the Admiralty on the defence of the Thames.   In it he stated that the coast of Sussex and of Kent to the westward of Dover should be well protected.   It was his opinion that London was the chief point aimed at by the French.

"From Boulogne, Calais, and even Havre," the communication runs, "the enemy will try and land in Sussex, or the lower part of Kent; and from Dunkirk, Ostend, and the other ports of Flanders, to land on the coast of Essex or Suffolk . . . added to this, the enemy will create a powerful diversion by the sailing of the combined fleet, and the either sailing, or creating of such an appearance of sailing, of the Dutch fleet, as will prevent Admiral Dickson[2] from sending anything from off the great Dutch ports, whilst the smaller ports spew forth its flotilla."   The Admiral's idea was that twenty thousand men would land on the west side of Dover, sixty or seventy miles from London, and the same number on the east side; "they are too knowing to let us have but one point of alarm for London."   He calculated that in calm weather the flotilla, with forty thousand men on board, could cover the distance from the

---

[1] *Nelson's Dispatches*, Vol. IV, p. 500.
[2] Commander-in-Chief in the North Sea.

French coast to the English shores in twelve hours. If this happened the British fleet and boats were to "get into the Channel and meet them as soon as possible : if not strong enough for the attack they must watch, and keep them company till a favourable opportunity offers. If a breeze springs up, our Ships are to deal *destruction :* no delicacy can be observed on this occasion. But should it remain calm, and our flotilla not fancy itself strong enough to attack the enemy on their passage, the moment that they begin to touch our shore, strong or weak, our Flotilla of boats[1] must attack as much of the enemy's Flotilla as they are able—say only one-half or two-thirds; it will create a most powerful diversion, for the bows of our Flotilla will be opposed to their unarmed sterns, and the courage of Britons will never, I believe, allow one Frenchman to leave the beach." He thought Solebay "not an improbable place" for the landing, and conceived the notion of having "a great number of Deal and Dover boats to be on board our vessels off the Port of Boulogne, to give notice of the direction taken by the enemy. If it is calm, vessels in the Channel can make signals of intelligence to our shores. . . ." Gunboats and flat-boats were to be kept near Margate and Ramsgate, a squadron was to lie between Orfordness and the North Foreland, and another in Hollesley Bay. After giving directions as to the movements of these divisions, Nelson goes on to say that "the more fast Rowing boats, called Thames Galleys, which can be secured the better, to carry orders, information, etc., etc. . . . Stationary Floating Batteries are not, from any apparent advantage, to be moved. . . ."

---

[1] "The Admiralty cannot build too many small craft, even if their armament interferes with that of the ships-of-the-line."—Dumouriez MS., p. 74.

AN ACCURATE REPRESENTATION of the FLOATING MACHINE
Invented by the FRENCH for INVADING ENGLAND and Acts
on the principals of both Wind & Water Mills. carries 60-000 Men & 600 Cannon

[1797-1801]

"Whatever plans may be adopted," he adds, "the moment the Enemy touch our Coast, be it where it may, they are to be attacked by every man afloat and on shore: this must be perfectly understood. *Never fear the event.* The Flat boats can probably be manned (partly, at least) with the Sea Fencibles[1] . . . but the Flat Boats they may man to be in grand and sub-divisions, commanded by their own Captains and Lieutenants, as far as is possible. . . . These are offered as merely the rude ideas of the moment," he concludes, "and are only meant as a Sea plan of defence for the City of London ; but I believe other parts may likewise be menaced, if the Brest Fleet, and those from Rochefort and Holland put to sea ; although I feel confident that the Fleets of the Enemy will meet the same fate which has always attended them, yet their sailing will facilitate the coming over of their Flotilla, as they will naturally suppose our attention will be called only to the Fleets."[2]

Lord St. Vincent was then at the head of the Admiralty, and he found himself unable to agree with all the propositions put forward by Nelson. "Our great reliance is on the vigilance and activity of our cruisers at sea, any reduction in the number of which, by applying them to guard our ports, inlets, and beaches, would in my judgment tend to our destruction."[3]

While Addington thought of nothing but peace, Commander-in-Chief the Duke of York evidently regarded

[1] A volunteer force consisting of fishermen and others connected with the sea, who had sworn to lend their aid in repelling the enemy.

[2] *The Dispatches and Letters of Vice-Admiral Lord Viscount Nelson,* with Notes by Sir Nicholas Harris Nicholas, G.C.M.G., Vol. IV, pp. 425-8.

[3] Mahan's *Influence of Sea Power upon the French Revolution,* Vol. II, p. 121.

war as a stern reality. A secret circular was issued on July 21st, 1801, by Colonel Brownrigg, Adjutant-General, to those in command of districts throughout the country. "I have the Commander-in-Chief's commands," it runs, "to acquaint you that from unquestionable intelligence there is the strongest reason that an immediate descent upon the coasts of the Channel is intended by the enemy. I am therefore to recommend you from His Royal Highness that you give orders for the utmost vigilance to be observed throughout your district, particularly by the troops stationed immediately upon the coast, and that in general they may be held in readiness to act with the greatest promptitude and effect against the enemy. . . ."[1] The same officer also informed Colonel Hope, Adjutant-General in Ireland, of the apparent danger, and called upon him to be prepared to send reinforcements to England, should the enemy "gain a footing in the country."[2] This was a tacit acknowledgment of lack of readiness, for Ireland was not overburdened with troops.[3] Had rebellion broken out as was anticipated, and a diversion made in that quarter by the French, as well as a landing effected in England, the consequences must have proved disastrous. But such urgent positive orders could not be disregarded, and Lord Gardner, commanding the fleet guarding the west of Ireland, was told that if the west of England was invaded, nearly 5000 men from Cork would have to be taken across. "If Scotland

---

[1] *Diary and Correspondence of Charles Abbot, Lord Colchester*, edited by Charles, Lord Colchester, Vol. I, p. 366.   [2] *Ibid.*, p. 367.

[3] "The regular forces in Ireland, including fencibles, during this period was about 30,000, and the militia 30,000 more; the yeomanry corps of infantry and cavalry were about 60,000; the cavalry part being about 12,000."—*Ibid.*, p. 276.

or the side of Liverpool was the point, a similar force might be sent from the North and Dublin. In this latter instance perhaps shipping for the purpose might be seized in Belfast and Dublin. . . ."[1]

Perhaps nothing did more to inspire Londoners with a sense of their responsibility to the nation than the frequent inspections and reviews of the volunteer and associated corps by the King or Commander-in-Chief the Duke of York. One of the most satisfactory of these was held in Hyde Park on the 22nd July, 1801, when 4,734 armed citizens assembled and went through various exercises and evolutions. "It was computed that, independent of the volunteers, upwards of 30,000 spectators attended. . . . Innumerable fair forms, sheltered from the scorching rays of the sun by the protecting parasol, were seen, escorted by their beaux, tripping over the turf. The surrounding walls were covered with men, women, and children. Every eye sparkled with animation, every heart beat with loyal fervour; the proud name of Briton was vaunted with self-congratulation; and if the chimerical idea of invasion occurred, not a man present but, contemplating this brilliant display of the ' Amor Patriæ,' was enthusiastically eager to exclaim :—

> 'And if their *flat bottoms in darkness get o'er,*
> We soon shall find means to receive them on shore."[2]

Nelson issued a Proclamation to the Sea Fencibles, urging them to man the coast-defence vessels, but few responded to his appeal. They were half-hearted, lacked spirit and vim, and thought more of keeping their jobs than of defending their country. "Of the 2600 Sea-

[1] *Ibid.*, p. 367.
[2] *Gentleman's Magazine,* Vol. LXXI, part ii, p. 662.

Fencibles enrolled between Orfordness and Beachy Head,"
the Admiral complains to St. Vincent, "only 385 have
offered themselves to go on board a Ship, and serve at the
Sand-heads, &c.; the Sea-Fencibles of Margate, for
instance consist of 118 men, their occupation is pier-men
belonging to the Margate hoys, and some few who assist
Ships up and down the River. These men say, 'our
employment will not allow us to go from our homes beyond
a day or two, and for actual service': but they profess
their readiness to fly on board, or any other duty ordered,
when the Enemy are announced as actually coming on the
sea. This, my Dear Lord, we must take for granted is the
situation of all other Sea-Fencibles: when we cannot do
all we wish, we must do as well as we can. Our Ships
fitted for the service, on both shores, between Orfordness
and the North Foreland, want 1900 men, the River-barges
two or three hundred. . . . I am sure that the French are
trying to get from Boulogne; yet the least wind at W.N.W.
and they are lost. I pronounce that no embarkation can
take place at Boulogne ; whenever it comes forth, it will be
from Flanders, and what a forlorn undertaking! consider
cross tides, &c. &c. As for rowing, that is impossible. It
is perfectly right to be prepared against a mad Government; but with the active force your Lordship has given
me, I may pronounce it almost impracticable."[1]

On the 4th August, 1801, Nelson relentlessly bombarded
the French flotilla, which was outside the harbour, for
sixteen hours. The hills near Boulogne and the heights
around Dover were almost black with a swarming mass of

---

[1] To Admiral the Earl of St. Vincent, K.B., dated from Margate Roads,
7th August, 1801. *The Dispatches and Letters of Vice-Admiral Lord Viscount
Nelson*, Vol. IV, p. 446.

spectators, and as it was a particularly clear day they were able to watch the conflict whenever the smoke from the guns and batteries cleared off a little. The action, however, was not a success, and comparatively slight damage was done to Bonaparte's miniature fleet. Nelson was not to be daunted, and he wrote on the 12th inst. to Mr. Addington: " In my command I can tell you with truth, that I find much zeal and good humour; and should Mr. Bonaparte put himself in our way, I believe he will wish himself even in Corsica. I only hope, if he means to come, that it will be before the 14th of September, for my stamina is but ill-suited for equinoctial gales and cold weather." [1]

Eleven days after the attack narrated above Nelson renewed the struggle, his fleet consisting of thirty sail and many small boats. He determined to attack the crews of the flotilla at night, and all would have been well had not the French profited by their recent experience and been on the alert as a consequence. A number of boats were let down from the English men-of-war, filled with tried and trusty sailors, and formed in four divisions. With muffled oars the seamen drew near to the ships lying off Boulogne. These were defended by long poles, at the head of which were sharp spikes of iron, while strong netting had been placed round the hulls, very similar to the torpedo netting used in modern naval warfare. Each of the enemy's vessels contained from 150 to 200 soldiers. It has been repeatedly stated that the clever scheme had been conceived of fastening the ships to the shore by means of iron chains, so that no prizes could be taken; but La Touche Tréville denies that

---

[1] *Dispatches and Letters of Vice-Admiral Lord Viscount Nelson*, Vol. IV, p. 456.

such was the case,[1] although in the week and a half which had elapsed since the last engagement the French had placed batteries and cannon wherever it was thought they could be used to advantage. On the heights of Boulogne a line of soldiers fired ceaselessly on the intrepid British bluejackets, whose firearms had been left behind for reasons of prudence; Nelson knowing full well that one shot fired at the wrong moment would bring down a veritable hail of bullets from the men on shore. Jack Tar suffered severely as a result, although the howitzer-boats did some damage.

The second division of boats, under the command of Captain Parker, was the first to close with the enemy. The French commander refused to order his men to fire until he had given the crews of the approaching boats an opportunity to withdraw. Going to the side of his vessel, he shouted in the best English he could muster: "Let me advise you . . . to keep your distance. You can do nothing here, and it is only useless shedding the blood of brave men to make the attempt."[2]

The British tars, however, did not flinch in the face of duty, and so the unequal contest began. One hundred and seventy-two were either killed or placed *hors de combat*, while Parker lost a leg and thigh. The French casualties were comparatively slight, being returned at ten killed and thirty wounded. Marks of distinction were conferred on twenty-two soldiers and sailors for their bravery during the action, and from this date the First Consul began to think seriously of Boulogne as the most suitable place for congregating the flotilla.

[1] Desbrière, Vol. II, p. 344.
[2] *Annual Register*, 1801, p. 269.

In a letter to Mr. Evan Nepean, Secretary of the Admiralty, dated August 16th, 1801, Nelson states that the darkness of the night, with the tide and half-tide, separated the divisions; and to all not arriving at the same happy moment was to be attributed the failure of the attack, which Nelson put on his own shoulders. It is characteristic of the writer that he adds, " more determined, persevering courage I never witnessed." Captain Parker died at Deal on the 28th of the following month.[1] Deeply attached as he was to his senior officer, the latter showed that the feeling was even more deeply reciprocated, for he paid the dead commander's creditors in full when he heard that he had involved himself in debt. Parker's opinion of Nelson is summed up in his own words : " He is the cleverest and quickest man and the most zealous in the world. In the short time we were in Sheerness "—that is, before embarking—"he regulated and gave orders for thirty of the ships under his command, made everyone pleased, filled them with emulation, and set them all on the *qui vive*." The Admiral's correspondence about this time shows very clearly the indomitable courage of the man who was destined to put an end at Trafalgar to Napoleon's attempt to make France a great maritime Power. His letters and despatches are full of witty remarks and brilliant metaphor, as spontaneous as the genius of the writer, and they show the soul of a hero. Thus on the 17th August he tells Lord St. Vincent, " I

---

[1] The death of Parker was a cause of deep grief throughout the fleet. Hardy speaks feelingly on the subject in his letters (see *The Three Dorset Captains at Trafalgar*, p. 114, by A. M. Broadley and R. G. Bartelot, M.A.). Since the publication of that book the tomb of Parker, a somewhat ponderous structure of stone, has been discovered in one of the disused cemeteries at Deal. It bears a lengthy inscription. See Appendix II.

own I shall never bring myself to allow any attack to go forward, when I am not personally concerned ; my mind suffers much more than if I had a leg shot off in this late business. Had our force arrived as I intended, 'twas not all the chains in France that could have prevented our folks from bringing off the whole of the vessels. . . ." [1] The French stated that their repulse of the enemy at Boulogne was as glorious a victory as the English triumph at Aboukir.

Shortly afterwards Nelson proposed an expedition to Flushing with between four and five thousand troops. He felt sure that if he were able to strike a blow in that quarter, Napoleon would, at any rate for a time, be forced to give up his projected invasion. The First Lord of the Admiralty, however, vetoed the idea, and thereby aroused Nelson's ire. " Lord St. Vincent is for keeping the Enemy closely blockaded," he complains to Addington, " but I see they get alongshore inside their sand banks, and under their guns, which line the coast of France. Lord Hood is for keeping our squadrons of defence stationary on our own shore (except light cutters to give information of every movement of the enemy). . . . When men of such good sense, such great sea-officers, differ so widely, is it not natural that I should wish the mode of Defence to be well arranged by the mature consideration of men of judgment ?" The last sentence was a sarcastic reference to Lord St. Vincent, who had refused a consultation with Nelson on the subject. The letter concludes with a defence of his own mode of conducting operations : "I mean not to detract from my judgment ; even as it is, it is well known : but I

[1] *Dispatches and Letters of Vice-Admiral Lord Viscount Nelson*, Vol. IV, p. 470.

boast of nothing but my zeal; in that I will give way to no man upon earth."[1]

Nelson begged repeatedly to be relieved of his command owing to ill-health, but the Admiralty only turned a deaf ear to his complaints and a "No" to his applications. "None of them cares a d——n for me and my sufferings," he comments in vexation.

Lord Howe, the "Father of the Navy," and the hero of the victory off Ushant on the "Glorious first of June," 1794, also differed with St. Vincent as to the wisdom of tightly bottling up the squadrons of the enemy in their home ports. He foresaw the difficulty which confronted Lord Melville[2] on his succeeding to the head of affairs at the Admiralty, when "he found a fleet of worn-out ships utterly inadequate to meet the combined fleets of France and Spain,"[3] necessitating much patching-up of a more or less temporary nature to enable them to keep the sea. As regards the sailors themselves, they were then, as now, believers that "there is nothing the British Navy cannot do," but a certain proportion of them were far from competent. Four months after the breaking out of the war in 1793, Collingwood had discerned that "we do not manage our ships with that alacrity and promptness that used to distinguish our navy. There is a tardiness everywhere in the preparation, and a sluggishness in the execution that is quite new. The effect is obvious to everybody, and the moment the ships are put in motion they feel it. After recording two disasters due to this lack of adequate training, he adds : " This was not the fault of the weather,

---

[1] *Ibid.*, p. 475.

[2] Henry Dundas. He became First Lord of the Admiralty on the 15th May, 1804.   [3] *Life of Lord Howe*, p. 217.

I.—O

but must ever be the case when young men are made officers who have neither skill nor attention, and there is scarce a ship in the navy that has not an instance that political interest is a better argument for promotion than any skill. . . ."[1] Writing from the *Barfleur*, at Torbay, on April 8th, 1800, he shows that this disgraceful state of things in the fleet is scarcely, if at all, improved. "The truth is," he says, "in this great extensive navy, we find a great many indolent, half-qualified people, to which may be attributed most of the accidents which happen."[2] But if this was true of British sailors, the remark applied with double force to those who manned the French fleets. If history has proved anything, it is that fighting efficiency does not depend solely upon the heaviest armament, that the general morale of the men is of more importance. Sheer weight of metal never did nor never will counter-balance inefficiency in the working of a ship. It is as true in this age of steam and steel as it was in the days of the three-decker. What Trafalgar proved in 1805, the battle of the Sea of Japan seconded a century later. Discipline and courage are not analogous terms, but they ought to be in a country whose very existence depends upon the command of the sea, and whose boundaries in time of war are the enemy's coasts.

---

[1] *Collingwood*, p. 24, by W. Clark Russell. This letter is dated from Spithead, July 22nd, 1793, and is to Sir Edward Blackett, Mrs. Collingwood's uncle.   [2] *Ibid.*, p. 93.

CHAPTER VII

THE LITERARY AND ARTISTIC LANDMARKS OF THE
GREAT TERROR, WITH SPECIAL REFERENCE TO THE
POPULAR PAMPHLETS, SONGS, BROADSIDES, AND CARI-
CATURES PUBLISHED BETWEEN THE FIRST FRENCH
EXPEDITION TO IRELAND AND THE CONCLUSION OF
THE TREATY OF AMIENS (1796–1802)

> Does haughty Gaul invasion threat?
> Then let the louns beware, Sir.
> There's wooden walls upon our seas,
> And volunteers on shore, Sir.—ROBERT BURNS.

THERE is a very marked divergence between the state of public opinion in England during the two phases of the Great Terror, divided from each other by the Treaty of Amiens and the brief cessation of hostilities which ensued. In 1796, when the invasion projects of the French Directory began to assume a tangible shape, and the energy and ability of Lazare Hoche were paving the way for the phenomenal activity and genius of Napoleon Bonaparte, the aftermath of the French Revolution still exercised an appreciable influence in English politics. Richard Price had died two years before the execution of Louis XVI, and Joseph Priestley had migrated to America; but Thomas Paine (who had only escaped the guillotine by the accident of Robespierre's downfall) was still active for evil, and his *Age of Reason*, published in 1793, gave a fillip to the waning

enthusiasm of the *habitués* of the "Crown and Anchor."
The Corresponding Society, the Constitutional Club, and
other kindred associations had not as yet closed their
doors; and the "sentiments" of "The Democrats throughout the World" and "The Friends of Freedom; and may
our Liberties never be swallowed in a Pitt" were as popular
toasts with one section of the community as those of "May
some plans be formed to save a sinking State" and "May
Britain never want sons to volunteer their services" were
with another.

Edmund Burke was from the days of his youth an
uncompromising foe to Democracy and even to the
moderate measures of Parliamentary Reform advocated
by Pitt, whose brother-in-law, the Earl of Stanhope, one of
the mainsprings of the democratic associations of 1788,
had now, in despair, turned his attention to the perfecting
of steam vessels, stereotyping, and microscopic lenses,
because his fellow-peers steadily refused to listen to his
motions for non-interference in Continental complications.
Fox, Sheridan, Grey, and many of their friends still
pleaded in vain for peace with France, and it thus came
to pass that they one and all fell under the merciless
lash of James Gillray, the Juvenal of eighteenth-century
caricaturists, who, as an ardent Whig, had once regarded
the proceedings of the Paris mob as the dawn of
universal freedom, but who now, like Burns, Southey,
Coleridge, and Wordsworth[1] amongst the poets, and

---

[1] It was the French invasion of Switzerland in 1798 which inspired
Wordsworth's sublime sonnet, commonly known as "The Two Voices."
There is an echo of the Great Terror in its last lines:—

> "For high-souled maid, what sorrow would it be
> That mountain floods should thunder as before,
> And ocean bellow from his rocky shore,
> And neither awful voice be heard by thee?"

Mackintosh amongst the politicians, frankly acknowledged his mistake and embraced, to some extent at least, the opinions of Pitt. From the commencement of the Great Terror the pencil of Gillray was at the service of George Canning and the *Anti-Jacobin.* As we shall presently see, the English Premier had no more powerful ally, and Bonaparte no more relentless foe. It took, however, some time to bring about that absolute unanimity of public opinion on the subject of French aggression which characterized the popular movements of 1803, 1804, and 1805. The prevailing feelings of 1796 and 1797 were half-hearted and lukewarm, compared to those which took complete possession of the British mind at the sudden termination of the "experimental" peace which no man believed in less than George III.[1]

In 1796 the office of Poet Laureate was by no means a sinecure. It was then held by a worthy Berkshire gentleman who rejoiced in the name of Pye, and is now described on high authority as "Poetaster and Poet Laureate." It was the duty of Henry James Pye, as it had been that of Thomas Warton, William Whitehead, and Colley Cibber before him, to compose odes for New Year's Day, the King's birthday, and other occasions, which, being duly set to music by the Court band-conductor, were performed in the presence of the Royal Family and their guests.[2] As far back as January 1st, 1795, the fear of foreign invasion took possession of the mind of Pye, and we find it reflected in the last verse of the ode "performed that day at St. James's":—

[1] See p. 266.
[2] At Sir William Fraser's sale a volume was sold containing copies of these effusions from 1715, when Nahum Tate was Laureate, culled from contemporary sources and entitled *Laureated Leaves and Rhymes for Royalty.*

Yet if the stern vindictive foe,
Insulting aim the hostile blow;
Britain in martial terrors dight,
Lifts high th' avenging sword, and courts the fight;
On every side, behold her swains,
Crowd eager from her fertile plains;
With breasts undaunted, lo ! they stand,
Firm bulwarks of their native land;
And proud, her floating castles round,
The guardians of her happy coast,
Bid their terrific thunder sound
Dismay, to Gallia's scatter'd host;
While still Britannia's navies reign
Triumphant o'er the subject main.

George III was a "stalwart" from the first. He had celebrated his fifty-sixth birthday some months before he applauded Pye's first "invasion" ode (harmonized by Sir W. Parsons), and several years afterwards was still anxious to lead his troops, sword in hand, against the "Corsican Usurper."[1] But Pye's task was not yet complete. A verse was promptly added to the National Anthem.

Thou who rul'st sea and land,
Stretch forth thy guardian hand,
    Potent to save;
Lead forth our Monarch's Host,
Check proud Invasion's boast
Crush'd on our warlike Coast,
    'Whelm'd by our wave.

Pye did his best also to "invasionize" "Rule, Britannia"; but Anna Maria Seward took the public fancy with the lines—

Thee, haughty tyrants ne'er shall tame,
All their attempts to bend thee down,
Shall but arouse thy gen'rous flame,
And work their woe, and thy renown.
                Rule, Britannia, etc.

[1] See Introduction, p. xvii.

Before the close of the year (1796) the volunteers were arming for the coming struggle, and the first abortive attempt "to get to London by way of Ireland" had brought ridicule on its contrivers. Amongst the early recruits was Robert Burns, who penned the Song of the Dumfries Volunteers when the shadow of death had already fallen upon him. It was early in 1795 that Burns donned the blue coat and nankeen breeches of his company, and just three months after the performance of Pye's first invasion ode his comrades-in-arms were singing to the heart-stirring tune of "Push about the jorum":—

> Does haughty Gaul invasion threat?
> Then let the louns beware, Sir.
> There's wooden walls upon the seas,
> And volunteers on shore, Sir.
> The Nith shall run to Corsincon,[1]
> And Criffel[2] sink to Solway,
> Ere we permit a foreign foe
> On British ground to rally.
>
> Fal de lal, etc.
>
> O let us not like snarling tykes[3]
> In wrangling be divided;
> Till slap come in an unco loon[4]
> And with a rung[5] decide it.
> Be Britain still to Britain true,
> Amang ourselves united;
> But never but by British hands
> Maun British wrangs be righted.
>
> Fal de lal, etc.
>
> The kettle o' the kirk and state,
> Perhaps a claut may fail in't;
> But deil a foreign tinkler loon
> Shall ever ca'[6] a nail in't;

[1] A high hill at the source of the Nith.
[2] A mountain at the mouth of the same river.
Dogs.   [4] Ragamuffin.   [5] Cudgel.   [6] Drive.

Our fathers' bluid the kettle bought,
And wha wad dare to spoil it ;—
By heaven, the sacrilegious dog
Shall fuel be to boil it.

        Fal de lal, etc.

The wretch that wad a tyrant own,
And the wretch, his true-born brother,
Who would set the mob aboon the throne,
May they be d——d together !
Who will not sing " God save the King,"
Shall hang as high's the steeple ;
But while we sing " God save the King,"
We'll ne'er forget the People.[1]

        Fal de lal, etc.

We have more to learn of the machinations of the " foreign tinklers " and their English friends in 1795–6. Playing at treason was not then quite so unfashionable as it became seven years later, and Burns was evidently a keen politician as well as a true poet. He for one had, at any rate, no sympathy with the specious pretexts for foreign invasion which found a few advocates in the early days of the Great Terror. It is sad to relate that the last days of Burns were harassed by pressing applications for the settlement of a debt of £7. 4s. incurred for his volunteer uniform. Allan Cunningham tells us that when the singer of this wonderful swan-song was brought home to die, he was " dressed in a blue coat with the undress nankeen pantaloons of the volunteers, and that his neck,

---

[1] The war-song does not appear in the *Anti-Gallican* of 1803–4, but another martial hymn written by Burns is published. The last verse runs thus :—

In the field of proud honour—our swords in our hands,
Our King and our Country to save—
While victory shines on life's last ebbing sands,
Oh ! who would not rest with the brave ?

which was inclining to be short, caused his hat to turn up behind in the manner of the shovel hats of the episcopal clergy. Truth obliges me to add, that he was not fastidious about his dress; and that an officer, curious in the personal appearance and equipments of his company, might have questioned the military nicety of the poet's clothes and arms."[1] Cunningham also relates that when one of his comrades came to visit him during his last illness, Burns smiled and said, "John, don't let the awkward squad fire over me." Whether this was a jest or a request will never be known, but the national poet of Scotland was buried with military honours. On the 25th July, 1796, the Dumfries warriors fired three volleys over his grave. The Invasion Parnassus is, it must be confessed, distinguished by quantity rather than quality, although Burns, Scott, Coleridge, and Wordsworth all contributed to it.

The year 1796 had begun with a remarkable but now entirely forgotten trial which threw considerable light on the state of public opinion concerning the all-absorbing question of the threatened invasion. On the 28th January a certain Mr. William Stone, a gentleman both by birth and education, appeared before Lord Kenyon and the full Court of King's Bench at Westminster Hall to answer an indictment for high treason. He was also charged with conspiring with his brother, John Henry Stone ("a domiciliated Frenchman"), and William Jackson, an Irish American, to commit that crime. It was clear that under the feigned names of Benjamin Beresford, Thomas Popkins, and William Enots they had carried on an extensive correspondence with the object of gaining such reliable intelligence as would enable them to judge of the expediency

[1] *The Casket of Literature,* Vol. I, p. 40, edited by Charles Gibbon.

or otherwise of a descent on these shores. Lord Lauder-
dale, Mr. Sheridan, Samuel Rogers, the banker-poet, and
others gave evidence. In the course of his examination
Mr. Sheridan said that the accused had been "introduced
to him by a Mr. Wilson, who said, that he (Mr. Stone)
wanted to communicate to him what might be of advantage to the country ; and then (the prisoner) said, that he
had had frequent communications with his brother at Paris,
and he understood, from this communication, that the idea of
attempting an invasion of this country was a plan seriously
and peremptorily resolved upon by the government of
France ; that this idea was adopted, and likely to be pursued, upon an opinion, which was very ill formed, of the
general state of the public mind, and the prevalence of
general discontent in this country. He then stated, that
the service he thought he could effect, would be the
means, through this circuitous channel of communication,
to undeceive the government of France upon this subject,
and by giving them the real state of the country, and
convincing them how little could be expected from anything like assistance, or co-operation, from any description
of men in this country, he conceived and hoped the consequence might be, their abandoning a project evidently
taken up upon false information." The whole question
turned on the real object of Mr. Stone's inquiries, and
after three hours' deliberation the jury acquitted him ; but
there can be no doubt that foreign emissaries were endeavouring to assist the would-be invaders of England
by sowing the seed of sedition throughout the country and
exciting discontent amongst our soldiers and sailors.

In April and May of the following year (1797) dangerous
mutinies declared themselves on board the King's ships at

Portsmouth and the Nore, and notwithstanding the victory off Cape St. Vincent on the 14th February, and the discomfiture of Tate's banditti at Fishguard ten days later, widespread anxiety prevailed.[1] In May the following handbill was distributed broadcast in every barrack throughout England :—

TO THE BRITISH ARMY.

COMRADES,

Are we not men? Is it not high time we should prove that we know ourselves to be such?

Are we anywhere respected as men, and why are we not?

Have not wrong notions of discipline led us to our present despised condition? Is there a man among us, who does not wish to defend his country and who would not willingly do it without being subject to the insolence and cruelty of effeminite puppies?

Were not the sailors, like us mocked for want of thought, though not so much despised for poverty as we are? Have they not proved that they can think and act for themselves and preserve every useful point of discipline, full as well, or better than when under the tyranny of their officers?

What 'makes this difference between a commissioned officer and a private or non-commissioned?

Are they better men? You must laugh at the thought! Do they know discipline half so well as our Serjeants? Don't they owe their promotions to their connections with placemen and pensioners, and a mock parliament which pretends to represent the people?

When we think of the people ought not each of us to think of a father, or a brother, as a part of them? Can you think a parliament speaking like fathers and brothers, would treat us as we are treated?

Would they mock us with a pretended addition to our pay, and then lock us up in barracks, to cheat us and keep us in ignorance? Would they not rather considering the price of every thing wanting for our families at least double our pay?

Why is every regiment harrassed with long marches, from one end of the country to the other, but to keep them strangers to the people and to each other?

Are we so well cloathed as soldiers used to be? Ask the old pensioners at Chelsea College, whether horse or foot? Ask them too, if it was usual when there were fewer regiments, for colonels to make a profit out of soldiers cloathes? Don't colonels now draw half their income from what we ought to have, but of which we are robbed?

[1] See *ante*, pp. 31–66.

THESE COMRADES, are a few of our Grievances and but a few; WHAT SHALL WE DO? The tyranny of what is falsely called discipline, prevents us from acting like other men. We cannot even join in petition for that which common honesty would freely have given us long ago. WE HAVE ONLY TWO CHOICES, either to submit to the present impositions, or demand the treatment proper for men.

THE POWER IS ALL OUR OWN! The regiments which send you this, are willing to do their part. They will shew their countrymen, they can be soldiers without being slaves, and will make their demands as soon as they know you will not draw the trigger against them. Of this we will judge, when we know you have distributed this Bill, not only among your comrades, but to every soldier whom you know in any part of the country.

BE SOBER, BE READY.

The reply of the soldiers in every branch of the service was reassuring. Regulars and volunteers vied with one another in the force and energy with which they expressed their hatred of treason and loathing for traitors. The broadsides issued by the men of the various corps, generally offering rewards at their own expense for the detection of the author or authors of this detestable incitation to rebellion, were placarded in every garrison town. A short time ago a complete series[1] of these characteristic relics of the events of 1797 was in existence, but it has now been dispersed, several of them having been purchased for regimental collections. The broadside now reproduced from Sir George White's Bristol collection may be regarded as typical of the ideas expressed in nearly all of them :—

[1] Thirty-three of the originals and all the correspondence as to the dispersal of this interesting series of military broadsides are in Mr. Broadley's collection of Invasion MSS.

AN ANSWER

TO THE INFAMOUS

HAND-BILL WHICH WAS READ BY **LIEUT. GEN. ROOKE,**

On MONDAY, the 22d of MAY 1797,

TO THE TROOPS UNDER HIS COMMAND AT BRISTOL.

LIEUTENANT-GENERAL ROOKE having had the Goodneſs to read to us an infamous Hand-bill, pretended to be an Addreſs from our Brother Soldiers, but which we are convinced is the Production of ſome deſigning Villains, who wiſh to overturn our excellent Conſtitution, under which we have ſo long lived happily; and having heard the Anſwer of the Marines at Chatham to a ſimilar Hand-bill found in the Barracks there, we moſt certainly approve of the ſame; but cannot paſs over in Silence ſuch atrocious Endeavours to ſubvert Order and Diſcipline, which none but the weakeſt and moſt profligate of Mankind would ever Attempt. WE, THE NON-COMMISSIONED OFFICERS AND PRIVATES OF THE ROYAL BUCKS OR KING'S OWN REGIMENT OF MILITIA, do moſt ſolemnly promiſe our Fellow-citizens and Soldiers, that we will uſe our utmoſt Endeavours to find out ſome of thoſe Villains who, under Pretence of eſpouſing our Cauſe and pointing out Grievances that never have exiſted and Oppreſſions that we never have laboured under, endeavour to withdraw us from our Allegiance to the beſt of Kings, our Duty to our Officers, and to throw the Country into Confuſion; and that, ſhould we meet with any ſuch wicked Wretches, we will deliver them over to the Magiſtrates that they may be brought to condign Puniſhment. We further take this Opportunity of declaring, that, ſo far from complaining of our Pay, we have had it increaſed without being petitioned for; and we are perfectly ſatisfied and moſt grateful for His Majeſty's paternal Goodneſs in ordering us ſuch Addition as he has been graciouſly pleaſed to do ſince we have been called out in our Country's Defence againſt its foreign and ſtill more dangerous Enemies at home, amongſt whom we look on the infamous Writer and Diſtributors of the above Hand-bill.

With Sentiments of the higheſt Veneration and Eſteem for the General who now commands us, and to whom we beg to offer our ſincereſt Thanks for the Confidence he ſhewed he had in our Loyalty by reading the Hand-bill to us, and alſo for our own Officers, we do moſt ſolemnly declare, that we will always be ready and willing to ſerve when commanded, and that we will protect our Country againſt all its Enemies to the laſt Drop of our Blood.

On Behalf of ourſelves and the Men of our reſpective Companies,

Thomas Newbery, Acting Serjeant Major	Robert Gudgeon	Charles Warren
John Dyos, Quar. Maſt. Serj.	William Chapman	William Hamp
Thomas Meehan, Serj.	John Moore	Charles Waſhington
Joſeph Thompſon, Serj.	Robert Simmons	Henry Perry
John Knapper, Serj.	Daniel Aldrage	George Hardwell
Abraham Lines, Serj.	John Humphreys	Francis Perkins
Wm. Heath, Serj. and Reg.CL	Thomas Poſter	Joſeph Baldwin
Wm. Davis, Drum Major.	John Chantrill	John Phillips
SERJEANTS.	W. Toms	Joſeph Peyton
John Loveredge	Thomas Hencher	George Sanders
John Perkins	Thomas Collingwood	Jonas Wiſe
James Hill	William Goodwin	James Wingrove
M. Weſtley	William Ariſs	Daniel Pearce
William Treacher	James Webb	William Biſhop
John Roberts	James Fawcett	Richard Leuſley
George Vickers	John Field	Richard Brown
Thomas Harmon	Thomas Griffiths	Thomas Garrett
William Carter	Nathaniel Safwell	James Jones
William Wageſfield	CORPORALS.	Joſeph Rane
	John Lines	Stephen Hatch

The deep interest felt by George III in the attempt made to shake the fidelity of the "Gunners" at Woolwich has been mentioned in the Introduction to these volumes (see page xviii), which contains several hitherto unknown letters written by the King to the Duke of York on the subject of the prevailing "unrest." Two days before the first of these communications was penned the following hand-bill had been circulated :—

100 Guineas Reward

Woolwich, May 26, 1797.

IT being believed that some disaffected Persons are endeavouring to corrupt the Loyalty of the Soldiers of the Royal Artillery in this Garrison by distributing Seditious Writings, and other improper Means :

WE, the non-commissioned Officers of the Regiment, quartered at Woolwich, from our Loyalty to His Majesty, and Zeal for the internal Peace and Happiness of the Country, do hereby offer a Reward of ONE HUNDRED GUINEAS out of our Subsistence, to any Soldier of the Regiment, who will give Information of any such seditious Attempts, so that the Person offending may be brought to Justice.

Signed on behalf of 150 *non-commissioned Officers,*

ALEXANDER JAMES,	
JAMES NIVEN,	
JAMES WILSON,	
THOMAS ATKINSON,	Serjeant
JOHN HAY,	Majors.
ANDREW BRAID,	
THOMAS FORTUNE,	
ANTHONY HAIG,	
GEORGE LIDDLE,	

GOD SAVE THE KING.

Printed by DELAHOY, at the Kent Printing-Office, Deptford Bridge.

In June, 1797, the June before Camperdown, the state of things on board the King's ships at Portsmouth and the Nore caused numerous loyal addresses to be presented to the King, many of which were placarded in public places and circulated as hand-bills to influence popular opinion. Here is a broadside reproducing the loyal address from the Trinity House:—

To the King's Most Excellent MAJESTY

The humble address of the Master, Wardens, Assistants and Elder Brethren of the Corporation of the Trinity House of Deptford-Strond.

Most Gracious Sovereign,

We, your Majesty's most dutiful and loyal Subjects, the antient Body Corporate of the Seamen of England, humbly beg Leave to approach your Majesty, to express the deep Concern, which, in common with all your Majesty's faithful Subjects, We feel at the present disgraceful conduct of some of the Seamen of your Majesty's Fleet, who, instigated, no Doubt, by the wicked Insinuations of some evil-disposed Persons, Enemies alike of your Majesty's Royal Person, and to their Country, have been betrayed into Acts of Insubordination and Outrage, degrading to the Character of British Seamen, hitherto so highly distinguished for Loyalty and good Conduct, as for Intrepidity in vanquishing their Enemies: Impelled therefore by the Duty We owe to your Majesty, and to our Country, We step forward at this alarming Crisis to declare our Readiness to support with our Lives, such Measures as your Majesty in your Wisdom may think most expedient to adopt for the Restoration of good Order and Subordination among the Seamen of your Majesty's Fleet.

Given under our Common Seal this Second Day of June, 1797.

The newspapers of 1796–1805 were, comparatively speaking, few and dear. A heavy stamp-tax rendered their price prohibitive as far as the great majority of the King's subjects were concerned, and their circulation was seriously restricted by the slowness of the post and the inadequacy of all means of communication. The influence exercised to-day by the Press (using the term in its widest sense) was then shared by the pedlars and other itinerant vendors, who brought to the doors of the tavern-keeper, the farmer, the tradesman, and the cottager a selection of broadsides and ballads, pamphlets, primers, and sermons, portraits and caricatures, song-books and story-books, together with the latest issues of a formidable array of monthly magazines like the *Gentleman's*, the *Universal*, the *London*, the *Town and Country*, and many others, all of them dealing with the topical questions of the day, and reproducing the New Year's and birthday odes, together with other popular and patriotic effusions. The age of steam and electricity, destined to effect such remarkable changes, was as yet undreamt of by the mass of the people, although Lord Stanhope, Fulton, and a small body of scientific students may possibly have foreseen its advent.[1] The word telegraph was used to indicate a complicated apparatus of wooden arms and shutters which by certain concerted movements communicated news from hill-top to hill-top until it reached Portsmouth, and later on other more distant parts of the country. The roof of the Admiralty office at Whitehall was utilized as a *point de depart* for all official messages,[2] and the extension of this primitive system of news-conveyance to Weymouth, when the visits of the King and Royal Family to that delightful Dorset watering-place became frequent, was regarded as an event of no small importance. The French used a very similar

---

[1] See *ante*, p. 196, and *post*, p. 302.   [2] See illustration, p. 125.

machine for the purpose of conveying intelligence between the coast and the capital.

Invasion broadsides and songs go back to the stormy days of 1715 and 1745, if not still further, and Peg Woffington won the plaudits of the town by appearing in the garb of a volunteer and singing :—

> In Freedom's cause, ye Patriot Fair, arise,
> Exert the sacred Influence of your Eyes,
> On Valiant Merit deign alone to smile,
> And Vindicate the Glory of our Isle ;
> To no base coward prostitute your charms,
> Disband the Lover who deserts his Arms :
> So shall you fire each Hero to his Duty
> And British Rights be Sav'd by British Beauty.[1]

But up till 1790 ghost stories, fairy tales, love songs, murder trials, and dying speeches and confessions proved more saleable than political pamphlets or caricatures of " Charlie " Fox and " Billy " Pitt. It was, however, now deemed advisable to counteract the poisonous doctrines and pernicious practices of our Gallic neighbours which culminated in the tragic death of their King and Queen, and to a woman, Hannah More,[2] belongs, to a great extent, the credit of supplanting the forms of popular literature above alluded to by scattering broadcast throughout the land a myriad of small tracts (of which *Village Politics by Will Chip* may be taken as an example) that, principally through the itinerant vendors, reached and influenced an immense public of all classes. It was in 1794, when the earlier threats of invasion began to make themselves heard, that she wrote thus to her friend

---

[1] The scene is depicted in a very scarce illustrated sheet printed and published by M. Moore in Paternoster Row, 1746.

[2] Hannah More, b. 1745; d. 1833.

I.—P

Elizabeth Montagu,[1] whose career was now nearing its
end: " I have been so long accustomed to receive favour,
kindness, and assistance from you on every occasion,
that I am encouraged to recommend the enclosed little
plan to your patronage.   It is not one of the wild
theories for which this age is so famous, but the fruit
of real experience.   I have long seen and lamented the
evil it is proposed to counteract.   In all the villages
I know, it is surprising to see with what impatience
the periodical visit of the hawker is expected, and with
what avidity his poison was swallowed.   You would be
diverted at the immense quantity of trash I have collected; even those papers which are written with better
intentions are in general calculated to do more harm
than good, consisting chiefly of ghosts, dreams, visions,
witches, and devils.   When we consider the zeal with
which the writings of Priestley, etc., are now brought
within the compass of penny books, circulated with great
industry, and even translated into Welsh, I begin to fear
that *our* workmen and porters will become *philosophers*
too, and that an endeavour to amend the morals and the
principles of the poor is the most probable method to
preserve us from the crimes and calamities of France.   In
this view, I am not above becoming the compiler and
composer of halfpenny papers.   If, my dear Madam, any
impressive story falls in your way, pray treasure it up for
me."   Thus originated Hannah More's *Cheap Repository*
of popular anti-revolutionary literature, which paved the
way for the wholesale dissemination of those pamphlets,
tracts, broadsheets, songs, and caricatures which, between
1796 and 1805, did so much to rouse public spirit, and

[1] Mr. Broadley's MSS.

make every man, woman, and child in Great Britain a personal hater of the Corsican invader, as well as to facilitate the carrying out of the defensive measures of which George III, quite as much as his ministers, generals, and admirals, was the life and soul. The literature and iconography[1] of the first period of the Great Terror is abundant enough, but between 1803 and 1805 the all-important question of resistance-to-death seems almost to have absorbed all contemporary topics.

The beautiful colour-plate books dealing with the uniforms and drill of every arm represented amongst the volunteers of 1796–8 have already been described,[2] and much has been said of the liberality and enthusiasm with which the national defence funds were augmented by private donations. The unanimity with which the appeal for pecuniary help was met is the more remarkable, when it is remembered that the second year of the Great Terror witnessed the mutinies at Portsmouth and the Nore, and other visible signs of general unrest. Help came from many unexpected quarters. In the minutes of our English Masonic Lodges, both for 1797 and 1798, frequent reference is made to contributions in aid of national defence. Goodly sums came from the brethren of Bristol and Bath, while a certain Dr. Richard Linnecar, who presided over the still-existing Lodge of "Unanimity" at Wakefield, Yorkshire, now bearing the number 154, appears to have sent an appeal for aid to other Masonic bodies all over the country. The following record[3] of the proceedings at the Bull Inn, Wakefield, on the 2nd April, 1798, is character-istic of the times :—

[1] By this convenient term portraits, views, caricatures, and every species of pictorial illustration dealing with a given subject are denoted.

[2] See *ante*, pp. 135-6.   [3] Mr. Broadley's MSS.

"Notice having been previously given to the Brethren of the Master's Intentions

"The Right Worshipful Master LINNECAR
"In the Chair,

"*Moved*   To take into Consideration the Expediency of a Masonic Contribution in aid of Government at the present alarming Crisis, when the following Resolutions were severally put, and unanimously agreed to.

"*Resolved*,

" 1. That it is the grand and leading Characteristic of Free and Accepted Masons, in every Clime and under every Form of Government, to be obedient to the Powers that are, and grateful to the laws by which they are protected.

" 2. That, accustomed as they *everywhere* are to the Study of whatever is most perfect in the sublime Science of *Architecture*, they are led to admire Beauty under all its forms and various Appearances.   And that *We* the inhabitants of this happy Isle do most especially contemplate with enthusiastic Fondness and Admiration the nice Symmetry and Proportion of that *Glorious Structure, the British Constitution ;* consisting of King, Lords, and Commons.

" 3. That the Cause and Interests of our most ancient Institution *are more particularly maintained by, and have ever been most prosperous under the Monarchical Form of Government :*—That this, and other weighty Reasons and Considerations moving us, We do avow an unfeigned love of the King, our Sovereign—the Friend and Father of his People ;—and look upon no Sacrifices to be too great, which have for their Object the Dignity of his Crown, the Safety of his Person, and the Stability of our incomparable Constitution and Laws.

" 4. That we are decidedly amongst the foremost of our patriotic Fellow-Subjects *to approve and adopt any Measure,* that may (by our competent Rulers) be thought most conducive to the general Welfare, and the Prosperity of the State.

"5. That in our *exclusive Capacity* of Free and Accepted Masons, We do *now* gladly embrace the Opportunity of acquiescing in the proposed Expediency of *A Masonic Donation to Government* in Support of its vigorous Exertions to confound the Enemies of the Land we live in :— and that we reserve to ourselves, at the same Time such other Portion of pecuniary Assistance as may be reasonably Expected in *a more general Parochial Contribution.*

"6. That the Secretary be empowered immediately to receive the Donations of the Brethren present, and without Loss of Time to collect the Contributions of absent Brethren :—that their Names together with the Amount of the respective Sums be. entered in the Books of their Society, and carefully preserved as a lasting Memorial of their Spirit and Patriotism and that the whole Sum thus contributed (together with a Copy of these Resolutions) be transmitted in the Name of the Wakefield Brethren Lodge of Unanimity (under cover to Francis Freeling, Esq.) to the Mansion House Committee now sitting in the Metropolis for the Receipt of *Voluntary Patriotic Contributions.*

"7. That We do most Sincerely hope and believe that these our Proceedings will not long be permitted to appear a Solitary Instance of Masonic Love of their King, Constitution and Country.

"8. That a Copy of these Resolutions together with an Account of the Sum voluntarily contributed be respectfully presented to the Grand Lodge of England, and that the Resolutions be twice inserted in the Leeds Intelligencer.

"*That lastly*, most emphatically and unreservedly We do desire to be understood as 'hating with a perfect Hatred' all treasonable and revolutionary Practices ;—and to solemnly deprecate that impious and atheistic System which now desolates the Continent of Europe, and which will, if it continue to gain Ground, not only disappoint the exalted Ends and benevolent Purposes of *the Cross*, but also do away the Fear and Love of the *Supreme Being*, and root out the moral and social Virtues from the Hearts and Souls of Men.

"MAY THE GRAND ARCHITECT OF THE UNIVERSE PRESIDE OVER THIS AND ALL OTHER LODGES ROUND THE GLOBE! *So mote it be!*"

Copies of these resolutions were extensively circulated with the accompanying commendatory letter :—

"WAKEFIELD, 17*th May*, 1798.

"These Resolutions, which we are extremely anxious should meet your approbation and support, we are now busied in circulating throughout the dominions of George the Third, whom God preserve.

"May every good attend your Lodge. Praise!

"(Signed)   RICHARD LINNECAR."

The activity displayed in the collection of contributions to the Defence Fund was by no means confined to the sterner sex. In his *History of Caricature under the Republic, the Empire, and the Restoration*,[1] Champfleury gives a very amusing plate, described as of English origin, but which has eluded the diligent search of the writers, in which an elderly and obese lady, pointing to a huge subscription book, is portrayed as addressing a crowd of her female friends, and in the act of uttering the words, "Ladies, let us show our patriotism. If the Bonapartes and the Sans-Culottes come we shall be all carried off and sacrificed"; to which there is a general response of "They will kill us," "Let our liberality equal our patriotism," "I have seen Bonaparte in my tea," and other lines scarcely translat-

---

[1] Champfleury, Vol. IV, p. 272.

able. The idea is rather French than English, but the costumes belong to the early days of the Great Terror.

The ardour of the mothers communicated itself to the sons, and in 1797 we are informed that a gentleman of Exeter, Michael Dicker Sanders by name, residing in Magdalen Street, " enrolled a troop of sixty boys, trained in military manners. They wore a blue uniform with yellow facings. Their muskets at first were mounted with tin barrels, subsequently changed to small light fusils. A drill-sergeant was employed, and they had the usual non-commissioned officers as in the regular regiments. They had also drums and fifes. It was not all pastime, as they were placed under a schoolmaster in a room somewhere adjacent to the Black Lion Inn in South Street, from which they marched on Sundays in full uniform, morning and afternoon, to Trinity Church, sitting in the gallery. If any boy behaved badly in church he was reported and confined in the school-room, with a sentry at the door. On one occasion the corps was reviewed in the Castle Yard by the officers of a regiment stationed here at the time, and in this special inspection the boys' heads were powdered and queued, as was the military fashion of the day. After the review the boys were entertained at dinner at the Queen's Head, outside Southgate. Mr. Sanders married subsequently, and his lady not approving of these young soldiers, they were disbanded ; each boy was presented with a gratuity, and all his clothes and books. The complete uniform of these young soldiers was a blue jacket trimmed with yellow, breeches and leggings, cap (probably mitre shape), with a tin plate on which was painted a star, and a bit of horse-hair hung from the top."[1]

[1] The " Boys Brigade " is in 1907 one of Exeter's most popular institutions.

The first period of the Great Terror, as might be expected, had also its echo in the "pulpit utterances" of the period. On Trinity Monday, May 23rd, 1796, the Rt. Honble. William Pitt, Master, and the Elder Brethren of the Trinity House went in state to St. Nicholas Church, Deptford, to hear Dr. Thomas Rennell preach a sermon on "Great Britain's Insular Situation, Naval Strength, and Commercial Opulence, a source of gratitude to God, loyalty to the King, and concord among ourselves." It was resolved to print it on the very day the loyal address[1] to the King, already described, was voted. The "invasion" charges of Richard Watson, Bishop of Llandaff (June, 1798), were printed and disseminated by order of the local Court of Quarter Sessions, and attained almost as much popularity as his "Address to the People of England." While the Volunteers of South London went to hear the Rev. Rowland Hill discourse eloquently on the iniquities of Bonaparte and his followers, the Fawley "Fencibles" crowded St. Thomas's Church, Winchester, where the Warden of St. Mary's, Dr. George Isaac Huntingford, preached from the text "Remember the Lord, which is great and terrible, and fight for your brethren, your sons, and your daughters, your wives, and your houses."[2] The Irish divines were commendably active in "improving the occasion" of the attempted invasions of their country, both in the form of supplication and thanksgiving, and for a time little else was preached about but "Reflections in this Season of Danger," "The Duty of Loving our Country," and "Christian Patriotism." One can understand the stentorian tones in which the assembled members of the Armed Associations of Middlesex made the walls of the

---

[1] See *ante*, p. 207.   [2] Nehemiah IV. 14.

WILLIAM PITT AS A VOLUNTEER. [MAY, 1798]

old parish church at Stoke Newington[1] re-echo with the
hymn :—

> The Sword of Gideon and the Lord,
>   The Shield of Righteousness,
> Aid to the Cause that's just afford,
>   And crown it with success.
>
> The Sons of Peace in such a cause
>   Assume the port of war,
> Arm for their Liberties and Laws,
>   And every danger dare.
>
> Was it the lust of pow'r or pride
>   That rous'd the patriot band?
> No ;—wrong received, and right deny'd,
>   And Justice arm'd their hand.
>
> It was Jehovah's name reviled,
>   His altars overthrown,
> His Holy Place with Blood defil'd,
>   His Vineyard trodden down.
>
> The enemies of God are ours,—
>   O may His help abound
> To quell the foe, and all the pow'rs
>   Of Darkness to confound.
>
> Behold 'tis done, and Egypt's shore
>   Scoffs at the vanquished Host,
> Sees his proud banners wave no more,
>   Sees all his triumphs lost.
>
> If distant Realms, and distant Seas,
>   O Lord, Thy mercies prove,
> GIVE US ONE HEART AT HOME,—AND PEACE
>   AND CHARITY,—AND LOVE.

On April 28th, 1798, the following resolutions were
passed unanimously at a meeting of the two Archbishops[2]
and eleven Bishops :—

---

[1] The Stoke Newington sermon was preached by Dr. Gaskin, Rector of
the parish, on October 21st, 1798.

[2] Dr. John Moore and Dr. William Markham.

1st. "That it would not conduce in any considerable degree to the Defence and Safety of the Kingdom, and would interfere with the proper Duties of the Profession, if the Clergy were to accept Commissions in the Army, be enrolled in any Military Corps, or be trained to the Use of Arms."

2nd. "That, in the Case of actual Invasion or dangerous Insurrection, it will be the duty of every Clergyman, to give his assistance in repelling both, in any way that the urgency of the case may require."

On the following day (April 29th) a circular was addressed

"To the Reverend the Clergy of the Diocese, and the Peculiars of the See of Canterbury.

"Reverend Brother,

"In the present situation of the Country expecting without undue alarm, but not without just anxiety, the appearance of a desperate and malignant enemy on our coasts, there is perhaps no circumstance, singly taken, on which more may depend, with Regard to the interests of Religion, the credit of our order, and the public safety, than the discretion with which the conduct of the Clergy ought to be distinguished in these moments of general and necessary exertion; when all good men are called upon to come forward and to repel the attempts of an enemy, breathing revenge against this Kingdom in general; revenge not for wrongs on our part done, but for wrongs on their part by us resisted, and fraught with particular Malice against our Holy Religion and its Ministers. Under this pursuasion [sic], I have thought it my duty to call a Meeting of the Bishops in order to consider in what way the Parochial Clergy may most effectually promote the common cause without neglecting the proper Duties of our

Holy Calling, of which we must never lose sight, and least of all, in times of public danger.

"The Meeting consisted of the two Archbishops and eleven other Bishops, the occasion being thought too pressing to await the arrival of others from the remote dioceses. The two resolutions which I now transmit to you were agreed upon unanimously. In them we warn you not to abandon the proper business of your profession in order to take up the soldier's occupation, in which your actual service can be but very limited, and at last may not be wanted. We assure ourselves you will in all circumstances naturally wish to make your exertions in those services in which you feel yourselves the most capable; and those will generally be such as will least interfere with your sacred functions. But, if the danger should be realized, and the enemy set his foot upon our shores, our hand with that of every man, must in every way be against those who come for purposes of rapine and desolation, the vowed champions of anarchy and irreligion, defying the Living God.

"We are servants of God; and God's servants in God's cause must take an equal share with their fellow subjects, in such an emergency against the blasphemers of His Holy Name. But one service in particular amongst many others, for which the country amidst the din of arms will naturally look to the wisdom and piety of the Clergy, will be, that by your pursuasion, your exhortations and your good example, you will be the instruments of maintaining internal harmony and subordination, in a crisis when harmony and subordination, even with the best general disposition of the people, are most difficult to be maintained.

"I commend you to God's high and holy protection, with good hope and confidence of your discretion and zeal in this time of trial.

"I am your affectionate brother,

"(Sd.) J. CANTUAR."

Three days later the Bishop of Rochester (Dr. Samuel Horsley) thus addresses the clerical brethren :—

" Revd Brother,

"I have observed with much satisfaction the zeal which is displayed by the Clergy of my Diocese in common with our Brethren in all parts of the Kingdom, to take an active part in the Defence of the Country against an Enemy, who threatens to come with a prodigious army, to depose our King, to plunder our Property, to enslave our Persons, and to overturn our Altars ; instigated in addition to the common motives of Ambition and Revenge which have ordinarily inflamed the animosities of contending nations, by that desperate Malignity against the Faith he has abandoned, which in all ages has marked the character of the vile Apostate. The readiness of the Clergy, to unite in the defence of objects so dear to all, against such a foe, is highly laudable and consistent with that character of rational Piety which hath ever distinguished the tried sons of the Church of England.

.   .   .   .

" Gird yourself therefore without scruple for the Battle, in this holy cause, when the occasion shall call, nothing doubting, but that the God whom we serve and our Enemies defy, will teach the hands of his servants to war, and their fingers to fight. Offering our earnest prayers to God to give us all grace in the hour of trial which seems to be coming upon the Christian World, to hold fast the profession of our faith without wavering and to do and suffer valiantly whatever we may be ordained to do and suffer for his sake ;

" We remain, your loving Brother,

"SAMUEL ROFFEN."

Ecclesiastical admonitions and sermons undoubtedly figured largely amongst the wares of the *colporteurs* who carried on the work of patriotic excitation and enthusing set on foot by Hannah More.

The stage aided the patriotic trend of public opinion quite as systematically as the pulpit. Old pieces which appealed to the rallying cry of national defence were revived and new ones written *ad hoc*. The same thing had happened in the earlier crises of the eighteenth century. The three Dibdins each did yeoman work for the good cause. In 1796 Charles Dibdin the elder was fifty-one; his sons, Charles and Thomas John, were respectively twenty-eight and twenty-five. As song-writers and playwrights they helped to stir the heart of the nation as effectually as Gillray, Rowlandson, and Woodward did with their caricatures and illustrated broadsides. In the spring of 1797 the word "invasion" was on everybody's lips. The news of Fishguard and the naval victory of the same eventful February had not lost its savour when Thomas John Dibdin wrote *The British Raft*, ridiculing the threatened descent on our shores, and its one song, "The Snug Little Island," attained astonishing popularity throughout the length and breadth of the United Kingdom and for years occupied a prominent position in all patriotic anthologies. It was first sung by "Jew" Davis at Sadler's Wells on Easter Monday, 1797, while Dibdin himself was acting at Maidstone, where he himself sang it before Lord Romney[1] and it won him the friendship of the Duke of Leeds. It ran as follows :—

[1] Lord Romney took a prominent part in organizing the defence movement in Kent. See *ante*, p. 136, and illustration.

THE SNUG LITTLE ISLAND

OR

THE MARCH OF INVASION.

TUNE— *"The Rogue's March."*

Daddy Neptune one day to Freedom did say,
If ever I live upon dry land,
The spot I should hit on wou'd be little Britain,
Says Freedom, " Why that's my own island ! "
   O, it's a snug little island !
   A right little, tight little island,
   Search the globe round, none can be found
So happy as this little island.

Julius Cæsar the Roman, who yielded to no man,
Came by water,—he couldn't come by land ;
And Dane, Pict and Saxon, their homes turn'd their backs on,
And all for the sake of our island.
   O ! what a snug little island !
   They'd all have a touch at the island ;
   Some were shot dead, some of them fled,
   And some staid to live on the island.

Then a very great man, call'd Billy the Norman,
Cried d——n it, I never lik'd my land ;
It would be much more handy to leave this Normandy,
And live on yon beautiful island.
   Says he, 'tis a snug little island ;
   Shan't us go visit the island,
   Hop, skip and jump, there he was plump,
   And he kicked up a dust in the island.

But party-deceit help'd the Norman to beat,
Of the traitors they managed to buy land ;
By Dane, Saxon or Pict, Britons ne'er had been licked,
Had they stuck to the King of their island.
   Poor Harold, the King of the island !
   He lost both his life and his island,
   That's very true, what more could he do ?
   Like a Briton he died for his island !

The SPANISH ARMADA set out to invade her,
Quite sure, if they ever came nigh land,
They couldn't do less than tuck up QUEEN BESS,
And take their full swing in the island.
 Oh, the poor Queen of the island!
 The Dons came to plunder the island;
 But, snug in the hive, the QUEEN was alive
 And buz was the word in the island.

These proud puff'd up cakes thought to make ducks and drakes
Of our wealth; but they hardly could spy land,
When our DRAKE had the luck to make their pride *duck*
And stoop to the lads of the island!
 The good wooden walls of the island!
 Devil or Don, let 'em come on;
 And would they come off at the island?

Since Freedom and Neptune have hitherto kept time,
In each saying "this shall be my land";
Should the army of ENGLAND, or all they could bring land,
We'd show 'em some play for the island.
 We'll fight for our right to the island,
 We'll give them enough of the island,
 Invaders should just, bite at the dust,
 But not a bit more of the island!

At the commencement of the season of 1798–9[1] Thomas John Dibdin contrived in the space of a few hours to elaborate a pantomimic entertainment of song, dance, and dialogue, which was produced on October 25th, "in celebration of the glorious victory of the Nile." Of this we shall speak presently, but on February 8th of the same year it is recorded that "the Manager of Covent Garden Theatre,[2] with a laudable spirit of patriotism, devoted the

[1] *Annals of Covent Garden Theatre from 1732 to 1897*, Vol. I, p. 270, by H. S. Wyndham, London, 1896.
[2] *Gent. Mag.*, Vol. LXVIII, part i, 1798, pp. 165–6.

profits of this night's entertainment to the voluntary subscription for the defence of the country. The dramatic piece represented on this occasion was the historical play of 'England Preserved,' brought forward three or four years ago, and written by Mr. Watson, first clerk of the Irish House of Commons. After the Play, an interlude, consisting of loyal and patriotic songs, was given. There was not a crowded house, but a large and elegant audience; and as the price of admission to the boxes and pit was advanced, and all the performers and servants of the house played gratuitously, the profits must have been considerable."

OCCASIONAL PROLOGUE

To the Play of "England Preserved," performed
at Covent Garden Theatre, Feb. 8th, 1798, in Aid of
the Voluntary Contribution for the Defence of
The Country.

———

Oh! then let each prepare with dauntless heart,
At Britain's call, to act a Briton's part!
Ye gen'rous Youths, whom active vigour fires,
Stand forth, and emulate our glorious Sires!
Like them, inspir'd your country's rights to shield,
Remember Agincourt and Blenheim's field!
Ye titled Great, display your native worth!
Let valour vindicate the claims of birth!
Ye sons of Wealth with bounty cheer the train
Who guard our shores or thunder on the main!
Ye Fair, for whom we toil, for whom we bleed,
With smiles reward each bright heroic deed!
So shall one heart, one soul inspirit all,
Bravely to conquer, or as bravely fall:
So crown'd [with] glory may our perils cease,
And reap their harvest, a Triumphant Peace.

To revert to the later performance of the same year.

A French Invasion — on the Fashionable Dress of 1798

A POPULAR INVASION CARICATURE OF 1798

In *The Times* of October 24th, 1798, appeared the following advertisement :—

"THEATRE ROYAL, COVENT GARDEN.

"To-morrow, Lover's Vows, with (1st time) a new Serio-Comic Intermezzo of Pantomime, Song, Dance and Dialogue, called 'The Mouth of the Nile'; the Overture and Music composed by Mr. Attwood, with some favourite Selections from the Works of Dibdin and Mazzinghi. On Friday, Lover's Vows, after which, for the last time, Mrs. Mills will perform 'Little Pickle' in the 'Spoil'd Child.'"

The *Mouth of the Nile* proved an enormous success, being played no less than thirty-five times, and earning a command night from the King. On the previous evening (October 24th) there had evidently been a patriotic performance of some sort at Covent Garden, for we read in *The Times* of October 25th :—

"Their Majesties and four Princesses went to Covent Garden for first time this season. They were received by the most brilliant and numerous audience we have ever witnessed at this House, with the liveliest effusions of heart-felt joy. The ardent loyalty displayed on the occasion appeared to be animated by the late glorious successes of our Navy, and expressed itself in reiterated and unanimous bursts of patriotic exultation. The free congratulations of a free people were never more zealously and more appropriately offered to the GUARDIAN of their civil and religious liberties. His MAJESTY seemed deeply affected by these testimonies of the fervent affection which Britons must ever entertain for his Royal person. The Play went off with repeated plaudits; and the lines in the Epilogue, which allude to Lord NELSON'S victory, and Sir JOHN WARREN'S recent success, produced the happiest effects. Every part of the House, except his MAJESTY'S box and the seats reserved for his suite, were filled in little more than a quarter of an hour after the doors were opened."

From *The Times* of October 26th, under the heading of Covent Garden Theatre, we learn that "a new Entertainment, composed of pantomime, song, dance, and dialogue, called *The Mouth of the Nile*, was performed for the first time at this Theatre last night. As this motley composition is brought forward from the most laudable motives, and on the spur of the occasion, we are inclined to treat it in an indulgent manner. It consists of two parts, the one entirely pantomimic, the other relates to the ever memorable Victory of the Gallant NELSON. Two parts so extremely dissimilar were perhaps never yet joined to form an entire theatrical exhibition. The Pantomime, or what is dignified by the name of a *Grand Ballet of Action*, is altogether serious, and is founded on the trite, but inexhaustible subject of the disappointments and happiness of lovers. It does not bear the least relation to the title of the piece, and is so tedious and unimportant in representation, as to tire the patience of the audience, who are naturally led to expect something analogous to the glorious event which suggested the entertainment.

"The incidents in the second part are, for the most part, clumsily contrived, but the Dialogue and the Songs, written by Mr. DIBDIN, Jun. possess considerable merit. The latter abound in humour and epigrammatic point, and the poetry is above the mediocrity which is generally observed in hasty sketches of this kind.

"The Songs given by FAWCETT and TOWNSEND, in

the characters of British Seamen, were deservedly en-
cored.

" The representation of the engagement between the
two fleets was well managed, and the explosion of the
French Admiral's ship, *L'Orient*, proved the most satisfactory incident in the piece.

" Several passages in the Overture were in the best style
of Attwood, but he has not been happy in his selections.

" Were the Ballet entirely omitted, the *Mouth of the
Nile* might, with a few alterations, become a popular
Interlude."

Possibly the success of the *Mouth of the Nile* encouraged
the management to put on *The Raft*, and on March 31st
it was performed after Sheridan's *School for Scandal*. The
success was only a qualified one, for one reads in *The
Times* of April 2nd :—

" After the Comedy, a new After-piece called the *Raft*
was performed for the first time. As a fugitive · trifle,
it possesses some merit, and abounds with loyal sentiments
so well adapted to the circumstances and spirit of the
times, that a few *Blackheads* in the Pit and Gallery showed
every possible discountenance to the piece. A model of a
raft was introduced, the folly of which caused a great deal
of laughter. A song by TOWNSEND was admirably sung,
and the composition does great credit to the author. We
hope it will not be lost to the public. The house was not
quite full, though very respectably attended." It was
taken off a fortnight later, but " The Snug Little Island "
lived throughout the Great Terror, and survived for many
a long year afterwards. It even figures in many of the early
Victorian song-books.

A few months later we hear that a piece entitled *Descent*

upon England: a Prophecy in two acts, is being played at
the Paris Théatre des Varietés.[1]   The scene is laid at
Dover, where a young Frenchman who has escaped from
prison takes refuge in the house of Fergusson, a tavern-
keeper in the town, and is concealed and fed by his
daughter Clementina, who, of course, falls in love with him.
Fergusson is a "patriot," and in conjunction with some other
"patriots," one of whom is the colonel of a regiment in the
garrison at the Castle, forms a plan for emancipating his
fellow-citizens by favouring the descent of the French and
assisting them in getting possession of the port.   Murai,
"a traitor sold to the party of Pitt," has the profligacy
to detect the conspiracy and to give intelligence of it to the
Governor of the Castle ; the persons of the conspirators
are, in consequence, secured ; and having been appre-
hended, tried, cast, and condemned, in the course of the
evening they are ordered for execution in the night, but
the French land apropos to rescue their friends from the
gallows.   The Castle is taken, the Governor blows out his
brains, and the united "patriots" of France and England
determine to march to London to complete the business
so happily begun.

So much for the fable, of which we may say to the
author, "*Ah! quel conte!*"   Now for a specimen of the
dialogue.   The scene is in Fergusson's house ; the
"patriots" are all met, Gordon at their head.

"*Gordon.* My friends, I will not remind you of the
crimes of the English Government ; the long tyranny
which it has exercised over the seas ; the disasters which
it has carried into the Colonies ; the perfidious means
which it employs for perpetuating the war ;—I will not

---

[1] *Anti-Jacobin Review and Magazine*, Vol. III, p. 572.

talk of Pitt. You all know that cunning is his instrument, delusion his element, and that his infernal policy would sacrifice all the belligerent nations to his ambition.

"*Fergusson.* Yes, 'tis time to put a stop to the homicidal plots of that destroyer of the human race.

"*A Conspirator.* Philosophy has already devoted him to the execration of the people.

"*Gordon.* You have all heard the thundering eloquence of Fox. English 'Patriots,' he calls on you to assert your Rights.

"*Fergusson.* We shall know how to defend them.

"*Gordon.* His voice invokes liberty.

"*Fergusson.* We will obtain it at the expense of our lives.

"*Gordon.* But let us not waste our time in idle words, but think of executing our plan.—You are all resolved to favour the descent of the French, to burst your chains, and give liberty to your degraded country?

"*The Conspirators.* Yes! Yes!

"*Fergusson.* We swear it.

"*Gordon.* Our pledges of victory are Fox and his friends, yours Courage, and Buonaparte. The genius of liberty watches over the people, and will soon crush their tyrants. (He reads a paper.) In two hours the descent will be made. The regiment in garrison is commanded by the brave Houssey—on him we may rely;—but we may have everything to dread from the Commander of the Port; he is sold to Pitt and his infamous agents. We must anticipate him and strike the first blow.

"*Fergusson.* That is my opinion. Is it yours?

"*Conspirators.* Yes! Yes!

"*Gordon.* At the very moment when we shall make our attack on Dover the conspiracy will break out in the heart of London. Let the Cabinet of St. James' tremble;— Fox is quite ready. His powerful hand has made Scotland and Ireland rise—and while the sea is covered with a forest of masts, Republican phalanxes will come forth as out of the bowels of the earth, to exterminate at once the oppressors of my country.—Friends, this day will decide our Fate."

In the last scene the author gives a gentle hint to the merchants of Paris, which was very seasonable at a time when the Directory was raising *a loan upon England.*

"*Alphonse.* How happy are my brave comrades! They followed you.—They say, General, that all the people in France wished to embark in the expedition; and that the trading part of Paris, not being able to partake of its glory, all the merchants hastened to contribute to its success, by offering their treasures to the Republic.

"*The French General.* In that generous act I recognise my nation.—Englishmen! Now is your time to destroy the British Government which has caused all your misfortunes, desolated your neighbours, and set Europe on fire. It is time that the fate of the people should no longer depend on the caprice of an individual."

The army sets forth quick march *au pas redoublé* for Canterbury, and the curtain falls.

The author was neither a prophet nor a dramatist; but his play, for a time at least, doubtless did the same work with the *badauds* of Paris as the following contemporary broadsheet accomplished a year or so later (1801) on the other side of the Channel:—

Substance of the
CORSICAN BoNAPARTE'S HAND-BILLS;
or a
Charming Prospect for John Bull & his Family.
Britons AWAKE!

And though it be galling to your feelings, and make your blood boil with indignation, to read that which is to follow, it is surely far better that you should experience this, than the direful effects of that ruin and destruction with which you are now menaced, and which must inevitably be your lot, should you not rouse and meet the danger with one hand and one heart.

KNoW THEN

That the Corsican Buonaparte, the Grand Subjugator of the French Nation, has at length thrown off the mask. This relentless Tyrant, this insatiable monster of cruelty and ambition, this eternal enemy to the repose and happiness of all mankind, no longer conceals his long buried rancorous designs of annihilating this truly happy country, the envy of all Europe. This atrocious intention he has not only made known to M. Marcoff, the Russian Ambassador at Paris in an affected fit of merriment but he has proclaimed it by handbills in every hole and corner of France.

There is not a Town or Village, between Paris and Calais where may not be read hand-bills to the following effect :—

ROAD to England.

But now mark my brave countrymen what follows. It is an invitation to every dastardly Frenchman whose courage is only to be roused by the hopes of plunder, to enlist for the Army of England; which country, the haughty Tyrant boastingly tells them, shall be devoted to its Conquerers as their just reward. Behold! says this rapacious Plunderer and Assassin, the Paradise of the World! the richest and most flourishing Nation the Sun ever blessed with its beams! Nature and art seem here to have combined to leave nothing wanting to it's happiness.—Observe the riches of her plains : not an acre but what is covered with grain and matchless cattle. Towns, villages, stately mansions, beautiful country seats, villas, gardens, orchards.—Was there ever beheld so enchanting, so lovely a scene! Brave Frenchmen! Could you but see the interior of these invaluable towns and happy dwellings, you would find there not only every desirable comfort of life, even among the very lowest classes of the people, (I mean compared with your own wretched hovels) but go but one or two steps higher, and there you would discover almost every article that industry can produce, or luxury ever thought of. But from whence flow all these superabundant riches ? The answer is plain—'tis their industry and their commerce ; 'tis their manufacturing towns that are her inexhaustible mines ; and these are the true seed of her boasted British Oak, that insolent and inconquerable navy, which has set all Europe at defiance for ages past.—

But let England boast her Sheffield and her Birmingham ; her Liverpool and her Bristol ; her Newcastle and her other numberless rich towns and cities !—All these brave Frenchmen shall be your's— Aye I repeat it, they shall be your's—Nay, your reward shall not end here ; for though the haughty Britons must bite the dust, their wives and daughters must he spared—for what purpose—I need not tell you. Rouse, rouse then, brave and heroic Frenchmen ; brave all dangers and look to your reward ; for, spite of that ridiculous lying song, Rule Britannia, I now announce to you, that Britains shall be slaves ; and what is more, they shall be most abject slaves, to all powerful, and all- conquering France.

Such, Britons, is the boast of the Corsican Tyrant, the grand Sub- jugator of the great French Nation ; and such are the Hand-bills spread throughout France. I do not say that the above are the very words ; but I say such are their true sense and meaning.

What answer my Gallant Countrymen shall we give to this ? Surely there can be but one ; and that thank Heaven ! will be found engraven on the bottom of your hearts.—" Or Death or Freedom ; or in other words, Annihilation to every Frenchman who shall dare to set his cloven-foot on these happy and matchless shores. Let this bloody-minded Corsican then dare to land on British ground, with his thousands and hundreds of thousands of hell-hounds at his back, and he shall find that that same spirit and bravery that enabled our gallant Egyptian Army to compel double its numbers of French to lay down their arms, shall now again, with the blessing of the Almighty, drive our enemies into the Sea, whenever their rapacity or temerity may tempt them to reach our shores.

A true Friend to Old England.

N.B. It is earnestly recommended to the Editors of the Sunday Papers to insert the above Hand-bill.

The invasion pamphlets were, as a rule, of a more serious character than the invasion broadsheets and ballads. There is a good deal of common sense in *Thoughts on a French Invasion with Reference to its Success and the*

Proper Means of Resisting it, by Havilland Le Mesurier, Commissary-General of the southern district of England, published in 1798. The earlier tract of Mr. Morton Pitt has already been dealt with, and Mr. Le Mesurier advocates a very similar policy as regards the attitude of the rural population.

"After distressing the enemy," he writes, "the next point for every individual to consider, is how best to assist the armed force and join in the common defence. Whenever troops are on their march towards the enemy, every hand will surely be active in procuring bread for them. There our generous countrywomen will be found to share in the laurels, which their husbands, their brothers, and their friends, are seeking to gather; they will be ready to provide for their refreshment and every necessary support on the march, and at every halt-; the farmers will assist with their teams and waggons in transporting artillery and forage, and every one will be careful to keep the roads as clear of incumbrances as possible; for, that is a point of the utmost importance, which they, who have never seen great movements, are not sufficiently aware of.

"That the French army, if ever it should land, will come with erroneous opinions of the people, and that it will meet with confusion and dismay at landing, in consequence of that error, is evident from the declaration of their rulers; their boastings must to every firm mind appear ridiculous, and, but for the wickedness of degenerate men in our own country, would be perfectly despicable."

Another poet scarcely less famous than Burns was now to take the field with the invasion as his theme. In the spring of 1798 (while *The Raft* and *The Mouth of the*

Nile occupied the boards at Covent Garden) Samuel Taylor Coleridge, in the inspiring quietude of Nether Stowey, penned *Fears in Solitude*, dated 28th April, 1798, and stated to be written "during the alarm of an invasion."[1] It is far too lengthy for quotation in its entirety, but the following lines give a good idea of the poet's feelings on the now all-pervading topic :—

> My God ! it is a melancholy thing
> For such a man, who would full fain preserve
> His soul in calmness, yet perforce must feel
> For all his human brethren—O my God !
> It weighs upon the heart, that he must think
> What uproar and what strife may now be stirring
> This way or that way o'er these silent hills—
> Invasion, and the thunder and the shout,
> And all the crash of onset ; fear and rage,
> And undetermined conflict—even now,
> Even now, perchance, and in his native isle.

   .   .   .   .   .   .

Richard Cumberland at this time entered the lists as a writer of the now eagerly sought for martial lyrics. Some years later he wrote as follows to a friend :—[2]

" 19*th September*, (1804 ?)

" TUNBRIDGE WELLS.

" My dear Sir,

    "When your letter reach'd this place I was at Ramsgate, whence I am just return'd, and at present too much occupied with a variety of affairs to solicit Invention for any thing new ; but that I may show my obedience to every wish of your's, I have rummag'd my old MSS. for what I can find, and send you yᵉ following, rather as a mark of my good will, than as flattering myself it will be worthy yᵉ genius of your friend to set to music.

---

[1] *The Poetical Works of S. T. Coleridge* (Warne's edition), pp. 139-40.
[2] Mr. Broadley's Invasion MSS.

THE VOLUNTEERS' SONG

" Captain, Captain, see before you
" Phalanx firm, that pants for glory,
" Dauntless souls, that flout at death :
" We are stout and we are steady,
" Give the word and we are ready, ⎫
" Loyal to our latest breath. ⎭

" Thund'ring blasts around us roaring,
" Fiery floods of sulphur pouring,
" Firm amidst yᵉ storm we stand :
" Truth and Honour thus combining,
" Steady, steady !—now be joining ⎫
" Heart to Heart and Hand to Hand ! ⎭

Chorus.

" Steady ! Steady !—&c. &c."

THE RIFLE-CORPS' SONG

(GLEE)

" To arms, to arms ! Now give the bugle breath ;
" Sound, sound yᵉ note of victory or death !
  " To the echoing woods,
  " To the mountainous floods
" Around let it go, and around :
  " Down the terrible Steep
  " To the bellowing Deep,
" When the Host of Invaders are drown'd,
" Around let it go, and around !

Solo.

" Hark, hark ! I hear the hollow blast,
" Sighing it comes, as 'twere the last ;
" I hear the wounded victims groan,
" The sympathetic echoes moan—
" And now it sinks, and now 'tis past.

Full.

" See, see ! the vaunting braggarts fly,
" Their fleet is wreckt, their hopes are lost,
" Their floating bodies strew yᵉ coast,
  " Now raise your voices high ;
  " Let notes of triumph rend the sky ! "

" RICHD. CUMBERLAND."

"Ever-Faithful Exeter," true to her great traditions, was, as might be anticipated, a foremost centre of resistance. The Exeter Volunteers (1797) "bespoke" at their theatre a performance of the historical drama of *Arviragus, or the Roman Invasion,* and insisted on encoring more than once with deafening cheers the war-song of Clewillin :—[1]

> If to the battle ye shall go,
> All rush upon th' invading foe :
> Rush on the foe without dismay,
> Like roaring lions on their prey ;
> Or wolves, that from the mountain rock,
> Descend upon the fleecy flock.
> Let your arrows' numerous flight
> Intercept the rays of light :
> Sling the javelins,—hurl the darts—
> Infix them in the Roman hearts ;
> And advanc'd to nearer fight,
> Britons ! exert your steadfast might :
> Each meet his Roman in the field,
> With spear to spear, and shield to shield,
> And thou, Arviragus ! in scythed car,
> Break through the firmest ranks of war :
> Vengeance and terror at thy side,
> O'er warriors, shields and helmets, ride ;
> Increase the torrent of the crimson flood,
> And bathe thy horses' hoofs and rapid wheels in blood.

As will be seen by the illustration reproduced from Sir George White's collection in these volumes, "Royal and Free" Bristol (the objective of Hoche's Black Legion expedition[2]) proved herself worthy of the occasion. Below the picture of her volunteers are the following MS. lines :—

[1] *Gentleman's Magazine,* Vol. LXVI, part i, 1797.
[2] See *ante,* p. 39.

Oh ! Alla, or what remains of thee,
Thou darling of posterity,
Whether to curb the Warhorse be thy guide,
Or draw the falchion glitt'ring from thy side,
To check the daring foe.

Let Bristow's Fifty be thy care,
Whose Volunteers in sweet Queen Square
Go forth to taste the morning air
And deal destruction mid the fair,
Whose charms before had laid them low.

Let other Laurels grace their brows,
Laurels obtained by good hard blows,
To show us that an ardour glows
Within their breast to check their foes
Who dare to soil their fame.

So shall the blood-stained Frenchmen know
Such sprigs of Liberty as his won't grow,
Where native freedom's lovely blossoms blow
Bright as a star and purer than the snow
To gild a freeborn Briton's name.

(1797.)

This was in 1797, and it was in the month of February
of the same year that the following effusion appeared,
which may be taken as a type of hundreds of similar productions :—

Sweet is the talk to strike the loyal string
To gallant Rodney's well earn'd praise,
Round him shall Fame eternal garlands fling,
Whose verdure shall increase till time decays !
But sweeter still, our living boasts to view
And sing how Warren and Pellew have fought,
    The oft-repeated theme renew,
And dwell on deeds immortal Howe has wrought.
These fill with joy the ravish'd heart,
These to each Briton's breast impart
The glow of conscious pride ;

Yet oft the tear is seen to flow,
E'en amid Conquest's gorgeous show,
For those who bravely fought and bravely died.
But now no mortal hand repels alarms,
In Britain's rightful cause e'en Heaven appears in arms.
Fame with her hundred tongues proclaims,
That France again will tempt the Ocean's rage ;
That yet Invasion's hope her breast inflames,
And sad experience fails to make her sage.
Thee, Caledonia ! thee she vows to tear
With harpy-talons, and thy sons destroy ;
Or Albion must her ireful efforts bear,
To dash with bitterness the cup of joy.
And shall we fear?   Shall Britons know dismay?
Shall Christians from the godless Heathen flee?
Forbid it, Heaven !   Avert the direful day !
For still our Hope supports itself on thee.
Then, Gallia, come ; a larger navy bring ;
And to Britannia's isle insulting haste ;
But know, one breath of Heaven's insulted King
Shall whelm thy pride and thee beneath the watery wave.[1]

(*February 24th,* 1797.)

In the autumn of 1798 the Court, according to its wont, migrate to Weymouth.   There was a "command" night at the theatre, and the following communication is sent to the *Gentleman's Magazine* :—[2]

"Mr. Urban,

"The following stanzas from Tasker's Ode to the Spirit of Alfred, the Founder of the British Constitution, were lately recited at the Weymouth Theatre, by Mr. Sandford, before their Majesties and received with universal applause.

[1] *Gentleman's Magazine*, Vol. LXVII, part ii, 783.
[2] *Gentleman's Magazine,* Vol. LXIX, part ii, October 12th, 1798, p. 884.

Stanza I.

O Muse ! dispel the mists, which Time
Hath spread round glory's lucid clime ;
While to the mental vision bright,
Ethereal objects strike my sight,
Rapt in poetic extasy,
Alfred, thy princely form I see
'Mid heroes, sages, patriots old
Who, (rising from their seats of gold,)
To thee supreme their gratulations pay,
While choral harps around attune the grateful lay.

Stanza II.

My humbler song, immortal Alfred ! hear,
If such weak strains may reach thy polish'd ear ;
Restorer of the sacred fane !
Expeller of the bloody Dane !
Hark ! with applause the distant regions ring !
Hail ! legislator wise !   Hail warrior, patriot King !

Stanza III.

Still shall the glorious bulwark rise,
By nations view'd with envious eyes ;
The genius of thy favoured Isle,
All clad in adamantine mail,
(While storms of Anarchy assail,
And Faction's tumults idly roar,
Like waves against a rocky shore,)
Shall with a flaming sword defend the pile,
Preserve its strength entire, and pillar'd height,
'Till fades the dome of Heaven, and every orb of light.

The deluge of patriotic verse continues, and Lord
Howe's successes are greeted with :—

Let Gallia threaten with contemptuous smile
To rear her Standard on our sea girt isle,
To ravish, murder, and confusion spread,
And rear her hellish democratic head :
If Neptune here his feat of empire keep,
And yield to us the Empire of the Deep,
Britannia's navies shall triumphant reign,
And Gallic foes know Howe to rule the main.

DE WILLOWBY.

The manifest loyalty of the next "invasion" song alone excuses the badness of the rhymes :—

SONG

TUNE.—" *To Anacreon in Heav'n.*"

To learn Johnny Bull *à la mode de Paris*
Some half-starv'd Republicans made declaration
That they would instruct him like them to be free ;
When this answer return'd from our loyal Old Nation ;
  " Ye ragged banditti
  " Your freedom we pity,
" And mean to live happy while frantic you sing
  " Your fav'rite *Ça ira*
  " And hymn *Marseillois*
" For the true Briton's song shall be ' God save the King.'"

If we fall in the conflict how noble the cause,
The stone will record it that stands on our grave ;
Here lies one who defended his country and laws ;
And died his religion and monarch to save.
  This and more shall be said ;
  But thank Heav'n we're not dead ;
We can all of us yet with one heart and voice sing
  Not the Frenchman's *Ça ira*
  Or Hymn *Marseillois*
But the true Briton's song, huzza, " God save the King."

Almost each corps had its march or camp-song. The following one, only existing in MS., was used by the volunteers of Burton Bradstock, a picturesque coast-village near Bridport, in Dorset, where Sir T. M. Hardy's first Captain Roberts lived and many gallant sea-dogs also resided :—[1]

[1] See *The Three Dorset Captains at Trafalgar*, p. 3.

SAYER'S CARICATURE OF THE "DEVIL'S OWN" [INNS OF COURT VOLUN-
TEERS] IN 1799

THE SONG OF THE LOYAL VOLUNTEERS OF BURTON BRADSTOCK

1. Come my lads of courage true
   Ripe for martial glory;
   See the standard waves for you
   And leads the way before ye.

   Chorus.
   To the field of Mars advance
   Join in bold alliance,
   Tell the blood-stain'd sons of France
   We bid them all defiance.

2. Burton's sons were always brave
   On the land or ocean;
   Ready for to kill or save
   Where honour's the promotion.
   Chorus.

3. Burton long has had a boast
   And right well deserving;
   For pretty maids a standing toast
   Of Nature's sweet preserving.
   Chorus.

4. Gallia's sons invasion plan,
   Threat'ning to destroy us;
   Seize our maidens, houses, land,
   And as slaves employ us.
   Chorus.

5. We must fight or starve or fly,
   Hope, nought else remaining,
   Or wives may faint and children die
   With no hand sustaining.
   Chorus.

6. Lives are lent for laws and King,
   When that they may need 'em;
   Let us then in chorus sing,
   Give us death or freedom?
   Chorus.

Even the proctors of the Ecclesiastical and Admiralty Courts appear to have loyally responded to the cry to

I.—R

arms, and amongst the broadsides of 1799 is the following :—

To the R^t Honble SIR WILLIAM SCOTT[1]

MAJOR COMMANDANT

OF THE

ASSOCIATED CORPS OF CIVILIANS

Pro Aris et Focis.

A Nation, great in Commerce, Arts and Arms
Hears with disdain the insolence of Foes ;
Firm in herself, She *fears* not War's Alarms,
Nor seeks *unwisely*, all it's direful Woes.

But when *new Doctrines* have Mankind misled,
When peaceful States in Anarchy are hurl'd,
When pow'rful Nations bend their mighty Head,
THEN ENGLAND RISES AND PROTECTS THE WORLD.

Then shall her FLEETS such glorious Vict'ries gain,
While dire disgrace the Foe infernal guides
That *Arabs* shout astonish'd, and the Main
Heaves its proud bosom, where a Nelson rides.

And still by Wisdom led RELIGION's Dome,
On its firm Basis will unshaken stand,
While CORPS of LOYALTY protect a Home
The Blessings which enrich this happy Land.

But one PECULIAR CORPS demands the Song—
Vers'd in the Law of NATIONS, well they know
The Rights inherent that to *all* belong,
When all OBEY the Law from which they flow.

ASSOCIATES CIVIL ! Eloquent and Sage
Who plead for Justice, and for Virtue fight,
Or Law declare, from Learning's ancient Page,
And soften Rigour, with maintaining Right.

[1] William Scott, Lord Stowell, 1745–1836. Judge of the Consistory Court of London, 1788–1820 ; Judge of High Court of Admiralty, 1798–1820 ; Privy Councillor, 1798.

While YOUNGER SONS of this distinguish'd Band
In vigour strong, with martial Genius soar
Eager to take the honourable Stand
Of active Soldiers in the CIVIL CORPS.

(1799.)

The colour-prints and aquatints relating to the first five years of the Great Terror are more numerous than one would have expected, and now fetch very high prices. Amongst them may be mentioned a pair of fine colour-prints, engraved by L. J. and N. Schiavonetti after paintings by R. K. Porter, portraying the presentation of colours to the Loyal Associated Ward and Volunteer Corps of the City of London and those of the City of Westminster. They were published May 30th, 1799. J. C. Stadler's aquatint of the " Hans Town Association exercising in their Ground at Knightsbridge " is also much prized. It was executed after a design in which S. Woolley was responsible for the landscape and J. C. Barrow for the figures. A series of four interesting plates deals with Isle of Wight volunteer subjects. These aquatints, by J. Wells after R. Livesay, depict the " Grand Review at Sandown Bay " (June 4th, 1798), the " Grand Review near Freshwater Bay " (June 17th, 1798), " West Cowes with the Volunteers on the Parade," and " Volunteers receiving the Island Banner at Carisbrooke Castle " (June 24th, 1798).[1] W.

---

[1] The Isle of Wight has been a favourite objective of the foreign invader ever since the days of Henry VIII. A book of great interest to future historians was recently sold in London. It is thus described :—

"ISLE OF WIGHT.—Worsley (Sir Richard), History of the Isle of Wight. *London*, 1781. 4to, *with map and* 31 *plates*.

"Inserted in the volume is an Original Despatch from the Council of State to the Governor of the Isle of Wight respecting the designs of the Dutch on the Island, warning him to take all precautions for its safety, signed J. Thurlow, and endorsed by Col. Sydenham, dated Aug. 27, 1652. Also an autograph letter from the Author to Sir G. Savile, and 22 ADDITIONAL ENGRAVINGS, including a large folding view of the Camp in the Isle of Wight, 1741, Prospect of Portsmouth, 1740, etc."

Alexander is responsible both for the drawing and engraving of the view of Lord Romney's mammoth dinner to 5319 Kentish Volunteers,[1] reproduced in these volumes. One of the most remarkable of these invasion colour-prints is J. Collyer's charming view of George III reviewing the Armed Associations in Hyde Park on his sixty-second birthday (June 4th, 1799), now given in facsimile by way of illustration. George Cruikshank gives an account of this striking military spectacle in his "Pop Gun"—a crushing retort to General Sir W. Napier, who in 1859 had stigmatized the volunteers of 1797-8 as "unwieldy, untaught, ill-commanded mobs." During the march past he repeated over and over again Bonaparte's gibe at the "shopkeepers" in tones of undisguised exultation, and it was on this occasion he suggested for the Bloomsbury and Inns of Court Volunteers the nickname of "Devil's Own," which bids fair to be immortal. J. Wells's aquatint after Guest of "The Situation of the Volunteer Corps assembled at Portsmouth in commemoration of His Majesty's Birthday on 4th June, 1799," relates to the events of the same memorable day. Another much-prized aquatint engraved by Pollard after a drawing by W. Mason perpetuates one of George III's numerous reviews of the troops—volunteers as well as regulars—on Black-heath, and J. C. Stadler's aquatint from R. Livesay's picture of the "Review of the Guards in Hatfield Park" belongs to the same period, although not published until January 18th, 1802.

It is manifestly impossible within the necessary limits of the present work to deal with the pictorial satire of the Great Terror in the detail one would wish. Of the 3200

---

[1] See *ante*, p. 136.

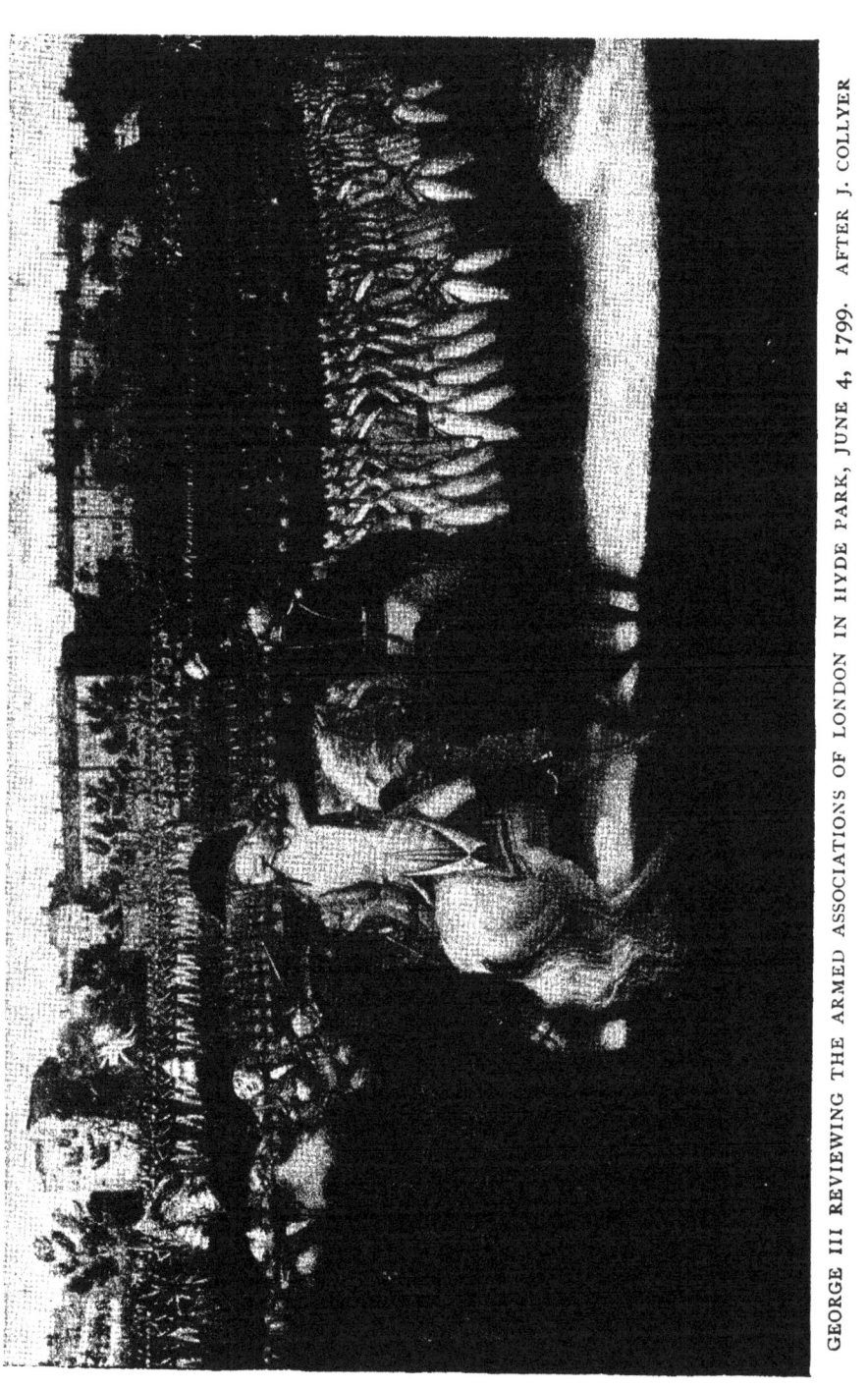

GEORGE III REVIEWING THE ARMED ASSOCIATIONS OF LONDON IN HYDE PARK, JUNE 4, 1799.   AFTER J. COLLYER

Napoleonic caricatures supposed to exist, about 300 refer directly or indirectly to the topic now under consideration. Many of them (especially those by anonymous artists of foreign origin) are exceedingly rare, but the better-known and comparatively familiar productions of James Gillray and Thomas Rowlandson on the subject of the invasion, published between 1796 and 1805, have been chronicled and described by Mr. Thomas Wright and Mr. Joseph Grego.[1] Nothing like a complete list exists of the Invasion caricatures of Isaac Cruikshank (born in 1756) or of George Murgatroyd Woodward,[2] four years his junior. At the commencement of the Great Terror, George Cruikshank (the "Glorious" George of the Elba, Hundred Days, Waterloo, and St. Helena epoch of Napoleonic history) was four years old, and his brother Robert only three years his senior. As far as the invasion period is concerned, one is unable to fall back on the now quite unrivalled collection of George Cruikshank's works possessed by Captain R. J. H. Douglas,[3] of Rosslyn, Blackheath. The great majority of Henry William Bunbury's military sketches relate to events which happened before the acute stage of the invasion threats, and "Pitt's own Caricaturist," James Sayers or Sayer, (1748-1823), preferred the *otium cum*

---

[1] See *England under the House of Hanover*, Vol. II, pp. 269-425, by Thomas Wright, London, 1849. *Account of Gillray's Caricatures*, pp. 84-255, by Thomas Wright, London, 1851. *Works of James Gillray*, pp. 204-324, by Thomas Wright, 4to, London, n.d. *Rowlandson the Caricaturist*, Vol. I, p. 327 to end, Vol. II, pp. 1-57, by Thomas Wright, 4to, London, 1880. *English Satire on Napoleon I*, Vol. I, p. 42 to end, Vol. II, pp. 1-48, by John Ashton, 2 vols., London, 1884. *Histoire de la Caricature*, Vol. IV, chap. v, pp. 236-307, by Champfleury, Paris, n.d.

[2] The second name of Woodward is, curiously enough, given as "Moutard" in the *Dictionary of National Biography*.

[3] The able author of *The Works of George Cruikshank classified and arranged*, London, 1903.

dignitate of his well-earned marshalship in the Court of
Exchequer to dealing with the misdoings of Bonaparte
and the prowess or shortcomings of our national defenders.
Almost the only exception he made was in favour of the
" Devil's Own," gently satirized in the print now reproduced
amongst the illustrations.

Below it one reads the lines :—

> Templars of old were valiant Knights,
> Defenders of their country's Rights,
> 　　A consecrated Band ;
> If one superior Merit Shew'd
> On him the general Voice bestow'd
> 　　A Leader's high command :
> With equal Zeal in Britain's cause
> To guard her Liberty and Laws,
> 　　Our Volunteers unite.
>
> But who Shall head the Loyal Host ?
> Erskine steps forth and claims the Post
> 　　And Mansfield dubs him Knight.
> Sleep ! Sleep in Peace ye Templars brave
> Nor cast a look beyond the Grave
> 　　To mark our Inn's dishonour.
> Two Evils press upon our Ranks,
> Erskine's Command and Sherry's Thanks,
> 　　Sworn friends of tried O'Connor.

The Gillray plate " FRENCH TELEGRAPH making
SIGNALS in the Dark " is dated 26th January, 1795,[1]
and was published before the firm of H. Humphrey
moved from 37 New Bond Street to 27 St. James's Street.[2]
It is now given on account of the quaint illustration of the
operation of the primitive " telegraph," and the light it

---

[1] *Account of the Caricatures of James Gillray*, p. 59, by T. Wright.

[2] As far back as 1781 the firm of Humphrey was in existence at 227
Strand, and there published several caricatures on the invasion projects
entrusted to the Count de Grasse.

FRENCH—TELEGRAPH making SIGNALS in the Dark

FRENCH SYMPATHIZERS AT WORK.   GILLRAY'S CARICATURE OF 26 JANUARY, 1795

throws on the reputed sympathy of Fox and his Whig friends for the idea of foreign intervention before the invasion threats came within the sphere of practical politics. The earliest Gillray caricature on the subject of the invasion, in the strict sense of the term, appeared more than a year later (20th October, 1796). It is entitled " Promised Horrors of the French Invasion, or Forcible Reasons for negociating a Regicide Peace."[1] St. James's Palace is in flames ; the victorious invaders throng St. James's Street ; a massacre of the members of White's Club is in progress ; the dead bodies of the Princes who have taken refuge in the balcony are thrown down on the pavement below, and Pitt, stripped and prepared for instant execution, is bound to a pole crowned with the *bonnet rouge*, while Fox, a birch in either hand, soundly castigates his fallen foe. This may be regarded as the commencement of the system of influencing public opinion by satire and song which contributed so much to the universal enthusiasm of 1803 and the following years. A fortnight after the Fishguard fiasco (March 4th, 1797) Gillray dealt with it, as well as with Jervis's victory of 14th February, very felicitously, in " The Tables turned. Billy in the Devil's Claws. Billy sending the Devil Packing."[2] The conception of this caricature is remarkably clever. The Premier (Pitt) is held in the brawny grasp of Fox, disguised as a Republican fiend. " Ha, traitor !" he cries, "there's the French landed in Wales ! What d'ye think of that, traitor ? " " The Tables " are quickly turned by the arrival of the Gazette announcing the defeat of the Spanish fleet by Sir John Jervis. Pitt is

[1] *The Works of James Gillray, the Caricaturist*, p. 204, by T. Wright.
[2] *Ibid.*, p. 219, by T. Wright.

released from the grasp of his grim captor, who is escaping chagrined, while Pitt slyly exclaims, "Ah, Mr. Devil, we've beat the Spanish fleet! What d'ye think of that, Mr. Devil?" Nearly a year later, 1st February, 1798 (H. Humphrey had now migrated to 27 St. James's Street, where, during the continuance of the Great Terror, the dense crowd before the window filled with patriotic prints often made the pavement impassable), appeared one of Gillray's veritable masterpieces, "The Storm rising—or—the Republican FLOTILLA in danger," now given as an illustration in facsimile. Fox, Sheridan, Tierney, and His Grace of Bedford are assisting the threatened French "descent" by turning a mammoth windlass which brings over a still more gigantic raft filled with our foreign foes, an enormous tricolour flag surmounted by a cap of liberty at the prow. On the distant coast is seen the Evil One on the top of a guillotine playing the tune "Over the water to Charley" (Fox) on a fiddle. In most of the earlier caricatures no attempt is made to give anything like a portrait of Bonaparte, who very soon became the central figure and the all-absorbing point of interest. The *sobriquet* of "Little Boney," which stuck to him even when an exile at St. Helena, was the creation of James Gillray. It was at first considered sufficient to portray the arch-enemy as wearing a gigantic cocked hat, with boots and sword to match. This was not so in 1803, when there was at least an attempt at verisimilitude. It is curious to note this difference in the familiar series of Gillray's plates labelled "Consequences of a Successful Invasion" (I to VI), published March 1st, 1798, and other satiric prints bearing a like title which appeared in 1803 and 1804. To March, 1798, belongs a superb caricature by Thomas Rowlandson, en-

THE BRISTOL VOLUNTEERS AT DRILL IN QUE

THE STORM RISING—OR—THE REPUBLIC.
Pitt's naval armaments counteracting the sy

(1797).   FROM AN ORIGINAL CARICATURE DRAWING

WM PITT

LA IN DANGER.   BY GILLRAY.   FEB., 1798
ix, Sheridan, Tierney and the Duke of Bedford

FOX   SHERIDAN   TIERNEY   DUKE OF BEDFOR

titled "England Invaded, or Frenchmen Naturalized,"
with a companion print published a little later, and known
as "REHEARSAL of a FRENCH INVASION as performed
before the INVALIDS at the Island's [*sic*] of St. Marcou on
the morning of ye 7 of May, 1798." Rowlandson and Gillray were born in the same year; but the artist who made
the fortune of both Ackermann and Fores survived Mrs.
Humphrey's "lodger" for twelve years. One of the most
popular of Rowlandson's early invasion caricatures is that
entitled "High Fun for John Bull, or the Republicans put
to their last Shift." It was published by Ackermann, 12th
November, 1798.[1] Mr. Grego thus describes it: "The
victory gained by Nelson at Aboukir Bay, over the combined fleets, disconcerted the French enthusiasts, and
restored confidence at home; it was recognized that while
English admirals could sweep their enemies from the seas,
neither the dangers of invasion, nor the difficulties of contending with France, need be ranked of much consequence.
In the print John Bull is enjoying the High Fun of setting
his opponents to equip fresh fleets (or invading rafts), in
order that his sailors may carry them off captives as
trophies. . . . The Frenchmen are excited over their pros-
pects; the head baker has a fine batch ready for the oven;
' *Sacredieu Citoyens,* make a haste wit one *autre* fleet, den
we will shew you how to make one *grande Invasion,*'" and
so forth.

Throughout the Great Terror the personality of Pitt was
only second in importance to that of Bonaparte. In May,
1798, Mr. S. W. Fores, of 50 Piccadilly, made a great hit
with his cartoon of "The Royal Soldier In His Majesty's
Service."

---

[1] *Rowlandson, the Caricaturist,* Vol. I, p. 352, by Joseph Grego.

The first of all Swains
That gladden'd the Plains ;
All nature obey'd him—the sweet Willy O !

It excited much more interest than the contemporary plate labelled " A French Invasion, or the Fashionable Dress of 1798."

The French satirical prints of this period are by no means numerous, but in 1798 (An VI) M. Ruotte, of Paris, produced a highly finished caricature, which was sold at Rolland's, No. 35 Rue Neuve des Petits-Champs. The personages who figure in it are six, viz. Bonaparte, George III, the Austrian Emperor, the King of Spain, a Dutchman, and a Paris tavern waiter. The likenesses are admirable and entirely free from grotesque exaggeration. In the left-hand corner hangs a map of the Straits of Dover, showing the position of the Army of England, and the road from Paris to Calais, with the legend : " It is but one step." George III in an arm-chair is fast asleep, an empty punch-bowl, glasses, and wine-bottles on a table at his side. He murmurs, " Ah, Pitt ! I should have put a little water in my wine." The Dutchman is escaping through an open door; the Austrian and Spanish monarchs crouch behind Bonaparte. The waiter is importuning them violently for the settlement of the bill. " Who is to pay the score, gentlemen ? " " Go back, go back," says Bonaparte, gently pushing him, " George wanted it, and will pay for everything . . . when he wakes up." " Yes," whispers the Emperor, " it is he who will pay for all of us."

Before letting the curtain fall on this brief account of the literary and artistic landmarks, the song and satire of the first period of the Great Terror, we must return for a

HIGH FUN for JOHN BULL or THE REPUBLICANS PUT TO THEIR LAST SHIFT

ENGLAND LAUGHS AT THE COMBINED EFFORTS OF THE FRENCH AND DUTCH
AFTER THE BATTLE OF THE NILE. [NOVEMBER 12, 1798]

moment to the poet laureate whom we left, lyre in hand, on the Royal Birthday of 1797. Mr. Pye continued to display the same poetic activity in the years that followed, both at St. James's and in his native Berkshire. On January 1st, 1798, we must imagine the gentlemen and boys of the Chapel Royal singing lustily—

> While treach'rous friends and daring foes
> Around in horrid compact close ;—
> Their swarming barks' portentous shade
> With crowded sails the watery glade ;
> When lo ! imperial George commands—
> Rush to the waves Britannia's veteran bands—
> Unnumbered hosts usurp in vain
> Dominion o'er his briny reign.
> His fleets their Monarch's right proclaim
> With brazen throat, with breath of flame.

Six months later (June 4th, 1798) they chanted—

> While loud and near, round Britain's coasts
> The low'ring storm of battle roars,
> In proud array while numerous hosts
> Insulting threat her happy shores—

and so forth. Mr. Pye was prophetic. It was the year of the Battle of the Nile. In August it was the birthday of the heir-apparent, and the poet laureate must not be held responsible for the following effusion " by an officer and handed round amongst the upper circle " at Windsor :—

> With what firm grace he takes the lead,
> When mounted on his martial steed
> Not the Black Prince more graceful wav'd his sword,
> And with more thunder gave his troops the word.
> Mark the lightning of his eye,
> When squadrons charge, or squadrons fly !
> And Britons mark his tear, should one dismounted lie.
> For his country and his Sire,

If he e'er meet the foe,
Each Briton he'll fire
With his true Patriot glow
To send the invaders to Pluto below.
Great George, like Great Edward, will hallow his Son,
And cherish those laurels the hero has won.

George III was far too wise to entrust a military command to the man who a quarter of a century later firmly believed that his personal presence and prowess had mainly contributed to the winning of Waterloo.

At the next New Year's musical meeting Henry James Pye wins fresh laurels with :—:

Around her coast, fenc'd by her guardian main,
    Around Iërne's kindred shores,
Hark ! loud Invasion to her baffl'd train
    In yells of desperation roars.
Along the hostile deep they vainly try
From Britain's thundering barks to fly;
Their Fleets, the Victor's trophy, captur'd ride,
In future battles doom'd to combat on our side.

Seas, where deathless bards of yore,
    Singing to the silver tide,
Wafted loud from shore to shore
    Grecian Art and Roman Pride !
Say, when Carthage learn'd to veil
To mightier foes her lofty sail ;
Say, when the Man of Athens broke
With daring prow the Medean Tyrant's yoke ;
Saw ye so bold, so free a band,
As NELSON led by Nilus' strand ;
What time, at GEORGE'S high behest,
Dread in terrific vengeance dress'd,
Fierce as the whirlwind's stormy course,
They pour'd on Gallia's guilty force ;
And Egypt saw Britannia's flag unfurl'd
Wave high its Victor Cross, Deliverer of the World !

The King's next birthday (4th June, 1799) was not only signalized by the memorable review in Hyde Park,[1] but by the poet Pye producing, with Sir W. Parsons' assistance, an ode beginning with the lines :—

> Still shall the brazen tongue of War
> Drown every softer sound :
> Still shall AMBITION'S iron Car
> It's crimson axles whirl around !
> Shall the sweet Lyre and Flute no more
> With gentle descant soothe the shore,
> Pour in melodious strain the votive Lay—
> And hail in notes of Peace our MONARCH'S Natal Day?

And ending :—

> The shouts of War the Gallic Plund'rers hear,
> Th' avenging arm of JUSTICE learn to fear ;
> And low his crest th' insulting Despot vails,
> While their collected Navy's force
> Speeds o'er the Wave its desultory course.

For the harmonious ushering in of the year 1800—the last of the moribund eighteenth century—Mr. Pye, poet laureate, varies his programme by adding three verses to the National Anthem of a singularly bellicose character.

> God of our Fathers, rise,
> And through the thundering skies
> Thy vengeance urge,
> In awful justice red,
> By thy dread arrows sped,
> But guard our Monarch's head,
> GOD Save Great GEORGE !

> Still on our ALBION smile,
> Still o'er this favour'd Isle
> O spread thy wing ;
> To make each Blessing sure,
> To make our Fame endure,
> To make our Rights secure,
> GOD Save our KING !

[1] See *ante*, p. 133.

> To the loud Trumpet's throat,
> To the shrill Clarion's note,
>   Now jocund sing ;
> From every open Foe,
> From every Traitor's blow,
> Virtue defend his brow,
>   GOD guards our King !

Dr. Valpy's scholars at Reading subscribed for the erection of a naval pillar, and the poet laureate furnishes a prologue to *King John,* to be spoken by Mr. Valpy in the uniform of the Reading Association, "part of the Berkshire Volunteers reviewed by His Majesty on Bulmarsh Heath." It commences in the usual key :—

> To-night our scene from British Annal's shews
> How British warriors brav'd their Country's foes:
> Whether their hardy bands with martial toil
> Dar'd the proud Gaul upon his native soil,
> And by his ravag'd plains and prostrate towers
> Led in triumphant march their conq'ring powers,
> Or, on his own insulted fields, defied
> The whelming deluge of Invasion's tide.

On the 4th June, 1800, the Court listened to the inspiring strains of :—

> Yet far from ALBION'S tranquil Shores
> The storm of Desolation roars,
> And while o'er fair Liguria's Vales,
> Fann'd by FAVONIUS' tepid gales,
> O'er Alpine heights that proudly rise
> And shroud their summits in the skies,
> Or by the Rhine's majestic stream
> The hostile arms of GALLIA gleam.
> Fenc'd by her Naval Hosts that ride
> Triumphant o'er her circling tide ;
> BRITANNIA, jocund, pours the festive lay,
> And hails with duteous voice her GEORGE'S Natal Day.

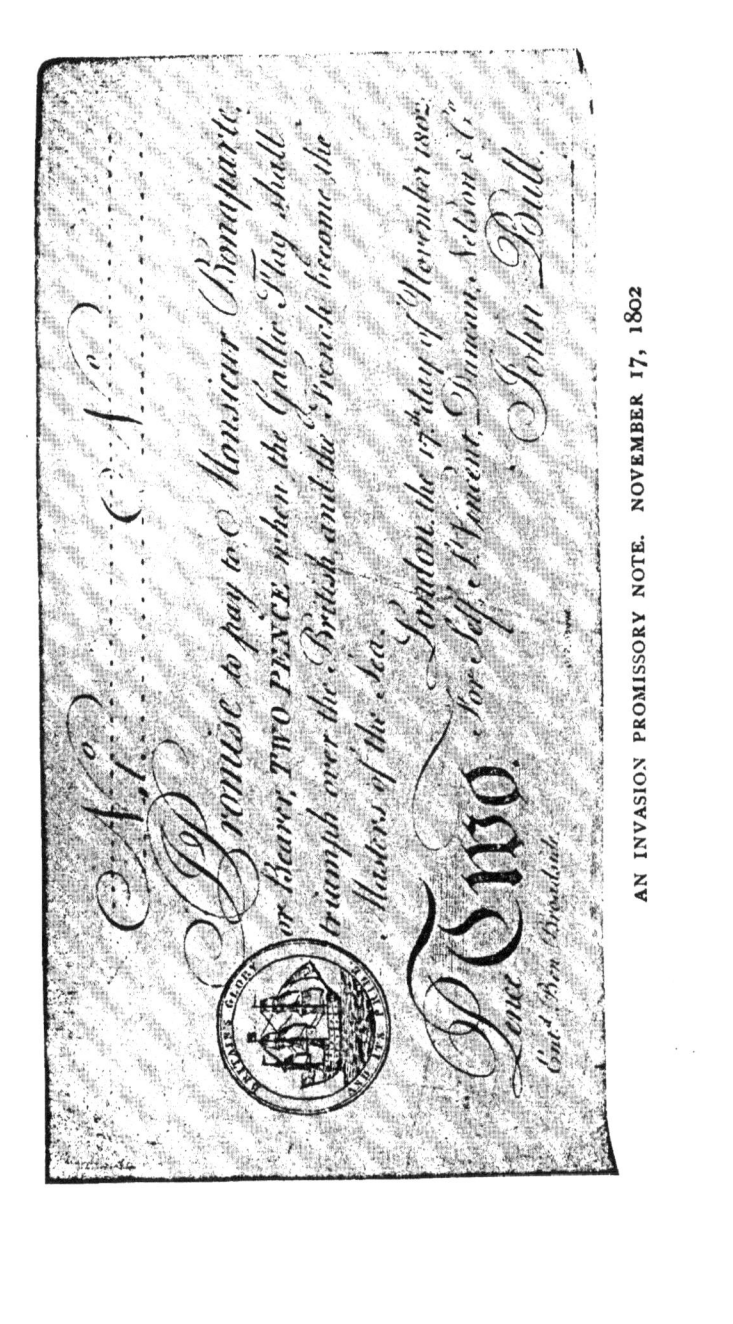

AN INVASION PROMISSORY NOTE. NOVEMBER 17, 1802

On the first day of the nineteenth century the Union interrupts for a moment the thread of the invasion theme.

> Albion and Erin's kindred Race
> Long as your sister Isles the seas embrace—
> Long as the circling Tides your shores that lave
> Waft your united Banners o'er the wave.

Ten generations of Pyes sleep in Farringdon Church, and in August, 1801, the Wantage Volunteers were favoured with :—

> When loud Invasion's will infuriate roar
> With boastful threat'nings shakes Britannia's shore,
> Should Alfred turn his sainted eyes to earth
> And view the hallow'd seats which gave him birth,
> How would he praise the patriot worth that calls
> Their manly sons from Vinitagia's walls.

For a time Mr. Pye's warlike notes are hushed. The Treaty of Amiens brings a temporary respite to both invaders and invaded. Mr. Pye is quite equal to the occasion, and the beginning of 1802 is celebrated with :—

> Lo, from Bellona's crimson car
>   At length the panting steeds unbound,
> At length the thunder of the War
>   In festive shouts of Peace is drown'd.

How short the dream of peace was to last we shall see in the following chapters. The continuity of the literary and artistic landmarks of the Great Terror was scarcely interrupted.

"An experimental peace."—GEORGE III.

THE first overtures for peace came through M. Otto, a French agent in London for the exchange of prisoners. The war had now dragged on for eight years at a fearful cost of blood and treasure, and the British National Debt stood at no less than £537,000,000. The Prime Minister certainly believed in the good faith of Bonaparte's pacific protestations, but how little Charles Yorke, the Secretary at War of Addington's administration, was able to support his Chief's views is revealed in a letter which he wrote to Charles Abbot, then Chief Secretary for Ireland and later Speaker of the House of Commons, on August 18th, 1801. He says :—

" . . . In the present state of France, I would not give a twelvemonths' purchase for any peace, however fair upon the face of it, that can be had with it. At the same time we certainly require breathing time, and the people will not be satisfied without the name of it. . . . France on her part, I mean the military despots of France, may possibly incline to a *truce*, with a view to throwing us off our guard, and procuring the laying up of our navy, and disbanding the greater part of our army. When this is done, Ambassador Bernadotte or Joseph Buonaparte is instructed to offer some insult, pick a quarrel, pass over to Calais, and in a week's time the garrisons of Flanders and the Netherlands embark on the Maese[1] and Scheldt, and are in the mouth of the Thames, perhaps on the coasts of Kent and Essex. The substance of this idea should be embodied in a few words, and written in large letters over the doors of both Houses of Parliament, and on the canopy of the King's throne.

" The question of our internal defence and preparation must indisputably be very different from what it was formerly, and a very serious and weighty question it will be. Every shilling that can be spared, or by any means scraped together, must be scrupulously and zealously devoted to this object. *Libertas et anima nostra in dubio est. . . .*"[2]

At last Otto and Lord Hawkesbury, the Secretary of State for Foreign Affairs, after much discussion and innumerable delays, were able to draw up the preliminaries of peace, which were signed in London on October 1st, 1801. At seven o'clock the following morning the joyful intelligence was communicated to the Lord Mayor of London, Sir W. Staines, who had risen from being an ordinary labouring bricklayer to the proud position of Chief Magistrate of the City. That evening a special courier left England with despatches for France, where he travelled with all speed to Malmaison, Bonaparte's country seat, arriving there in the forenoon of the following day. Nobody outside those directly concerned with the matter knew of the glad tidings until they were officially informed in a

---

[1] Meuse.
[2] *Diary and Correspondence of Charles Abbot, Lord Colchester*, Vol. I, p. 363.

" London Gazette Extraordinary.
" Friday, October 2nd.
" Downing Street, October 2nd.

" Preliminaries of Peace between His Majesty and the French Republic were signed last night at Lord Hawkesbury's Office, in Downing Street, by the Right Hon. Lord Hawkesbury, one of His Majesty's Principal Secretaries of State, on the part of His Majesty, and by M. Otto, on the part of the French Government."

An inkling of what was passing the day before managed to leak through the official barriers of Downing Street, with the result that stocks rose to a high figure. *The Times* in its issue of a day later noted that " many persons were actually duped by this rumour." The same journal saw occasion on the following Saturday (October 3rd) to remark in its leader that, "contrary to the general expectation and better than our hopes has it pleased Providence to order the issue of this great event. The fortitude of ministers has been crowned with success ; and in consequence of the accession of the Republican Government to their demands, and of full powers transmitted to M. Otto for that purpose, the Preliminaries of Peace were signed in Downing Street at seven o'clock in the evening of Thursday by that Minister and His Majesty's Secretary of State for the Foreign Department."

When the official news became known, a wag had the following rhyme printed and pasted up on a building near the Stock Exchange :—

> Peace —Ratified
> Bulls —Gratified;
> Bears —Mortified;
> Nation—Dissatisfied;
> Alley —Purified;
> All   —Electrified.

JOHN BULL SAYS, "HANDS OFF!" APRIL 16, 1802

M. Otto's house was most elaborately illuminated, the word "Concord" shining out in letters of fire above the heads of the people. A sailor misread the word, and immediately shouted out, "Conquered! Not so by a great deal. That will not do." His cry created a disturbance. Among the crowd were people as illiterate as himself, and soon a tumult ensued which brought the Frenchman to the balcony. After vainly endeavouring to get a hearing, he told his servants to take down the fixture at once, and substitute the word "Amity." This was done, and the hisses gave way to cheers. England was, on the surface at any rate, in an ecstasy of delight. Every mail coach was decorated with laurels, and on many of them labels were hung in a conspicuous place bearing the magic words, "Peace with France." Others carried banners on which the same pregnant sentence was inscribed. Even the drivers decked themselves with a sprig of laurel in their hats. Many of the largest provincial cities and towns were informed by means of circulars. When the coach which brought the glad tidings of peace arrived at Ipswich, some of the soldiers stationed at the barracks there came and kissed the wheels of the vehicle. In many cases the horses were taken out of the shafts and citizens dragged the coaches along, often for a considerable distance. At Hull, for instance, the sailors drew the mail coach through the various thoroughfares of the port for three hours, eventually overturning it in the market place, fatally injuring one man, and wounding several others. "The unexpected news of peace, which we might have hoped would have cheered every heart, was not the case at Sheerness," *The Times* facetiously remarks. "To have seen the slop-sellers and the Jews put on their long faces was truly ludicrous." At Great Yarmouth the ships in the harbour as well as the houses were decorated with flags, the church bells were set a-ringing, and the vessels fired guns at intervals. At Brighton the Steine was brilliantly lighted up, while the inhabitants of Plymouth gave vent to their feelings by raising a general subscription for a bonfire. A large sum of money was collected, and some idea of the size of the structure may be gathered from the fact that its base was two hundred and forty feet in circumference, and the height between seventy and eighty feet. When it was well alight the flames were visible upwards of forty miles.

The news of the signature of the preliminaries reached Paris at four o'clock on Saturday afternoon (3rd October). It was immediately communicated by the telegraph to every point of the Republic, and all parts of the frontiers. The Minister of the Interior forwarded the intelligence to the theatres. Discharges of artillery from the quay of the Tuileries, and on the esplanade of the National Hôtel des Invalides, announced it to other inhabitants, while a torchlight procession was arranged for the evening, in which the Commissaries of Police, escorted by detachments of light infantry and dragoons, took part. Many of the public bodies presented addresses to the First Consul, congratulating him on the conclusion of hostilities. He announced that the 9th November was to be observed as a general holiday.

Wild rumours of a contradictory nature spread with alarming rapidity throughout the metropolis. Thus, on the 5th inst., reports were in circulation that the ratification had actually arrived from Bonaparte, with the result that Piccadilly and Bond Street were "exceedingly brilliant." The house of a firm of tea dealers was the only exception in the latter thoroughfare, the inhabitants being prevented from illuminating by Lord Camelford, who lodged over the shop, and heartily disapproved of the Peace. An angry mob speedily collected, shouted for lights to appear, and began knocking violently at the door. Seizing a bludgeon which happened to be handy, his lordship flung open the door and prepared to defend himself against all comers. Brickbats began to fly his way, but he defended himself so ably, and put on such a bold front, that many of the mob turned and fled.

By this time the other people in the house thought fit to interfere, and forcibly dragged the irascible aristocrat out of the way. No sooner was the door shut than the crowd came back helter-skelter to the position they had evacuated. Seizing any missile they could put their hands on, they proceeded to fling stones, refuse, and mud at the windows. Enraged at finding his assailants still furious, Lord Camelford eluded the vigilance of his protectors, secured a pistol, and presented himself at one of the windows, fully intending to blow out the brains of at least a few of his enemies. For a second time his lordship's friends prevailed upon him to retire, and they then proceeded to light a few candles in the upper part of the house, the window-panes of which were too high to be broken. Having satisfied their "righteous" anger the rowdy gang dispersed. When the ratifications were actually exchanged, it was remarked that Lord Camelford had repented, for a few lamps were hung out in front of the building.

It was necessary for the treaty to be ratified by Bonaparte, and he attached his signature to it on the 5th inst. He had previously given orders for a superb gold box to be made in which to place the parchment. It was a beautiful piece of workmanship, most richly ornamented and enamelled, and secured with gold clasps, an appropriate inscription being engraved on the outside. General Lauriston, *Chef de Brigade* in the artillery and first aide-de-camp to Bonaparte, was sent to London with the valuable document. Owing to a delay in the making of the casket, he did not leave Paris until two days later,[1] and this postponement of his departure caused no little trepidation to the citizens of London. He arrived at M. Otto's house in Hereford Street at ten o'clock on the morning of the 10th inst. He would have reached London earlier had not his carriage broken down on the road. The two representatives of the Republic took breakfast together and afterwards proceeded in company with M. St. Jean, brother-in-law of M. Otto and a personal friend of the First Consul's, to Reddish's Hotel, in St. James's Street. A huge concourse of people had gathered to catch a sight of the two Frenchmen, and no sooner did they make their appearance than the horses were taken from the carriage and it was dragged along by the enthusiastic throng. "Gentlemen! Gentlemen!" shouted Lord St. Vincent from his garden gate, "let me request you to be as orderly as possible; and, if you are determined to draw the gentleman accompanied by Monsieur Otto, I request of you to be careful, and not overturn the carriage."[2] General Lauriston expressed

---

[1] October 7th, 1801.
[2] *Annual Register*, 1801, Chronicle, p. 33.

himself as being delighted with his reception, and on arrival at his destination he showed himself at a window and bowed to the populace, who cheered to the echo. After this the crowd shouted, "Long live Bonaparte!" till they were voiceless. As soon as the ratifications had been exchanged Lord Hawkesbury communicated with the Lord Mayor. The following interesting item appeared in a *Gazette Extraordinary* of the same date: "While General Lauriston, M. Otto, and M. St. Jean were exchanging the ratifications at the Foreign Office, such a mob collected in Downing Street, that those gentlemen were absolutely obliged to change their clothes and depart one by one through the back gate in the Park."

The illuminations on this occasion, although very fine, were completely extinguished by a violent thunderstorm which broke over London during the evening. The superstitious saw in this catastrophe the forecast of a short peace. As at the signing of the preliminary treaty, M. Otto's house was the cynosure of all eyes. A large P encircled by a wreath was displayed on one side of the building; while on the other side was a transparent inscription of "Peace and Universal Happiness," in the middle of which was a crown. An olive branch formed of lights hung underneath, with the initials G.R. and F.R. A many-coloured star was also conspicuous. All the theatres were illuminated, and we are told that no fewer than six thousand lamps were found necessary for the Post Office buildings. Not a few people were attracted by a large transparency representing Pitt, the First Consul, Windham, and Joseph Bonaparte dancing a fandango to a tune played on the "union bagpipes."

At length all parties pleased to yield,
A treaty was in London sealed ;
And Nap with pleasure had to say
That England own'd his Cons'lar sway.
The Royalists were vex'd at this,
They took the treaty much amiss ;
It seemed (as for a time it was)
Destructive of the Bourbon cause.
This Amiens treaty, as 'twas termed
Was in October month confirm'd.
And London, tho' so ill repaid,
Illuminations grand display'd.[1]

History was again repeating itself, and had Walpole been alive he would have assuredly once more uttered his oft-quoted remark, " They may ring the bells now; before long they will be wringing their hands." On hearing of the extravagant terms used by certain high officials with reference to the peace, and the unseemly conduct of the mob, Nelson waxed wroth. " There is no person in the world rejoices more in the peace than I do," he averred, " but I would burst sooner than let a d——d Frenchman know it. We have made peace with the French despotism, and we will, I hope, adhere to it whilst the French continue in due bounds ; but whenever they overstep that, and usurp a power which would degrade Europe, then I trust we shall join Europe in crushing her ambition; then I would with pleasure go forth and risk my life for to pull down the overgrown detestable power of France."[2]

It would be impossible to exaggerate the feeling of intense relief which was evident in the navy. After months of unceasing watchfulness, officers and men would be able to see their loved ones again, and " sleep in their

---

[1] *The Porcupine,* October 15th, 1801.
[2] *The Life of Nelson,* Vol. II, p. 144, by Captain A. T. Mahan.

beds with both eyes shut." Rear-Admiral Collingwood furnishes us with an excellent word-picture of what happened, in a letter written on board his ship the *Barfleur*, off Brest. It is dated October 16th, 1801, and runs as follows :—

"I cannot tell you how much joy the news of peace gave me ; the hope of returning to my family, and living in quiet and comfort among those I love, fills my heart with gladness. . . . The moment the French in Brest heard the preliminaries were signed, they sent out a flag of truce with the information to Admiral Cornwallis, and their congratulations on the approaching amity of the two countries. The British officer who was sent in with a return of the compliment was treated with the greatest hospitality and kindness, both by the French and Spanish. They feasted him all the time he stayed there, and carried him to the plays and places of entertainment. I hope now we have seen the end of the last war that will be in our days, and that I shall be able to turn my mind to peaceful occupations. . . . At present we know nothing of what is going on in England. . . . How glad will my heart be to see you all at my own home ! I look on the day to be at hand when I shall be very, very happy indeed."[1]

Pitt offered little opposition to the terms which Bonaparte dictated, although he strongly objected to eating humble pie, and said so in the speech quoted below. That they were humiliating terms, especially when our navy had proved itself so much in the ascendant, cannot be denied. The excesses of the Revolution, the claims of the Bourbon exiles—to whom England had given shelter—even the aggressive policy of Bonaparte, were

---

[1] *Correspondence and Memoir of Lord Collingwood* (third edition), p. 87, by G. L. Newnham Collingwood, F.R.S.

forgotten for the time, and the "usurper" of yesterday became the acknowledged ruler of to-day. George III, for all his fits of insanity, was never more sane than when he remarked to Lord Malmesbury: "Do you know what I call the peace? An experimental peace; for it is nothing else. I am sure you think so; and perhaps you do not give it so gentle a name: but it was unavoidable. I was abandoned by everybody: allies, and all." Sheridan put the matter even more forcibly when he declared in Parliament that "This is a peace which all men are glad of, but no man can be proud of."

Speaking on November 3rd, 1801, the day on which the preliminaries of peace were laid before Parliament, Pitt emphasized his belief in the proverb: "In times of peace prepare for war." "The object which must naturally first present itself to every minister," he said, "must be to give additional vigour to our maritime strength, and security to our colonial possessions. It was to them we were indebted for the unparalleled exertions which we have been enabled to make in the course of this long and eventful contest; it was by them that we were enabled, in the wreck of Europe, not only to effect our own security, but to hold out to our allies the means of safety, if they had been but true to themselves."

His optimism, usually so overpowering, extended no further than "to hope everything that was good, but he was bound to act as if he feared otherwise." He spoke of the common cause which had united the people of Great Britain and Ireland, "and led to that happy union which adds more to the power and strength of the British Empire, than all the conquests of one and indivisible France do to that country." Pitt concluded with another reference to the navy and an implied acknowledgment that it was the command of the sea which had alone enabled his country to dare and do: " If any additional proofs were wanting to prove her ability to protect her honour and maintain her interests, let gentlemen look to the last campaign, and they would see Great Britain contending against a powerful confederacy in the North; they would see her fighting for those objects at once in Egypt and in the Baltic, and they would see her successful in both. We had shewn that we were ready to meet the threatened invasion at home, and could send troops to triumph over the French in the barren sands of Egypt, before a man could escape from Toulon, to reinforce their blocked-up army; we had met the menaced invasion by attacking France on her own coasts, and we had seen those ships which were destined for the invasion of this country moored and chained to their shores, and finding protection only in their batteries. These were not only sources of justifiable pride, but grounds of solid security. What might be the future object of the Chief Consul of France he knew not, but if it were to exercise a military despotism, he would venture to predict that he would not select this country for the first object of his attack; and if we were true to ourselves we had little to fear from that attack, let it come when it would. But though he did not entertain apprehensions, yet he could not concur with those who thought we ought to lay aside all caution; if such policy were adopted, there would indeed be ground for most serious apprehensions: he hoped every measure would be adopted which prudence could suggest, to do away with animosity between the two countries, and to avoid every ground of irritation by sincerity on our part. This, however, on the

other hand, was not to be done by paying abject court to
France.   We must depend for security only upon ourselves.   If, however, the views of France were correspon-
dent with our own, we had every prospect of enjoying a
long peace.   He saw some symptoms that they were, though
upon this he had no certain knowledge; but he would
never rely upon personal character for the security of his
country.   He was inclined to hope everything was good,
but he was bound to act as if he feared otherwise."

This proves that although Pitt was willing to try the experiment of peace, he was far from sanguine as to the
good intentions of Bonaparte.   He confessed to Wilberforce that the terms were not all that he should have
wished, but that they were " on the whole highly honourable to the country and very advantageous.   The event is
most fortunate both for Government and the public, and
for the sake of both gives me infinite satisfaction."[1]   That
Pitt had a singularly clear conception of the First Consul's
character is evident; it was as though he had already
dreamed of Ulm and Austerlitz, and saw vaguely the com-
pensations of Trafalgar and Waterloo.

Lord Cornwallis, who was then over sixty years of age,
was sent to Paris as Ambassador Plenipotentiary to represent Great Britain in the drawing-up of the definitive
treaty.   The First Consul gave orders that he was to
be " received with the greatest distinction.   On his arrival
at Calais a salute must be fired, and he must have a
guard of honour to escort him on his journey." [2]   He had

---

[1] *Private Papers of William Wilberforce*, p. 30.   This communication is
addressed from Park Place, October 1st, 1801.

[2] To General Berthier.   Paris, 14th October, 1801.   Bingham, Vol. I,
p. 372.

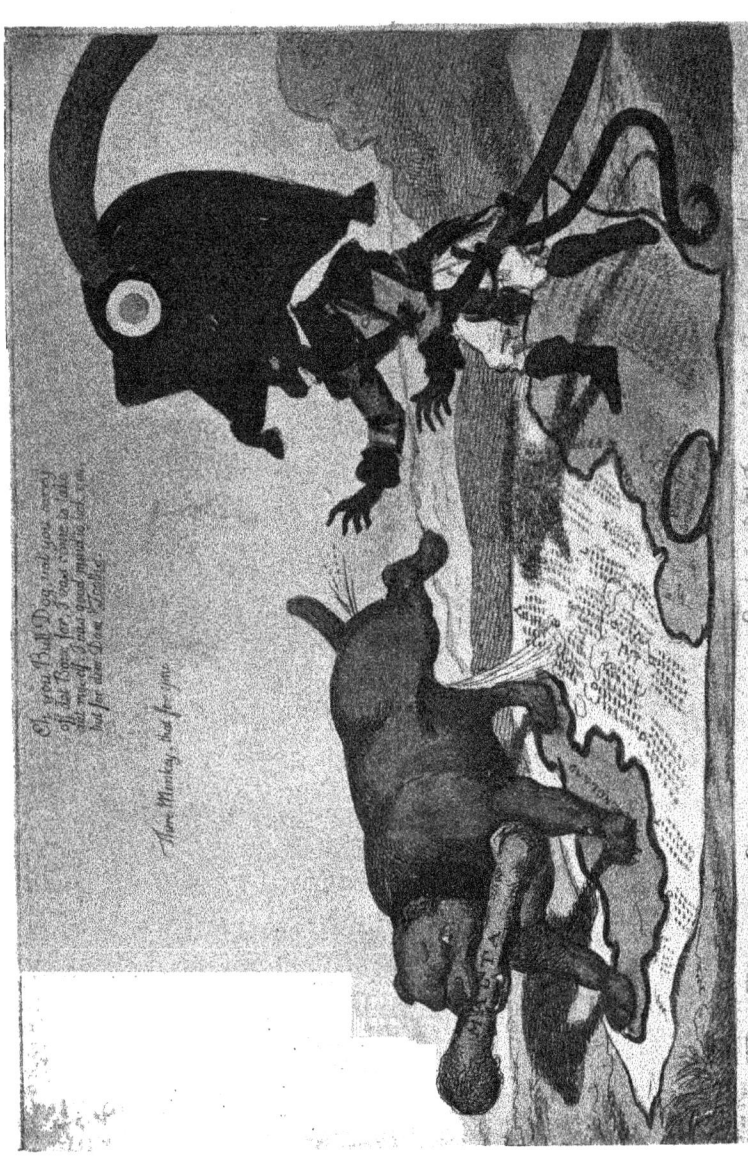

MALTA, THE BONE OF CONTENTION. JUNE 14, 1803

a long interview with the First Consul.   In his correspondence Cornwallis states that Bonaparte " affected a frank,
liberal, and conciliatory spirit." The conferences were
afterwards transferred to Amiens, a city which served the
purpose of a half-way house between London and Paris.
Talleyrand and Joseph Bonaparte represented France
while the matter was being discussed, the Chevalier
d'Azara looked after the interests of Spain, and M.
Schimmelpennick attended on behalf of Holland.   Lord
Cornwallis, it is to be feared, was as clay in the hands of
such skilful diplomatists.   For some months the negotiations went on, both countries haggling over comparatively
trivial details.   Eventually their differences were settled,
and on the 27th March, 1802, the Peace of Amiens was
signed.   Great Britain agreed to give up Egypt to the .
Sublime Porte ; the Cape of Good Hope was handed over
to Holland, along with Berbice, Demerara, Essequibo,
and Surinam ; Malta was to be evacuated and restored to
the Knights of the Order of St. John of Jerusalem ; and
all the French colonies taken in the war were to be given
back.   For these concessions Great Britain obtained
Ceylon and Trinidad, France also agreeing to withdraw
from Naples and the Roman States ; Portugal was to be
an independent kingdom, and the Newfoundland fisheries
were to be on exactly the same footing as before the outbreak of war.

The British Government lost no time in showing in a
practical manner its satisfaction at the harmonious relations
which now existed between England and France, and orders
were given for the disbanding of all the sea fencibles
and the discharge of the press-gangs.   The militia, which
had been nine years under arms, was disembodied, but

the services of certain of the volunteer yeomanry corps were retained in large centres. Shortly afterwards Nelson with his fleet quitted his station off Boulogne and anchored in the Downs.[1]

The Peace of Amiens stood Bonaparte in good stead so far as personal ambition went, for the Tribunate and Legislative Body decided that he should have some mark of esteem paid to him. A further ten years was therefore added to his consulate on the expiration of his term of office. Shortly afterwards he was made Consul for life, the second step leading to the imperial throne.

---

[1] At the end of the war Great Britain had sixty-seven more sail-of-the-line than when hostilities began, while in 1801 France had only thirty-nine sail-of-the-line against the eighty she possessed in 1793. See Mahan, *Influence of Sea Power upon the French Revolution and Empire*, Vol. II, p. 73.

CHAPTER IX

THE LULL BEFORE THE STORM, 1803

"England is not asleep, she is always on the watch."—NAPOLEON.

FOR a time Bonaparte devoted himself to national reforms, such as reinstating religion, furthering education, and encouraging commerce in every direction. He also paid particular attention to the construction of military roads and canals, and had a number of new ships put on the stocks. His aggressive schemes on the Continent were not, however, allowed to lapse for long. In an incredibly short period the First Consul became President of the Italian Republic, subdued Switzerland, seized Piedmont, occupied Parma and Piacenza, and obtained Elba from the King of Naples. He also desired a great colonial empire, and with this object in view he endeavoured to reorganize the island of St. Domingo ;[1] Louisiana was ceded to France by Spain in exchange for an extension of territory in Italy ; Guiana was also secured ; and India once more became the object of his solicitude. He again declared Europe was too small for him, and that the East and West contained vast tracts of land as yet unopened to the civilizing influ-

[1] In one of Napoleon's conversations with Gourgaud at St. Helena, he characterized "the Saint Domingo business" as the "greatest error that in all my government I ever committed." See *Talks of Napoleon at St. Helena with General Baron Gourgaud*, p. 112.

ence of commerce. Moderation was the one great attribute Bonaparte lacked; it would have consolidated his
interests and established his line; unfettered ambition
took away every shred of power, and left him at the
mercy of the country he had vowed to conquer. Tronchet
was right when he remarked to Cambacérès: "This young
man begins like Cæsar: I fear that he will end like
him."[1]

The Peace of Amiens lasted one year and sixteen days,
and its rupture plunged Europe into a twelve years' war.
Neither side kept strictly to the conditions set forth in
the treaty, and it was evident that before long swords
would leave their scabbards once more. In the words of
Hazlitt, the peace "was a sponge to wipe out old scores
and begin the game over again on new ground."[2] "You
know how much under all the circumstances I wished for
peace," writes Pitt to Wilberforce, "and my wishes remain
the same, if Bonaparte can be made to feel that he is not
to trample in succession on every nation in Europe. But
of this I fear there is little chance, and without it I see no
prospect but war."[3]

On the 18th February, 1803, Lord Whitworth, the
English Ambassador at Paris, had a long interview with
the First Consul in his cabinet at the Tuileries. The
First Consul asserted that his efforts to live on good terms
with England had met with no friendly response. He
also complained bitterly of the attacks which were continually made upon him by the Press, and persisted in

---

[1] Cambacérès was Second Consul, and afterwards became Arch-Chancellor
of the Empire.

[2] *Life of Napoleon Bonaparte*, Vol. II, p. 486, by William Hazlitt.

[3] This letter is dated from Bath, October 31st, 1802. *Private Papers
of William Wilberforce*, p. 34, collected and edited by A. M. Wilberforce.

THE POLITICAL SITUATION OF MAY, 1803. ADDINGTON ALARMED. SHERIDAN AS A PATRIOT

the statement that he had executed the Treaty of Amiens with scrupulous fidelity. "As a proof of his desire to maintain peace," runs Lord Whitworth's report,[1] "he wished to know what he had to gain by going to war with England? A descent was the only means of offence he had, and that he was determined to attempt, by putting himself at the head of the expedition. But how could it be supposed, that after having gained the height on which he stood, he would risk his life and reputation in such a hazardous attempt, unless forced to it by necessity, when the chances were that he and the greater part of the expedition would go to the bottom of the sea? . . . He acknowledged that there were one hundred chances to one against him; but still he was determined to attempt it, if war should be the consequence of the present discussion; and that such was the disposition of the troops, that army after army would be found for the enterprize. He then expatiated much on the force of the two countries. France, with an army of 480,000 men, for to this amount, it is, he said, to be immediately completed, all ready for the most desperate enterprize; and England with a fleet that made her mistress of the seas, and which he did not think he should be able to equal in less than ten years."

King George III informed Parliament on the 8th of March, 1803, that though there was still a chance for the peace to continue, the " very considerable military preparations" going on in the ports of France and Holland,

[1] Lord Whitworth to Lord Hawkesbury, Paris, February 21st, 1803. "War with France: Official Papers, presented by His Majesty's command to both Houses of Parliament, on Wednesday, the 18th of May, 1803, relative to the negociations between Great Britain and the French Government," p. 37, Dublin, 1803.

I.—T

though "avowedly directed to colonial service," called for further precautions to be taken for the defence of Great Britain. Accordingly an addition of 10,000 men to the naval force of the country and the calling out of the militia was voted. In 1802, owing to Bonaparte's restlessness, Parliament had sanctioned an addition of 20,000 men to the navy, and 66,000 men to the army in order to provide for the safety of Ireland, which it seemed probable would be invaded at the earliest favourable opportunity.[1]

The French preparations in Holland were, in theory at any rate, intended for Louisiana. Some 6500 troops were stationed at Helvoetsluis in accordance with articles . signed on February 1st, 1803, and of these 3040 were for the expedition.[2] But by the Treaty of Lunéville, which guaranteed the independence of the Batavian Republic, and also by the convention concluded at the Hague on the 29th August, 1801, five half-brigades and five companies of artillery were to be allowed to remain in Holland only "until the final conclusion of peace with England."[3] Napoleon had not thought it well to evacuate the country. The Cape of Good Hope had been but recently restored to the Dutch, and there was the probability that it might "at any time become the base of operations of French cruisers and privateers preying upon British East Indiamen,"[4] thus menacing Britain's Eastern Empire. An expedition under Decaen had been already sent to India with the express purpose of finding exactly what discontent there was

---

[1] *Cambridge Modern History*, Vol. IX, p. 102.
[2] Desbrière, Vol. III, p. 17.
[3] Coquelle's *Napoleon and England*, 1803–1813, p. 16.
[4] *Ibid.*, Introduction, p. xviii.

'Get it, my hearties—pump away!
for the honor of old England!'

Bonaparte's Head-Quarters in London.'

NAPOLEON'S RECEPTION IN THE ENGLISH CAPITAL, A CARICATURE OF MARCH, 1803

among the rajahs and princes, and the probable number of troops likely to be required to conquer the country. No child crying for the moon was ever more eager than the First Consul was for India. Bonaparte had done much the same kind of thing while he was at Cairo in 1799, when he had written to Tippoo Sahib announcing that he had arrived "on the shores of the Red Sea, with a numerous and invincible army, animated with the desire of delivering you from the iron yoke of England."[1] He then asked for news regarding the political position there; he was asking for the same information now. He suggested to Decaen that although "the English are masters of the continent of India," there was no reason why they should continue as such, provided he carefully followed out his instructions. The First Consul went so far as to plan Decaen's course of action "in the event of war," which he anticipated would not break out before September, 1804.[2] As to hostile naval preparations, Lord Whitworth clearly states in his despatch of March 17th, 1803, to Lord Hawkesbury, that no armaments of any consequence were being carried on in the French ports. A fortnight before, notice had been given "to equip what there was in the different ports; and the absence of by far the greater part of the naval force renders such an order almost nugatory."[3] The army was supposed to be on a peace footing, but troops were concentrating in the north-east of France; surely a warlike proceeding!

No commercial treaty existed between Great Britain and France, and Bonaparte had taken advantage of the

[1] Bingham, Vol. I, p. 244.
[2] *Cambridge Modern History*, Vol. IX, p. 209.
[3] *England and France in the Mediterranean*, p. 190.

truce to send over a number of so-called "agents" or
consuls, ostensibly for the purpose of furthering more
amicable relations in this respect, but really to spy out the
nakedness of the land.   In a declaration afterwards laid
before both Houses of Parliament, this double-dealing was
fully exposed.   The suspicion that these agents had more
than one object in view "was confirmed, not only by the
circumstance that some of them were military men, but
by the actual discovery that several of them were furnished
with instructions to obtain the soundings of the harbours,
and to procure military surveys of the places where it was
intended they should reside."[1]   A letter sent to Marès, the
French "consul" at Hull, was intercepted by the Post
Office authorities, and proved the perfidy of Bonaparte
beyond doubt.   It contained a plan of Hull harbour and
details of its approaches.   The agents were simply secret
service men, who spent their time in obtaining information
likely to be of service in effecting a descent upon the
British Isles.[2]

Sunday, March 13th, was the day fixed for a reception
at the Tuileries.   Bonaparte had been reading the despatches of his Ambassador at the Court of St. James's, and
also a verbatim copy of the King's message of March 8th.[3]
Entering the salon, in which some two hundred people

---

[1] *War with France: Official Papers*, p. 81.

[2] See *Correspondance de Napoléon*, Letter No. 6475.

[3] Napoleon's own statement of the 21st of February, 1803, to the French
Legislature was quite as capable of being turned into a declaration of war as
was the message read in the British Parliament. "The Government," it ran,
"guarantees to the nation peace on the Continent, and it may entertain hopes
for the maintenance of peace on the high seas.   The Government will make
every effort to preserve it, compatible with the national honour, which is bound
to maintain the literal execution of treaties. . . . Five hundred thousand men
must be in arms ready to defend their country and to avenge her."

BONAPARTE AND LORD WHITWORTH.   THE PEACE OF AMIENS IN DANGER

were assembled, he went straight up to Lord Whitworth and asked in an angry tone, "Why those preparations for war? Against whom are those precautionary measures taken? I have not a single ship-of-the-line in the ports of France; but if you will arm I shall also arm. If you will fight I shall also fight. You may possibly be able to destroy France but never to intimidate her." [1]

The prudent Ambassador made a bow, but did not venture to reply. The First Consul then went his round, and shortly afterwards withdrew to his cabinet. There was nothing of the violent "scene" mentioned in so many histories, but Bonaparte was certainly agitated. [2] Diplomatic notes were exchanged between the two Powers for some weeks. Important concessions were proposed by Great Britain; "explanations" of Sebastiani's report on the situation in Egypt were given which were not explanations, but a mere play upon words; finally Whitworth told Talleyrand that "actual war was preferable to the state of suspense in which England, and indeed all Europe, had been kept for so long a space of time." [3]

On May 16th, 1803, England declared war, and an embargo was laid on French ships, and those of other Powers under her jurisdiction, which happened to be in British ports or fell in with our men-of-war. Although a number of seamen were taken prisoners, no French civilian was interfered with. Bonaparte retaliated by issuing the following order from St. Cloud on the 22nd May, which duly appeared in the official *Moniteur* :—

---

[1] Lord Whitworth to Lord Hawkesbury, Paris, March 14th, 1803. *War with France: Official Papers*, p. 41.

[2] See *England and Napoleon in* 1803, by Oscar Browning.

[3] April 29th, 1803.

"The Government of the Republic, having heard read, by the Minister of Marine and Colonies, a despatch from the Maritime Prefect at Brest, announcing that two English frigates had taken two merchant vessels in the Bay of Audrieu, without any previous declaration of war, and in manifest violation of the law of nations:

"All the English, from the ages of eighteen to sixty, or holding any commission from His Britannic Majesty, who are at present in France, shall immediately be constituted prisoners of war, to answer for those citizens of the Republic who may have been arrested and made prisoners by the vessels or subjects of His Britannic Majesty previous to any declaration of hostilities.[1]

"(Signed)   BONAPARTE."

Junot was then Governor of Paris, and long before dawn a messenger arrived from the First Consul summoning him to his study immediately. "Junot," said the latter as soon as the General entered the room, "you must, before an hour elapses, take measures so that all the English, without one single exception, shall be arrested. The prisons will hold them; they must be seized. This measure must be executed at seven in the evening. I am resolved that in the obscurest theatre, or the lowest restaurant in Paris, not an Englishman shall this night be seen!" The result was that some thousands of British subjects in France, Italy, Switzerland, and Holland were seized and confined within the gloomy walls of the prisons of Lille, Valenciennes, and Verdun. Bonaparte's act was absolutely unjustifiable, for he had instructed Louis Gold-

---

[1] No prisoners were made previous to the declaration of war. The two ships mentioned were captured on May 18th. See *post*, Vol. II, p. 159.

MUTUAL RECRIMINATIONS.   JULY 10, 1803

smith, who, besides being the editor of the *Argus*, a French journal issued in London, was also one of the First Consul's confidential agents, to state in his paper that British tourists in France would have their rights respected, as that country, unlike its rival, respected the law of nations. The French prisoners in England were those legally taken in war.

The French army was now being actively mobilized, and in a couple of weeks the tramp of armed feet was heard throughout the length and breadth of France. General Mortier, at the head of 25,000 French troops, invaded Hanover, of which George III was Elector, and on the 13th June, 1803, His Britannic Majesty received the tidings of the loss of his hereditary continental possessions. The Hanoverian army certainly offered some resistance, and the Duke of Cambridge, who was Viceroy, and General Walmoden, endeavoured to call some of the German States to their aid. The appeal was disregarded, and consequently Hanover was surrendered to France. The Duke of Cambridge agreed that his troops should retire behind the Elbe and not serve again till exchanged, while General Walmoden disbanded his army and left his assailants with 30,000 muskets, many pieces of cannon, and 3500 horses. Thus Bonaparte was able to funish himself with a considerable supply of munitions of war at little expense of blood and treasure. A contribution of 8,000,000 livres was imposed on the newly annexed territory, and the timber in its extensive forests began to fall before the woodman's axe, ready to be conveyed to France to be made into boats for the conveyance of the soldiers destined for England.

An interesting description of the First Consul's personal

appearance was published in the *Moniteur*[1] a little while previous to the events just recorded, and gives a fairly reliable pen-portrait of the man who sought to use England as a step-ladder to universal Napoleonism :—

"The person of the First Consul is small, below the ordinary size of men. The consular garb does not become him ; he looks best in the plain uniform of the National Guard, which he, at present, generally wears. His face is strongly marked with melancholy, reflection, and deep thought ; the lines of premature age áre very visible upon it. He is said to be impenetrable even to his friends. His head is remarkably large, and his eyes are well formed and well set, animating a countenance which has been seldom known to smile. His voice is the deepest toned, and seems to issue as from a tomb. His head is large and handsome ; and, in general, it may be asserted there is that harmony of features which denotes an entire character. The various likenesses of him are tolerably exact; though they by no means do him justice, nor give his look, which is extremely interesting and impressive."

Bonaparte's colonial projects were far from successful. The St. Domingo expedition, which had left France late in December, 1801, and consisted of thirty-two men-of-war and thirty-one frigates, had met with disaster, and seeing that the time was not yet ripe for expansion across the seas, he sold Louisiana,[2] a colony then but little developed, to the United States for 60,000,000 francs. It must have cost him a bitter pang to part with that vast domain, so rich in promise. For hours on the night of

---

[1] January 5th, 1803.

[2] France received Louisiana in 1800 " in return for the cession of Tuscany to the heir of the Duke of Parma." See Rose's *Napoleon I*, Vol. I, p. 366.

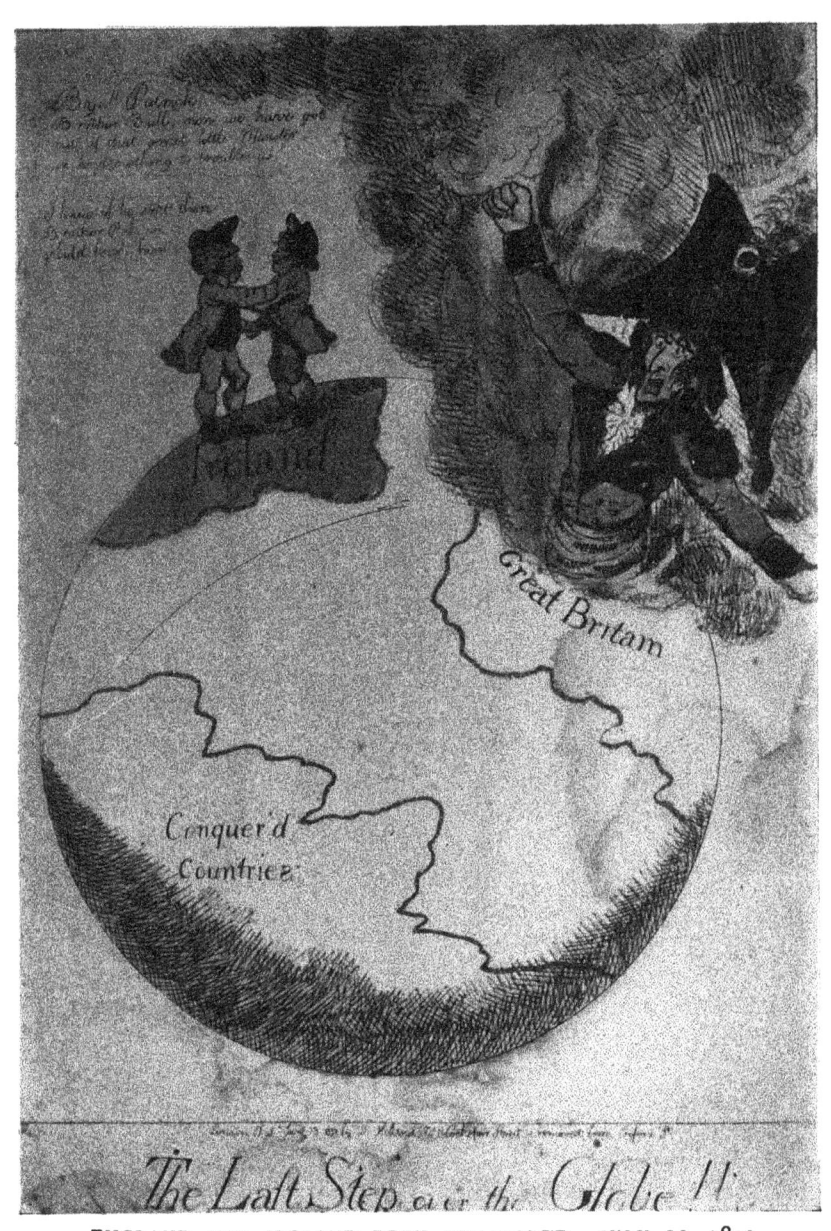

ENGLAND AND IRELAND DEFY BONAPARTE. JULY 13, 1803

Easter Sunday, 1803, Napoleon pondered, and it was not until dawn broke that he arrived at a decision. The despatches lying on his table told of England's preparations for a coming struggle. His mind was made up. " I renounce Louisiana," he said to Talleyrand on April 11th.[1] " It is not only New Orleans I will cede : it is the whole colony, without reserve ; I know the price of what I abandon. . . . I renounce it with the greatest regret : to attempt obstinately to retain it would be folly. I direct you to negotiate the affair." The treaty was signed and sealed May 4th, and much of the money received was spent on preparing for the execution of his third and greatest project for the long-talked-of invasion of England.

[1] *Ibid.*, p. 371.

CHAPTER X

*" What battle ever promised the results that we may look for from
a descent on England?"—NAPOLEON.*

BONAPARTE had candidly confessed to Lord
Whitworth that the invasion of England was a
perilous undertaking and fraught with difficulties, but "to extraordinary circumstances
we must apply extraordinary remedies," was a Napoleonic precept, and the First Consul certainly put it
in practice as soon as the British Ambassador had left
Paris. He made the most gigantic and determined efforts
to collect a formidable flotilla, revised the plans for its
organization a dozen times, built new docks and enlarged
existing ports, and when it was proved to him beyond the
shadow of a doubt that a temporary command of the sea
was indispensable, he worked towards that end with
almost superhuman energy. Bonaparte was a good hater,
and he loathed England with a fiercer intensity as each
year found her still unconquered. He wanted "ships,
colonies, and commerce." Great Britain destroyed the
first, captured the second, and fought for the third with a
doggedness unrivalled in the history of nations. Although

Trafalgar crushed the navies of France and Spain, circumstances alone vetoed the Emperor's later plans for the subjugation of his rival by striking a blow at her very heart. To him London was more important than Paris; for the greater includes the less. It is difficult therefore to understand the attitude taken by certain historians who have endeavoured to prove that Bonaparte's real object was not to invade England or Ireland, but to gather together an immense army to use against Austria and Russia. It seems highly improbable, however, that the First Consul would have spent millions of francs in building the flotilla had such been the case. He was not given to squandering money on castles in the air. The cost of the wars in which he had already engaged had told heavily on the resources of the French treasury, and the money could have been used for many other purposes than excavating harbours and constructing flat-bottomed boats.

At St. Helena the Emperor frequently and frankly discussed his plan of invasion, and always referred to it as a serious undertaking. Another weighty argument in favour of reality, as opposed to mere bluff, arises from the fact of his giving so much of his time to visiting the various ports and examining everything of importance personally, amazing those who were directly engaged in the work with his knowledge of apparently unimportant details. For three years he concentrated his mind and energies on the proposed expedition, perfecting designs, attending manœuvres, and accepting or rejecting schemes either originated by himself or submitted by others. His position as head of the Government was no sinecure. He was already the Emperor Napoleon without the crown and the royal purple. His court was as brilliant as that of any monarch by "Divine Right," while he gathered round him the master-minds of the nation. Pressing business calling for the most careful statesmanship was for ever intruding itself upon his restless brain. It is therefore scarcely feasible to think that such a man would dissipate his already overtaxed energies on a gigantic policy of sham.

During his stay at Elba, and especially while he was on his voyage to St. Helena, the projected invasion of England was a favourite topic of conversation at the dinner-table. The subject naturally appealed to naval men, and Napoleon never showed himself unwilling to gratify their curiosity. The Diaries of Admiral Sir Thomas Ussher, who conveyed the "King of Elba" to his last possession, and of John Glover, secretary to Rear-Admiral Cockburn, of the *Northumberland*, to which may be added that of Lady Malcolm at St. Helena, all bear witness to the rigid cross-examinations the Emperor voluntarily underwent on this particular subject. As Dr. J. Holland Rose remarks in his admirable introduction to *Napoleon's Last Voyages*, "those who note the enormous extent of his preparations on the northern coast in 1804–5, as set forth in his 'correspondence,' and the retentiveness of his memory, even of small details, as proved by the conversation with Ussher, *will find it difficult to believe that he did not really intend to strike at London.*"[1] Although in details he sometimes failed to accurately state the case, as when he told Colonel Campbell that the arming of the

---

[1] *Napoleon's Last Voyages*, being the Diaries of Admiral Sir Thomas Ussher, R.N., K.C.B. (on board the *Undaunted*), and John R. Glover, Secretary to Rear-Admiral Cockburn (on board the *Northumberland*), with Introduction and Notes by J. Holland Rose, LITT. D. (1906), p. 16.

JOHN BULL'S CHALLENGE TO BONAPARTE. APRIL 6, 1803

flotilla was merely to deceive the enemy, and that he never intended to cross without a superiority of fleet to protect it, a statement he reiterated to Admiral Cockburn,[1] he consistently maintained that it was always his intention to invade England. A certain allowance must also be made for the diarists. Bingham,[2] for instance, makes a curious error in asserting that "twenty thousand men [*sic*] were ready at Boulogne to embark at a moment's notice," and in the sentence immediately following renders the statement absurd by saying that Napoleon "could have debarked this army in twenty-four hours."[3]

Referring to his plan of September, 1804, for the conquest of Ireland, the Emperor told.Cockburn that "if he could have got safely over to it the force he intended sending, the party there was so strong in his favour that he had every reason to suppose they would have succeeded in possessing themselves of the whole island."[4]

A conversation which is briefly noted in Glover's Diary under dates September 10th and 11th, 1815, is narrated at greater length by Bingham as having occurred on Tuesday, 12th (September). According to the latter, the Admiral had told Napoleon that many English people had regarded his invasion scheme as a feint.

"'Mr. Pitt never thought so,' was the reply; 'I had well weighed the consequences, and I calculated that if I did not succeed the demonstrations would do me great dis-

---

[1] *Ibid.*, pp. 89, 140.

[2] Sir George Bingham, K.C.B., was on board the *Northumberland* with Napoleon. During the first year of Napoleon's captivity he commanded the second battalion of the 53rd Regiment at St. Helena, when he was appointed Brigadier-General on the Staff of the island.

[3] "More Light on St. Helena," in *Cornhill Magazine*, 1901, p. 22.

[4] *Napoleon's Last Voyages*, p. 194.

service, as it would make the English a military nation,
and at the same time would give the ministers a command of money, since no other measure could authorise
them to call for so large a sum as in this case was
requisite. I was very well pleased to see the preparations
the ·English made on the coast opposite Boulogne, at
which place it was never my intention to have attempted
a landing. I kept up this farce by frequent embarkations
and by the exercise of my flotilla. My real point of
attack would have been somewhere between Margate and
Deal. I calculated that I could have possessed myself
of the lines of Chatham as a point of retreat. I should
then have pushed for London, and, had I arrived there,
I should have offered very moderate terms of peace, taking
care, however, so far to cripple you that you could have
done no further mischief, nor have disturbed my future
plans. Whether I should have succeeded or not I can't
say, but such were my objects.'" The Emperor also
alluded to the Irish expedition: "My sole object was
to divide it from England, and to have occupied the
attention of the English in reconquering or tranquillising
it. Could the division once be effected, peace, and the
ultimate ruin and subjugation of both countries, would
have been the consequence." [1]

Dr. O'Meara, one of Napoleon's physicians at St.
Helena, asked his patient point-blank if he had really
intended to invade England, and if so, what were his
plans? The exiled Emperor replied: "*I would have
headed it myself.*" [2] After describing one of his projects,
he added: "I would have hastened over my flotilla

[1] *Cornhill Magazine*, 1901, pp. 28-9.
[2] *A Voice from St. Helena*, Vol. I, p. 349, by Dr. Barry O'Meara.

THE UPSHOT OF THE INVASION,

or BONY in a fair way for Davey's Locker.

Published in terror & bl-t Poultry.

FRONTISPIECE TO THE ANTI-GALLICAN 1803

with 200,000 men, landed as near Chatham as possible, and proceeded direct to London, where I calculated to arrive in four days from the time of my landing."[1] Again, Las Cases, who was nothing more or less than his master's mouthpiece, quotes him as saying : " It was supposed that my scheme was merely a vain threat, because it did not appear that I possessed any reasonable means of attempting its execution. But I had laid my plans deeply, and without being observed I had dispersed all our French ships ; and the English were sailing after them in different parts of the world. Our ships were to return suddenly and at the same time, and to assemble in a mass along the French coast. I would have had seventy or eighty French or Spanish vessels in the Channel, and I calculated that I should continue master of it for two months. Three or four thousand little boats were to be ready at a signal. A hundred thousand men were every day drilled in embarking and landing, as a part of their exercise. After landing my troops, I could calculate upon only one pitched battle, the result of which could not be doubtful ; and victory would have brought us to London."[2]

Count Balmain, the Russian Commissioner at St. Helena, relates a conversation on the same subject between Admiral Malcolm and the Emperor.[3]

" Malcolm : ' What was the real object of the great preparations you made at Boulogne ? '

---

[1] This statement exactly coincides with the details he gave to Sir George Cockburn. See *Napoleon's Last Voyages*, pp. 140–1.

[2] *Mémorial de Sainte Hélène*, Vol. I, Part II, p. 278 (English edition, 1823), by Las Cases.

[3] "Napoleon's Imprisonment : Memoirs of Count Balmain." Translated and edited by Alder Anderson. Published in the London *Daily Mail*, Nos. 2000-2028.

"Napoleon : 'To take my soldiers across the Channel, of course.'

"Malcolm : 'Did the conquest of England, then, appear to you to be such an easy undertaking?'

"Napoleon : 'No, but it was surely worth while attempting it.'

"Malcolm : 'Nobody was ever able to guess what your plan was.'

"Napoleon : 'It was quite simple. My fleet was despatched towards America, as if for the purpose of disembarking troops there ; I was convinced that the bulk of your fleet would follow it. Villeneuve, taking advantage of the first favourable opportunity—there are so many at sea—was to suddenly turn about and make for the Channel, reaching there a fortnight before the English Admiral, and was to cruise about while my boats were crossing.'"

A visitor to Elba in 1815 records an interview he had with the fallen Emperor, and adds : "I regretted much it had not occurred to me to touch upon a point on which there has always existed much diversity of opinion ;— whether he had ever contemplated the invasion of England. However, I took an opportunity on the following day of introducing the subject to Count Bertrand, during a conversation I had with him.—He reasoned for a considerable time, as if it had really been Bonaparte's intention to make the attempt ;—the Emperor, he said, had forty sail of the line collected in the Mediterranean and at Cadiz ; it was intended that the ships in the different ports should form a junction, and then proceed to the Channel, where the fleet would have been joined by ten sail of the line kept in readiness for that purpose. This force, he remarked, would probably have given them the

JOHN BULL AND THE FRENCH SHIPBUILDER. [EARLY IN 1803]

command of the Channel for a fortnight or three weeks, which time would, it was calculated, have elapsed before Nelson could have discovered their real destination, and reached the scene of action. When the combined fleet had once obtained the command of the Channel, a force of 100,000 men, or more, could have been assembled on the French coast in forty-eight hours, and might have been passed over before the arrival of the British fleet. The invading army, it was conceived, would have been sufficiently strong to overpower any opposition that could have been made to its progress before it had reached London, and taken possession of the seat of Government. I replied, that supposing all these plans had succeeded according to their wishes, their army must inevitably have been destroyed, as they could not have obtained reinforcements. He observed, that they could have kept possession of some small ports, and could have smuggled men over; for as the run is so short, this could not have been wholly prevented by any precautions on the part of the English. I said that the opinion in England was, that the threat of an invasion was a mere pretext for bringing a large force together in order to be prepared to pounce upon one or other of the Continental Powers, as in fact the Emperor had done in the case of Austria. He replied, ' *Cela est possible.*' Here the conversation ended. . . . Some of the Imperial Guard, with whom I conversed at Elba, were decidedly of opinion that, had the invasion of England been attempted, the enterprise would have failed."[1]

Thiers, the great French historian, who was probably

[1] *Minutes of a Conversation with Napoleon Bonaparte during his Residence in Elba, in January, 1815,* by J. H. Vivian. London: Ridgway, Piccadilly. 1839.

I.—U

the first writer to thoroughly peruse the State papers and other documents having reference to the invasion,[1] dismisses the question of whether the First Consul really meant to descend upon England in a single sentence. He says: ".... If the credulous who have questioned the reality of his [Napoleon's] project could read his private correspondence with the Minister of Marine, the infinite number of his orders, and the secret communication of his hopes to the Arch-Chancellor Cambacérès, they would no longer entertain any doubt as to the reality of that extraordinary resolution."[2] Captain Mahan also most emphatically asserts that the great commander certainly meant to attempt to cross the Straits; but Captain Édouard Desbrière, the most recent historian of this period, inclines to the belief that Napoleon was not serious, and largely bases his conclusions on the fact that there are strange discrepancies and oversights in his plan of maritime strategy. In other words, the organization is not worthy of the Emperor's genius, because it proves that he was sufficiently human to make mistakes. The campaign which ended at Trafalgar was a small affair when compared with the disasters which overtook the army and its head at Moscow. The latter was a colossal miscalculation on the part of the military man *par excellence;* the former, especially in the opening operations, was largely successful, although planned by the same mind, which never thoroughly grasped the difference between manœuvres on land and those at sea. There are few living naval authorities of equal eminence to Captain Mahan, who avers that

---

[1] Many of these letters are to be found in *Correspondance de Napoléon I,* thirty-two volumes, and also in Captain Desbrière's *Projets.*

[2] Thiers' *Consulate and Empire,* Vol. III, p. 241.

the last phase of the invasion projects was "profoundly conceived and laboriously prepared."[1] It seems to the present writers that the plan was right, but that the men who were charged with carrying it out were wrong. France had no admiral equal in activity to Nelson, who, like Napoleon, was without a compeer. Cornwallis, Collingwood, and Pellew were more than a match for Ganteaume, Villeneuve, and Missiessy. Coquelle sums up the bitterness of the blow to Napoleon's ambition in a single sentence: "The failure of his preparations for an invasion, and especially his defeat at Trafalgar, were wounds which never healed."[2]

Without going so far as the late Judge O'Connor Morris, who summarily dismisses the matter by saying: "It is useless to argue with those who have denied, or doubted Napoleon's real intention to invade England," we fully agree with him in his conclusion that the Emperor "hesitated more than once; but no one who has carefully read his correspondence can question his purpose."[3]

Captain A. Crawford, R.N., who served as a young man in the British frigate *Immortalité*, of the Downs squadron, and not only watched the goings on in Boulogne, but had many an encounter with sections of the flotilla from the beginning of the war until Trafalgar, says: "I am of opinion that Bonaparte fully intended the invasion of England, which only the rupture with Austria, and the mismanagement of Admiral Villeneuve, in 1805, prevented his attempting. In this opinion I am fortified by what I learned from Admiral Lacrosse, some years ago, at Bor-

---

[1] *Influence of Sea Power upon the French Revolution*, Vol. II, p. 181.
[2] *Napoleon and England, 1803-1813*, p. 273, by P. Coquelle.
[3] *The Great Campaigns of Nelson*, p. 106, by W. O'Connor Morris.

deaux. This Admiral was second in command under Admiral Bruix, at Boulogne, and in consequence of the latter's feeble state of health, had been nominated Director-General of the flotilla. In that situation, he had the entire management and arrangement of the naval force there and in the contiguous harbours ; and upon the death of Admiral Bruix, which took place in 1805, he succeeded to the chief command."[1]

Méneval, who was one of his secretaries at the time, is equally positive as to Napoleon's intentions. He further adds :—

"His habits changed : his genius, which had appeared to slumber, awoke, full of courage and daring. He raised himself to the height of the formidable circumstances which our eternal enemies had created, and indeed rose superior to them. His activity became prodigious, and was all-sufficient. From that time forward a new life began for him, a life of action, of combat, a life given up to the hardest labours, to dangers of every kind, to the most fruitful and the most audacious of conceptions; a life from which no diversions of any kind were even for a moment allowed to turn him aside. Like an intrepid athlete, he entered upon this gigantic struggle, which was to produce such marvels—to raise him so high, and to cast him down so low."[2]

But for the fact that Bourrienne's *Memoirs of Napoleon Bonaparte* is a much-quoted and widely read work, it would not be necessary to refer to the opinion of its alleged author as to the reality of Bonaparte's project. Referring to the Emperor's visit to Boulogne in 1804, the writer

---

[1] *Reminiscences of a Naval Officer during the Late War*, Vol. I, p. 192, by Captain A. Crawford, R.N.

[2] Méneval's *Memoirs of Napoleon I*, Vol. I, p. 219.

says: "At his departure, it was generally believed at Paris that the distribution of the decorations of the Legion of Honour was only a pretext, and that the grand object to be realized was the descent on England. It was indeed only a pretext. The Emperor wished to excite still more the enthusiasm of the army, and to show himself to the military invested with his new dignity; to be present at some grand manœuvres, and dispose the army to obey the first signal he might give." Having strained at this gnat we are asked to swallow a camel. "How, indeed, could it be supposed, after such extensive preparations—so many transports—and the whole army ready to embark—that it really was never intended to attempt a descent upon England? But so it was—the blow was to be struck in another quarter."[1]

There is abundant evidence that the book in question is not the work of a single individual, but of a number of collaborators, who were helped by a few incomplete notes of Bourrienne's, and much information culled from more or less accurate sources. Méneval gives the lie direct to the "pretext" supposition. "If M. de Bourrienne had written these memoirs himself," he says, "he would not have said that Napoleon had confided to him in 1805 that he had never had any serious intentions of an expedition against England, and that the project of a landing, the preparations of which were made with so much noise, was only a trick to amuse fools."[2]

Although Chancellor Pasquier does not deal with the matter at length in his *Memoirs*, he maintains that Britain's rule of the sea "compelled" Napoleon to fall

---

[1] Bourrienne's *Memoirs of Napoleon Bonaparte*, p. 290 (Crosby Lockwood's edition, 1888).   [2] Méneval, Vol. I, p. 132.

back on. the old method of invading England by means
of a flotilla in 1803. He regards the former attempt
made "during the interval which elapsed between the
Treaty of Lunéville and that of Amiens" as pretence,
"but this time it was taken up with far greater ardour. The
whole of France's resources were set in motion."[1]

Lanfrey,[2] who certainly holds no brief for Napoleon,
after showing that Bonaparte did not hesitate to risk a
war with the whole Continent, proceeds to call to task
"several very sensible writers" who have concluded "that
the project of the descent on England was only a feint,
intended to mask his plans of conquest upon the continent.
If this project was serious," he asks, "how can such reck-
less policy be explained? Why did he, who was about to
throw all our available forces upon England, with the
almost certain probability of being immediately surrounded there by the British fleets, set all the Continental
Powers at defiance, and put them into such a state of
irritation, that their first step would infallibly be to take
advantage of his absence to rush down upon France unarmed? If the descent was anything else than a feint,
the policy was that of a madman. If the policy was calculated, the descent was only a false demonstration. It is
impossible to escape this dilemma, and we can understand
how historians, penetrated above all with the sublimity of
Napoleon's genius, have preferred to solve the difficulty by
denying the reality of the project of expedition, rather
than suppose that this extraordinary genius wanted
common sense, and could not see things that would have
struck the intelligence of a child. But it is impossible to

---

[1] *Memoirs of Chancellor Pasquier*, Vol. I, pp. 176-7.
[2] *History of Napoleon*, Vol. II, p. 398, by P. Lanfrey (Eng. edition).

GEORGE III AND BONAPARTE.   AN INVASION FORECAST, JULY 20, 1803

retain the slightest doubt in regard to this, when we see the thousands of orders, of projects and counter-projects, which Napóleon's correspondence has revealed ; when we see the interest, the passion, the obstinacy, the incredible resources that he employed in the realization of his favourite enterprise, the profound and breathless anxiety with which he followed its various phases and definite failure, and history is forced to admit the amazing contrast that is presented to us in the same man, of marvellous faculties in action, associated with a weak and radically false judgment in the appreciation of general facts."

Reference is very frequently made to the Emperor's remarks to the Council of State in January, 1805, that the Boulogne organization was nothing but a demonstration to deceive the Continental Powers as to his real intentions. " I now have," he assured the Councillors, " the strongest possible army, a complete military organization, and am this moment on the footing which I generally have first to secure in case of actual war.   To raise such forces in time of peace—20,000 artillery, horses and trains complete— there was need of a pretext in order to levy and bring them all together without rousing suspicion in the other Continental Powers.   This pretext was afforded by the project for landing in England.   Two years ago I would not thus have spoken to you, but it was nevertheless my sole purpose.   I am well aware that to maintain such an equipment in time of peace means throwing thirty millions out of the window.   But in return I have the advantage of all my enemies by twenty days, and can take the field a whole month before Austria can even prepare the artillery. . . . You now know the| explanation of a great many things ; but we shall not have war, for I have just opened direct negotiations with the King of England with a view to conclude peace."[1]

We are inclined to think that the above statement is one of many which Napoleon made to meet the exigencies of the moment. It served the double purpose of announcing that peace with Great Britain was possible, and if it did not come about it would be through no fault of his, and it warned the Council of a probable war with Austria. Truth to tell, he was in a very awkward position. He knew that a third coalition was being formed against him. and as he was always the last man to acknowledge the failure of his own designs, the idea of pretending that the expedition was solely to throw dust in the eyes of his antagonists, to keep England on tenter-hooks while preparing for war against another Power, must have appealed very strongly to him.

In referring to Bonaparte's plans of 1803 Miot de Melito says: "He was making astonishingly active preparations for a descent on England. . . . Yet it is doubtful whether he ever seriously intended to attempt this great enterprise. He was too good a judge in matters of the kind not to have recognized how small were the chances of success, and in any case I do not believe that he ever intended to undertake the invasion in person, to risk his fortune and his life on so slight a probability of victory."[2] Miot goes on to suggest that the soldiers were at Boulogne for spectacular purposes; to fire the imagination of the people; or to enable Austria "to repair her losses, and to avenge the insults she had recently endured, by a sudden aggression in which victory would seem certain to her.

[1] Miot de Melito's *Memoirs*, Vol. II, p. 234.
[2] *Ibid.*, Vol. I, p. 580.

VUE DU PORT ET DE LA RADE DE BOULOGNE, AU MOMENT DU DÉPART DE LA FLOTTILLE LE 16 AOÛT 1804

BOULOGNE DURING THE EARLY DAYS OF THE SECOND PERIOD OF THE GREAT TERROR

Thus war, the object of all the First Consul's desires—war, which only could save him from the critical position in which he stood—would again break out on the Continent." These statements prove nothing, and are merely Miot's own criticisms. " It is doubtful," is not a fact, only a supposition, and a poor one at that. Strangely enough, almost his next mention of the invasion is a report of a conversation between Bonaparte and his brother Joseph, with whom the Count was on intimate terms. " I have made up my mind," said the First Consul, " I shall try a descent on England. Victory would enable me to carry out anything I wished ; while if, on the contrary, I should fail, it matters little to me what happens afterwards!"[1] Surely it must be admitted that this statement is as worthy of credence as Miot's own ideas on the subject, which they appear to contradict.

The Count only begs the question when he says: "Whether the Emperor had in reality prepared for an expedition against England, with the sole design of concealing his military preparations from Continental Powers, or whether he had given it up on perceiving the extreme difficulty of the undertaking, the fact remains that for a long time past all his measures for a war on land had been taken."[2] This leaves the reader in blissful ignorance as to the real solution of the problem. As to the preparations for a land war, the wretched state of the commissariat at the opening of the Austerlitz campaign proves that Bonaparte was not prepared in this respect for immediate hostilities, for most of the provisions were stowed in the boats of the flotilla. In 1814 the Emperor referred to Miot as an " imbecile," and it is worthy of note

[1] *Ibid.*, p. 589.   [2] *Ibid.*, Vol. II, p. 115.

that when any plan went amiss or failed, the Count, according to his *Memoirs*, appears to have always foretold, or at least foreseen, that such would be the case.

The Emperor's remarks to Metternich, which have been seized upon with such avidity by those who hold the view that the invasion was nothing more than a threat, seem to come under the same category as those of Miot de Melito. "By far the greater part of the political prophets," says the Prince, "the camp at Boulogne was regarded as a preparation for a landing in England. Some better-instructed observers saw in this camp a French army held in readiness to cross the Rhine, and that was my opinion. In one of my longer conversations with Napoleon on the journey to Cambrai, whither I accompanied the Emperor in 1810, the conversation turned upon the great military preparations which he had made in the years 1803–5 in Boulogne. I frankly confessed to him that even at the time I could not regard these offensive measures as directed against England. 'You are very right,' said the Emperor, smiling. 'Never would I have been such a fool as to make a descent upon England, unless, indeed, a revolution had taken place within the country. The army assembled at Boulogne was always an army against Austria. I could not place it anywhere else without giving offence; and, being obliged to form it somehow, I did so at Boulogne, where I could, whilst collecting it, also disquiet England. The very day of an insurrection in England I should have sent over a detachment of the army to support the insurrection. I should not the less have fallen on you, for my forces were echeloned for that purpose. Thus you saw, in 1805, how near Boulogne was to Vienna.'"[1]

[1] *Memoirs of Prince Metternich*, Vol. I, p. 48, note.

How does this passage support the contention which it is supposed to prove? Far from removing all doubts as to the unreality of a projected invasion, Napoleon admits half the truth to the crafty Austrian : " the very day of an insurrection in England I should have sent over a detachment of the army to support the insurrection." His agents tried to provoke a revolution in Ireland, that being the most unsettled and therefore the most likely place for the planting of the seeds of sedition, and had the crop been plentiful, a second harvest would probably have been gathered in England. Of course " the army assembled at Boulogne was always an army against Austria "—or any other country if it had served the Emperor's purpose. The time of this conversation must also be taken into account. Napoleon had only just married Marie Louise, and it is more than probable that he wished to flatter the Austrian Minister by allowing him to think that what he had surmised was really what had been intended.

Such cogent evidence as that furnished by the documents preserved in the French Archives, and which would seem to be irrefutable, cannot assuredly be explained away by the statement that Napoleon used the soldiers he had concentrated at Boulogne for another purpose. Neither does it seem reasonable to suppose that the orders which he issued were prevarications and the two exceptions cited—oral evidence, be it remembered—the only occasions on which he told the truth regarding his real intentions. With half a million of men preparing to oppose him—the armies of the alliance of Continental Powers which the skill of Pitt had brought about—the movement of his soldiers from the coast was one of necessity and not of choice. Before Austerlitz had been won Trafalgar had been lost, thereby necessitating the abandonment, for the time, of all thoughts of invasion. Obviously the matter had to be shelved until the French navy was reconstituted, which could not be for several years. We shall see in a later chapter that he cherished this hope of a successful descent on the British coasts in 1807, and again in 1811—the year after his conversation with Metternich—when his dream of a Russian campaign first took practical shape.

Again, if the enormous armament which he called into being was meant only as a threat, why did he set so much store by the carefully considered combination of fleets? There was certainly nothing to be gained by sending a number of vessels to the West Indies on what could be little else than a fool's errand unless the great *dénouement* of utilizing them to cover the passage of the flotilla was really intended. This was certainly not planned in the hope that his admirals would destroy the British squadrons, for they carefully evaded action whenever they could possibly do so. Sir W. Laird Clowes holds that the "elaborate mystification" theory is "untenable." "It is absolutely clear," he says, "from the testimony of many of the naval and military chiefs who were engaged in the preparations, that Napoleon did intend to cross the Straits of Dover, and that, if his plans had not been rendered palpably hopeless by Cornwallis, Calder, Villeneuve, and Nelson, he would have actually made the attempt."[1] More convincing still is the fact that from 1801 till the autumn of 1805 Napoleon's sword was sheathed as far as the great Continental Powers were concerned. All his energy was concentrated in pushing forward his naval measures, and

---

[1] *The Royal Navy*, Vol. V, p. 181, by W. Laird Clowes.

BONAPARTE AND DANIEL LAMBERT—A CONTRAST. THE INVASION POSTPONED.
MAY, 1806

preparing in other ways for the invasion of England. Napoleon's skill as a soldier reached its zenith almost at the same moment as his ambitious efforts as a naval tactician came to naught. Not until his hopes were shattered beyond possibility of revival by Villeneuve's retreat into Cadiz did Napoleon cross the Rhine on his victorious march to Vienna. Then it was that the dying Pitt with trembling finger pointed to the map of Europe on the walls of Bowling Green House, Putney, with the memorable words, "Roll up that map; it will not be wanted these ten years."[1]

[1] 12th January, 1806.

CHAPTER XI

FULTON AND HIS INVENTIONS IN RELATION TO NAPOLEON'S INVASION SCHEMES

"The project of Citizen Fulton may change the face of the world."

NAPOLEON.

WHY did not Napoleon utilize steam power for his projected expeditions? This question has been often asked by modern writers. The answer is simple enough. The great force of the near future had not then been sufficiently developed to be of any known practical use for the purpose of propelling craft on the sea.[1] Fulton's first complete steamboat was not in running order until the year 1807, and although the Emperor was then thinking of making yet another attempt at invading England, it would have taken far too long to build a sufficient number of these vessels to serve his purpose, even if he had been able to come to a working arrangement with the inventor. Writers have also commented on Bonaparte's apparent disregard of Fulton's other inventions, namely his diving ship and submarine torpedo. That the ruler of France took some interest in his experiments is proved

[1] The *Charlotte Dundas*, a tug built by William Symington, was running on the Forth and Clyde canal in 1802. It towed two loaded vessels nineteen miles in six hours against a strong wind.

by the fact that he not only advanced ten thousand francs to aid the enterprising American, but authorized the Minister of Marine to give him "certain sums by way of recompense."[1]   It is foolish to suggest that the immense army at Boulogne could have been conveyed across the Channel in the diving boats.   Fulton had only the germ of practicability in his contrivance.   When one remembers that it is only within recent years that submarines have proved their seaworthiness, and that in none too satisfactory a manner, Bonaparte's judgment is shown not to have been at fault.[2]   Nor were Fulton's torpedoes perfected at the time, although the inventor had such faith in them that he believed England would be compelled to surrender if they were placed in Torbay or outside Plymouth and Portsmouth.   When they were tried by the British Government against the Boulogne flotilla in October, 1804, they did little damage, although Admiral Lord Keith recognized that under different circumstances there was "a reasonable prospect of a successful result."

Fulton's plans were submitted to the Directory in 1797. Its members were disposed to take the matter up, and Bruix was called upon to form a Commission to report on their value.   The following unique letter bears at the top a curious device symbolizing the liberty of the seas, and the words "Liberty" and "Equality" on either side.

---

[1] 30th March, 1801.

[2] According to Admiral Fournier, the French manœuvres of 1906 in the Mediterranean showed that submarines were almost perfect for coast defence, and this would seem to imply that their services are necessarily restricted. Although the submarine is now a recognized engine of warfare, it is scarcely more suitable for the purposes of transport than was Fulton's diving boat.

" *Eustace Bruix,*
"*Vice-Admiral, to Citizen Adet,*
"810 RUE DU REGARD, PARIS.

" PARIS, 13*th Thermidor, Year VI* (JULY 31, 1798)
of the Republic One and Indivisible.
" Citizen,

"Citizen Robert Fulton having invented a machine
for the destruction of the enemy's marine forces, you are
informed that I have appointed you one of the commissioners for examining the same. I invite you in consequence to the residence of Citizen Fulton, No. 515 Rue du
Bacq on the 15th of this month at 11 a.m. The other
commissioners will also attend, and you will come to an
agreement with them as to the report which you will
make to me relative to Citizen Fulton's machine.

"(Signed)   E. BRUIX.[1]

" *The Minister of Marine and the Colonies, to Citizen Adet,*
"810 RUE DU REGARD, PARIS."

The Commission seems to have reported favourably,
but Bruix would have none of it. Fulton, who was an
American by birth, had no patriotic scruples, and approached the Dutch Government with no better success.
In France, however, he had one very good friend in
Forfait, who seems to have taken a special interest in
Fulton's schemes. He granted him a passport in 1801
allowing him to carry on his experiments "dans les divers
ports de la Manche ou de l'Océan par terre ou par mer," a
privilege which was made good use of by Fulton, who had
now built the *Nautilus.* He had spent the previous
summer at Havre, studying the intricate problems of

---

[1] Mr. Broadley's collection of MSS.

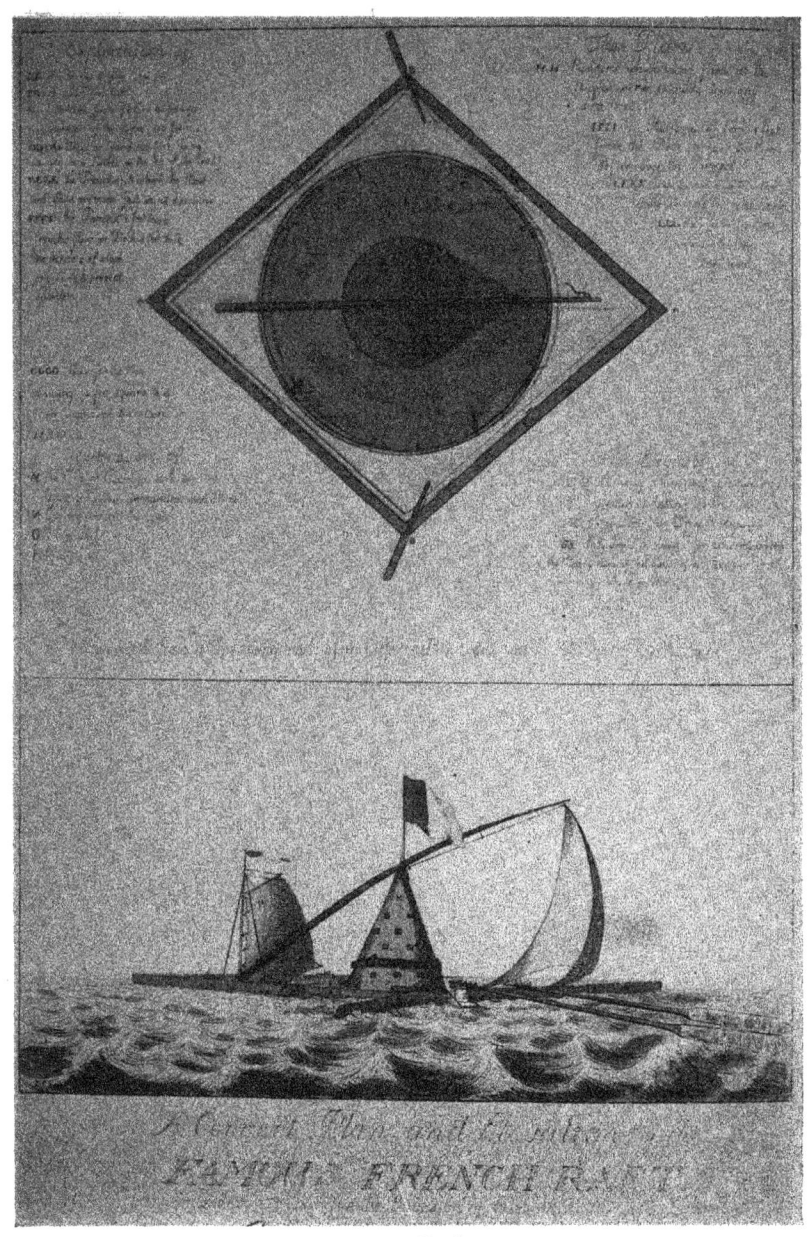

FAMOUS FRENCH RAFT

[1797-1801]

submarine navigation. His efforts had been attended with some success, for he writes: "You will learn with great pleasure that all my experiments in submarine navigation have fully succeeded." The inventor had overcome the initial difficulties of lowering and ascending, but was unable to make the *Nautilus* go backwards. For this purpose he fixed an Archimedean screw to the stern, but finding this did not answer so well as he had hoped, he "applied two wings, similar to the four wings of a windmill. The wings are four feet in length, their angle is about thirty degrees, they describe a circle in the water of four feet in diameter. . . ."[1] His next difficulty was to so balance the *Nautilus* when it was submerged and going astern that it would neither ascend to the surface nor sink to the bottom, but maintain any desired level. This trouble was overcome by means of a pair of horizontal wings which, when revolved, created a resistance and enabled the boat to keep at a depth of from four to six feet. Motive power was furnished by two men who, by turning the cranks attached to the wings, were able to proceed about seventy fathoms before the want of air necessitated the boat ascending to the surface.

Fulton's third, and perhaps greatest problem had now to be faced. How could he keep the *Nautilus* in the same position in the midst of the strongest currents? "For this purpose," he writes, " I made a cone-shaped anchor of lead, weighing 350 pounds. This anchor is attached to a cable twenty fathoms long, which is wound on a capstan, and passes from the interior of the ship to the bed of the sea. When this anchor is left at the bottom it lightens the *Nautilus* to the extent of 350 pounds. Therefore,

[1] Desbrière, Vol. III, p. 307.

when it is necessary to sink in the Channel, where the depth does not exceed twenty fathoms, let go the anchor, fill the *Nautilus* with water to the weight of 100 pounds, then turning the cable on the anchor it will have a strain of 250 pounds at the bottom, and the *Nautilus* will have a tendency of 100 pounds to rise. All danger is then taken away."[1] The boat was so far successful that on July 3rd, 1801, it descended to a depth of over twenty feet in Brest Harbour without mishap. Fulton and three friends remained below the surface for about an hour. As there was no means of allowing light to enter they were obliged to continue in darkness. Fulton subsequently remedied this defect by inserting " bull's eyes " in the conning tower.

In 1803 Robert Fulton came under the notice of Bonaparte. The inventor desired him to test his diving ship, but the matter was referred to Forfait, and that expert reported on the subject to the First Consul on the 2nd September, 1803, as follows : " By your orders I have seen M. Fulton, the American inventor of a plunging boat. He seems very much disposed to try fresh experiments, and assures me that he is confident of success ; but he makes a condition without which he will not work ; it is to have a short interview with you. He has, says he, political views to impart of the greatest importance." St. Aubin, a French officer, also spoke well of the invention. " In making his experiments," he said, " M. Fulton not only remained a whole hour under water with three of his companions, but had the boat parallel to the horizon at any given distance. He proved that the compass points as correctly under water as on the surface, and that while

---

[1] Desbrière, Vol. III, p. 308.

under water the boat made way at the rate of half a league an hour by means contrived for that purpose." Fulton felt himself justified in again approaching the French Government, and offered to sell his ship for 40,000 francs. He also made the suggestion that he should have a certain sum for every vessel he was able to destroy by means of his torpedoes, but he received no further encouragement. Disheartened, but persevering, the inventor then prepared plans for a submarine boat on a larger scale. This was to have a crew of eight men, and to be big enough to carry provisions for twenty days. By means of an air reservoir he calculated that they could remain submerged for at least eight hours. It was to be so solidly constructed that it would resist the pressure of the water at one hundred feet below the surface, and could travel when at that depth.

Although Fulton was now apparently concentrating his energy and resources on the perfection of his " plunging boat," he had already made experiments in the application of steam to navigation, and he designed a boiler which M. Calla, a mechanician living in the Rue du Faubourg Saint Denis, built under his directions. Unfortunately the hull of the boat on which the trials were made was not strong enough for the purpose; the bottom fell out, and the engine found a resting-place in the soft mud of the Seine. In July, 1803, after the machine had been recovered and the boat patched up, the predecessor of the *Lusitania* made a successful trip. It attained a speed of a little over two miles an hour. But it was nothing more than an experiment, and it was not until four years after, when Fulton had returned to America, that the *Clarmont*, his first practicable steamer, was launched. It travelled from New York to Albany, a distance of about 150 miles, in thirty-two hours.[1] Bonaparte lost little time in showing his appreciation of Fulton's efforts, and appointed a commission to go into the question. His faculty for seizing on the essential points of a novel idea was never better typified than in this instance. How keenly alive he was to the possibilities of the invention is shown by his wanting the whole matter settled within a week!

"I have just read the project of Citizen Fulton, engineer," writes the First Consul, "which you have sent me much too late, since it is one that may change the face of the world. Be that as it may, I desire that you immediately confide its examination to a commission of members chosen by you among the different classes of the Institute. There it is that learned Europe would seek for judges to solve the question under consideration. A great truth, a physical, palpable truth, is before my eyes. It will be for these gentlemen to try and seize it and see it. As soon as their report is made, it will be sent to you, and you will forward it to me. Try and let the whole be determined within eight days, as I am impatient."[2] The members of the Institute may or may not have formally reported to Napoleon, but no mention of the fact is to be found in the Archives, although the letter is registered as having been received on 20 Thermidor (8th August). The column headed "*Date des decisions de l'Institut*" is blank, and there is no other reference to Fulton's steamboat.[3] In November, 1803, however, Bonaparte's attention was drawn to the invention of a Swiss, upon whose idea he commented to

[1] The engines were designed by Boulton and Watt.
[2] 21st July, 1804. Desbrière, Vol. III, p. 312.
[3] *Ibid.*, Vol. III, p. 313.

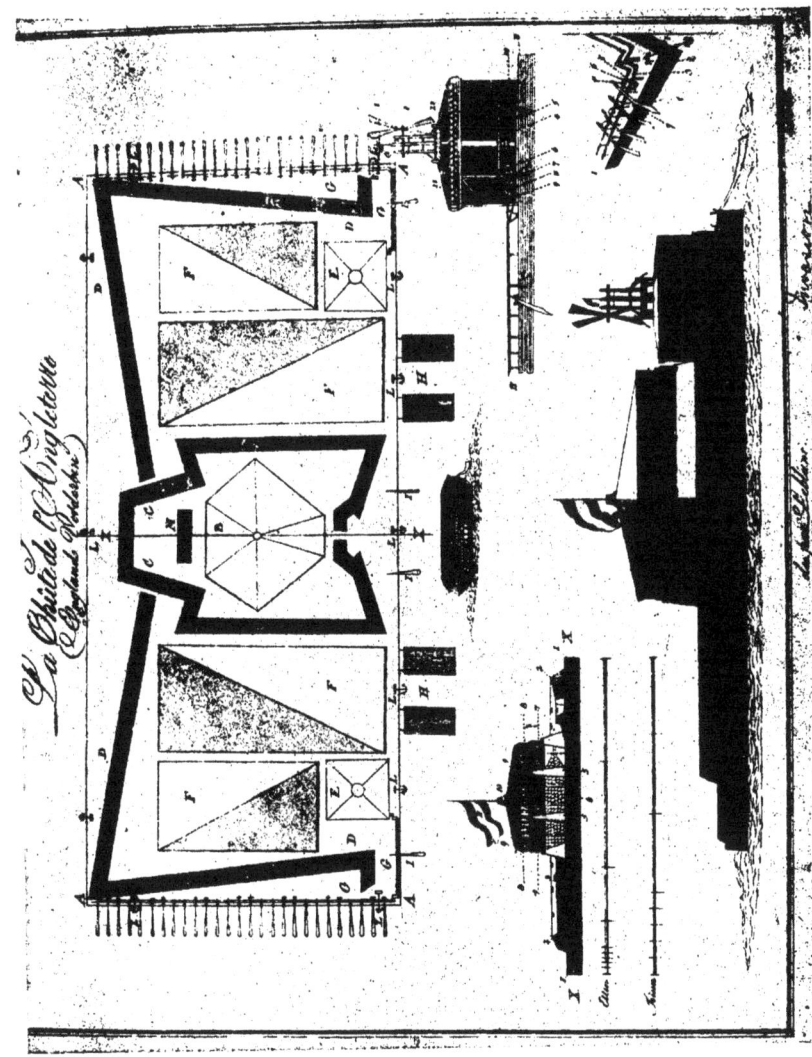

SECTION OF FRENCH INVASION RAFT. [1797-1801]

Talleyrand. "For a great length of time," he says, "people have occupied themselves with the means of propelling boats without men. The solution of this problem offers such immense advantages that it is improbable anything reasonable can have been imagined by a Swiss mountaineer." Pasquier calls Napoleon severely to task for not having received Fulton and his steamboat with enthusiasm.[1] "Its value was not recognized," he avers, "and it was disdainfully cast aside," but he ultimately does Napoleon justice, after stating that "never was he more badly served by his instinct," by doubting whether the "almost insurmountable difficulties" of manufacture could have been overcome at the time of his greatest attempt at invasion.

The British Government, on the other hand, viewed Fulton's experiments with alarm, and as the inventor was unable to obtain satisfaction from Bonaparte, he approached the First Consul's rivals with a view to their taking the matter up in a more business-like way.[2] He appears to have abandoned his application of steam to navigation and reverted to his old loves, the plunging boat and the torpedo.[3] A personal audience was arranged with Pitt

---

[1] *Memoirs of Chancellor Pasquier*, Vol. I, p. 178.

[2] On 8th May, 1794, Robert Fulton was granted an English patent, No. 1988, for "his new invented machine or engine for conveying boats and vessels, and their cargoes, to and from the different levels in and upon canals without the assistance of locks, or other means now known and used for that purpose." This is the only patent recorded in the official series.

[3] In the *Life of Brigadier-General Sir Samuel Bentham, K.S.G.*, who was Inspector-General of British Naval Works at this period, his widow gives an instance of the prejudice against steam and machinery which obtained among dockyard hands during the closing years of the eighteenth century and the beginning of the nineteenth : "In the spring of the year [1799] the steam engine and the pumps worked by it were put to use with all the success which the Inspector-General had anticipated in planning them. On the 7th of June Lord Hugh Seymour accompanied him to witness this novelty. To the surprise of all, the piston rod of the pump broke whilst at work. The millwright

and Lord Melville. Both statesmen came to the conclusion that the inventions were capable of development, and Fulton was encouraged to perfect them. A commission, consisting of the two Ministers, Lord Mulgrave, Lord Castlereagh, Sir Joseph Banks, Mr. Cavendish, Major Congreve, Sir Charles Rennie, and Admiral Sir Home Popham, was appointed. As the last named was the only naval representative, it cannot be said that the Commission was overburdened by the weight of expert advice. The report was as unfavourable as St. Vincent's view of the matter, which was one of contempt. He referred to Fulton as a "gimcrack," and endeavoured to dissuade Pitt from having anything to do with him, "for so he was laying the foundation for doing away with the Navy, on which depended the strength and prestige of Great Britain"—surely an illogical way of expressing an opinion. He went further, and called Pitt "the greatest fool that ever existed to encourage a mode of war which those who commanded the seas did not want, and which, if successful, would deprive them of it." Notwithstanding such ill-concealed aversion to the trial of a new invention, the Navy Board eventually consented to an experiment being made on the flotilla at Boulogne.

James thus describes Fulton's "torpedo":—[1]

who had charge of the machinery found a broken copper nail in the packing of the pump piston . . . ; the master blacksmith, a working blacksmith, and all others present, attributed the breaking of the rod to this nail. . . . It had been said by all, including the Navy Board, and perhaps some members of the Superior Board itself, that the introduction of a steam engine would cause risings of the workmen" (p. 155). Such was not the case, however, for the Inspector-General was careful that the men who worked at the pumps should have other duties given to them, and "a murmur amongst them was no longer heard" (p. 156).

[1] James's *Naval History*, Vol. III, p. 231.

"It consisted of a coffer of about twenty-one feet long and three and a quarter broad, resembling in appearance a log of mahogany, except that its extremities were formed like a wedge. Its covering was of thick plank, lined with lead, caulked and tarred. Outside this was a coat of canvas, laid over with hot pitch. The vessel weighed when filled (done, of course, before the covering was wholly put on) about two tons. The contents consisted, besides the apparatus, of as much ballast as would just keep the upper surface of the deck of the coffer even with the water's edge. Amidst a quantity of powder (about forty barrels) and other inflammable matter was a piece of clockwork, the mainspring of which, on the withdrawal of a peg placed on the outside, would at a given time (from six to ten minutes) draw the trigger of a block and explode the vessel. This "catamaran," as it was called, had no mast and was to be towed to the spot of its operation. On the opposite end to which the tow-rope was fixed was a line with a sort of grappling iron at its extremity, kept afloat by pieces of cork, and intended to hook itself to the cable of the object of destruction and swing the coffer alongside."

A favourable opportunity was presented towards the end of September, 1804, when from 150 to 160 boats were anchored in a double line outside Boulogne Harbour. Lord Keith, who had already experimented with various types of fire-ships, tells the result of his attack by means of Fulton's catamarans on Bonaparte's flotilla in the following despatch to the Admiralty :—

"'MONARCH,' OFF BOULOGNE,

"3rd October, 1804.
"Sir,
"Their Lordships are aware that my attention has for some time past been directed to the object of ascer-

taining the most effectual mode of annoying the enemy's flotillas at their anchorage in front of their ports under protection of their land-batteries. Having on the afternoon of the 1st instant arrived at the anchorage, and finding the weather promising, and about 150 of the enemy's flotilla on the outside of the pier, I resolved to make an experiment on a limited scale of the means of attack which had been provided.

"The first arrangements for this purpose were made on the morning of yesterday. The officers named on the other side were put in charge of the principal vessels which at this time were to be employed. Manned launches and other boats of the squadron were appointed to accompany and protect them. The *Castor*, *Greyhound*, and some smaller vessels were directed to take up an advanced and convenient anchorage for covering their retreat, giving protection to the men who might be wounded and boats that might be repelled, and for towing off the boats in general in the event of the wind freshening and blowing upon the coast. The operation commenced a quarter past nine o'clock last evening, and terminated a quarter past four this morning, during which time several vessels, prepared for the purpose, were exploded amongst or very close to the flotilla; but on account of the very great distance at which they lay from each other, no very extensive injury seems to have been sustained, although it is evident that there has been very considerable confusion among them, and that two of the brigs and several of the small vessels appear to be missing since yesterday. I have great satisfaction in reporting that, notwithstanding a very heavy discharge of shell, shot, and musketry was kept up by the enemy throughout the night, no casualty on our part has been sustained. The enemy made no attempt to oppose their rowing-boats to ours. Their lordships will not expect that at the present moment I am to enter much into details;

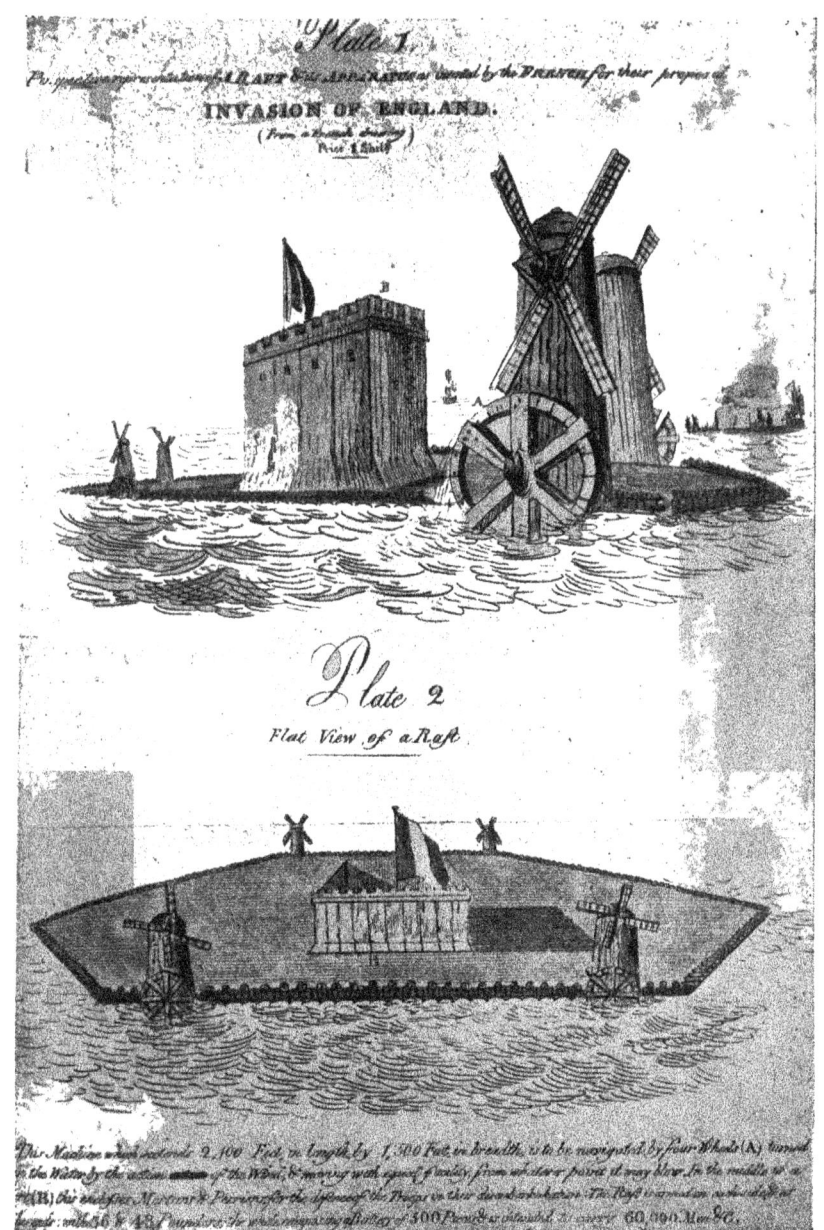

FRENCH INVASION RAFT, 1797-1801

but I think it my duty to state to them my conviction that in the event of any great accumulation of the enemy's force in their roadsteads, an extensive and combined operation of a similar nature will hold forth a reasonable prospect of a successful result. . . ."[1]

Further light on the subject is given in a letter written by an officer of one of Keith's ships :— [2]

"We took on board, from Dungeness, several large coffers, something of the shape of Hambro' chests, only rather longer ; they were filled with combustibles, and covered over with pitch about two inches thick. We also took on board a quantity of large casks filled up in the same manner, for the purpose of destroying the enemy's ships and gun boats in Boulogne roads. Different ships in the fleet had a number of these machines on board, on each one of which was affixed a machine somewhat of the nature of a clock ; out of it a pin was to be drawn, and at the expiration of ten minutes the machine would catch fire, when driven in by the tide. Last night being extremely dark, this scheme was attempted to be put in execution. No sooner had we approached near the shore, than the enemy spy'd us, and began to fire upon us from every quarter, when they saw the explosion of our machines, which they kept up from nine o'clock, till four this morning, and we on our part, kept sending in the machines at every opportunity. Had one of the enemy's shells fallen on our ship, and set the *infernals* (as they are termed by the fleet) on fire, there would have been an end of us. I am happy to inform you, there were no lives lost on our side ; and we have some reason to think, the enemy sustained very little, if any injury, our machines not

---

[1] *Memoir of Admiral Lord Keith*, p. 343, by Alexander Allardyce.

[2] This letter is dated October 3rd, 1804, and appeared in *The Times* of the 8th inst.

answering the purpose for which they were intended. We could perceive this morning some of them were driven on shore, without having either taken fire or exploded, and unfortunately fell into the enemy's hands, some thousands of whom were assembled on the beach to look at them. We expect to go to the Downs tomorrow, to return the remainder of the machines into store, from which, as a true friend to the service, I heartily wish we had never taken them."

Sir Evan Nepean, then Irish Secretary, and formerly Secretary of the Admiralty, was no more disposed to welcome Fulton's invention than was Lord St. Vincent. He writes :—[1]

"DUBLIN CASTLE,

"*9th October*, 1804.

"My dear King,

"I have received both your letters with the papers which accompany them containing the intelligence which has been obtained of the operations of the squadron employed against the enemy at Boulogne, and have communicated its contents with the Lord-Lieutenant, who has desired me to thank you. The newspapers of the same day, the 5th [October], represent that much greater injury has been done to the enemy's flotilla than your letters represent. I hope your relation is correct, not from any desire that the enemy's craft should be spared, but because I think we had better taken our chances of getting them at sea than to have used the means we have taken for destroying them. If the plan which I am told has been resorted to should have been carried into execution with success, we may expect that the enemy will some time or another retaliate,

---

[1] Mr. Broadley's collection of MSS.

and we have much more to lose than they have by such retaliation. In short it appears to me if navies are to be destroyed by such means as have been pursued, our naval strength can no longer be counted on. Believe me to be, my dear King,

" Ever sincerely yours,

" EVAN NEPEAN.

" JOHN KING."

The cause of the failure at Boulogne was partly due to a mistake in the construction of the torpedoes, and an attack against Fort Rouge, at Boulogne, by Sir Home Popham, acting under Keith's instructions, was decided upon in the following December. The affair was again a fiasco, and the frequent trials made did little damage to the flotilla; indeed, Bonaparte referred to the explosions as " breaking the windows of the good citizens of Boulogne with English guineas."[1]

The tenacity of the inventor is usually second only to his poverty. In October, 1805, Fulton persuaded Pitt to allow him to experiment in blowing up an old brig, the *Dorothea*, in the Downs. The vessel was anchored within sight of Walmer Castle, and the Prime Minister, Sir Sidney Smith, General Don, and other military and naval officers were eye-witnesses. Two torpedoes were used on this occasion, each charged with 170 lb. of gunpowder, and fired by clockwork. The boat was completely shattered, but the Admiralty would allow no further experiments.

This was apparently the inventor's last attempt in

---

[1] *Reminiscences of a Naval Officer during the Late War*, p. 128, by Captain A. Crawford, R.N. (1851).

England, for Trafalgar was fought and won six days afterwards, and the pressing need for such a contrivance was no longer the question of the hour. Fulton returned to America, where he survived until 1815, the year following the successful trial of his new vessel, the *Demologos*, which was the first warship to be driven by steam. It remained for the elder Brunel to propose the use of the great force in the British navy which, in the words of Napoleon, "may change the face of the world." It was not until 1822 that the *Comet*, a wooden paddle-steamer of 80 horse-power was added to our "first line of defence," thereby ringing the knell of the stately three-decker that was the pride and glory of England in the days of Nelson and his captains.

END OF VOL. I.